Living Nonduality

Enlightenment Teachings of Self-Realization

by Robert Wolfe

Karina Library, 2014
Ojai, California

A little more truth in the world.
Karina Library
PO Box 35
Ojai, California 93024
805.500.4535

www.karinalibrary.com
publisher@karinalibrary.com

Living Nonduality: Enlightenment Teachings of Self-Realization
ISBN: 978-0-9824491-0-3
2014, alphabetical title index

Cover: detail from painting by Robert Wolfe

The following monographs reprinted with the permission of Inner Directions:
Where I am Not, Suchness, Beginner's Mind.

Also by Robert Wolfe

<u>Print and ebook</u>

Abiding in Nondual Awareness:
exploring the further implications of living nonduality

The Gospel of Thomas:
The Enlightenment Teachings of Jesus

One Essence:
The Nondual Clarity of an Ancient Zen Poem

Science of the Sages:
Scientists Encountering Nonduality from Quantum Physics to
Cosmology to Consciousness

Elementary Cloudwatching:
31 Meditations on Living without Time

Always—Only—One:
A Dialogue with the Essence of Nondual India

<u>Smaller ebooks</u>

Enduring Enrichment

The Absolute Enigma

Where does infinity lead?

The heart of living: The Heart Sutra

www.livingnonduality.org

Table of Contents

Alphabetical Title Index

Acknowledgements
("to admit, confess")

This book did not come into print as a result of my own effort. Publication was made possible from the nonprofit So-Hum Foundation, whose director felt that it was time that these writings saw print.

Michael Lommel at Karina Library provided more than publication and distribution expertise, but encouragement as well.

And my gratitude extends to the men and women for whom, or to whom, these monographs were written: their discovery always enriches my discovery.

Preface

"Is there such a thing as the absolute, the immeasurable, and is there any relation between that immensity and our everyday living?"

~ J. Krishnamurti

These monographs are a selection concerning nondual realization. Some were written as a reply to letters from correspondents; others were written as a response to a specific inquiry, resulting from an in-person or telephone discussion, over the years since 1988.

They appear in no particular order. However, there is a (loose) arrangement in terms of complexity, with some on an earlier subject perhaps making a later subject clearer.

The teachings of nonduality have begun to come of age in the West, recognized (at last) as the central essence of Zen, Dzochen, Tao, Vedanta, Sufism, and of Christians such as Meister Eckhart. In particular, the recorded teachings of sages (such as Ramana Maharshi and Nisargadatta Maharaj) have paved the way for a contemporary generation of illuminating speakers and writers.

Due to the informal style of these monographs, quotations are sometimes abridged, or words emphasized; and English words may be substituted for Sanskrit, etc.

Since these monographs were written for persons of varied interest in the subject, and since each was written independently of the others, there is (regrettably) some unavoidable repetition. Nevertheless, each one has something unique to say, which is why it was selected for inclusion here.

As Ramesh Balsekar has said,

> "…even for those who have already understood something very clearly, a particular statement made in a particular context often brings out a subtle aspect which had earlier escaped their attention. It is therefore important not to take a repetition lightly, as a mere repetition."

Self-Realization is not Religion

There is probably no person alive who has not pondered that which some intellects have termed "ultimate reality"—the source of animation and activation that expresses the phenomenon that we call life. Because this noumenon is immaterial, to the senses, it is sometimes described as "spirit".

An interest in the *spirit*ual need not have any inherent relationship with what is defined as *religion*. It can be free of: required beliefs; worship of forms (or even the absence of form); dictates of regulated behavior; or ideas of right versus wrong. It can be free of all doctrine or dogma, allowing you to discern and verify for yourself what is true.

In the latter category, is an area of interest in ultimate reality (or the "spiritual") which is referred to as self-realization. This is a direct, unmediated confirmation of the nature of truth concerning the root questions of worldly existence: what can be said about this life?

There is a motivation for exploring this area, this personal investigation into our intrinsic essence. Each person, universally, possesses a sense of immediate and *unique* presence. This specialized sense of personification results in an experiential image or form which is characterized as our ego.

This ego plays a pivotal and crucial role in our relationships with other life forms. Resolving the questions about the nature of ultimate reality can have a profound effect on the isolation or alienation that we countenance from within the perspective of our encapsulating, or self-limiting, ego. It is this ego which is the progenitor of the bulk of the conflict which we daily experience, for the duration of a lifetime.

The consequence of the internal inquiry, into what you are that is in transcendence of the individual ego, is the revelatory awareness that is known as self-realization. This can be independent of any and all of the behaviors and attitudes that are associated with religion. This is not an inquiry into the supposed existence (or non-existence) of a god or gods, but an investigation into the relationship (if any) between the self, that you are conscious of, and the ultimate reality in which you are conscious of it. And this is a discovery which can be immediate and direct, without reliance on any religious propositions.

" It is right in your face.
This moment,
the whole thing is handed to you. "

– Zen master Yuanwu
(1063-1135)

"...A word to the wise

is sufficient."

– Cervantes

More than twenty years ago, my (second) wife and I divorced, after ten years of marriage. We both had, originally, looked forward to our years ahead with each other, and had planned for a comfortable retirement. I was in my early forties when we married, and I focused my attention on a career (as an insurance agent) so that we might further our goals. In so doing, I put aside what had been a primary interest prior to my marriage and this career: the "spiritual pursuit", for enlightenment.

After we divorced, I recognized that I had some unfinished business: it revolved around "the meaning of life", which is at the bottom of the spiritual pursuit—to which I returned.

As soon as our house was sold, I took my share of the equity and bought a fully-equipped camper van. I parked it on the property of an absentee friend in the redwood forest, near where I had been living in Northern California. I lived there in virtual solitude: reading, contemplating, taking walks for hours in the forest. At the end of three years, something suddenly fell into place. The spiritual quest resolutely came to an end. I discovered the actuality which is inescapable.

The inseparability of all things, which has been referred to persistently by mystic sages for 3,500 years of our written history, is commonly spoken of as "oneness" (or Oneness). There is an aspect of this oneness which is rather apparent to most any attentive mind. But the aspect which seems to give many of us some difficulty has to do with our personal, individual relationship to this oneness. This latter aspect is the matter which had now become clarified for me.

It was not that something was added to my fund of knowledge; it was that I saw the truth in what was already actually present but which had been overlooked or ignored. The situation is similar to one of those "optical illusions", which you have probably encountered: what appears to be, say, a black candlestick and its holder is displayed against a white background. But in addition to this apparent picture is a picture which is not so apparent; if the white portion is viewed as the foreground and the black, candlestick portion seen to be its background, an entirely different picture emerges: the outline of two matching profiles whose noses nearly touch.

My relationship to the whole of existence was now revealed in a radically different light. If you were to view a fish in an aquarium, for instance, directly head on, what you would perceive would be remarkably different from what you would perceive if you were to shift your perspective so as to observe it broadsided. It would not be a different fish than it had been—and nothing would have been added to it—but your perception of it would now be thoroughly different.

This radical, and sudden, shift in perspective was received like good news by me. Where before there had been confusion and perplexity concerning the relationship of the individual to the whole of existence, now there was a calming clarity. There was a profound resolution of the uneasy questing which had punctuated my prior years, a resolution which was not transitory because it has not since been apart from my general awareness.

I hoped to share the good news, particularly with those whom I knew to have quested concurrently with myself. I knew, from my own experience, that a certain element of this unitive understanding is communicable from one mind to another; the analogy is sometimes given of a flame leaping from one torch to another torch. Probably a more apt analogy is that of a center-fielder making a throw to home plate: if the catcher is not fully attentive, there is nothing within the center-fielder's power which will complete the transmission. But the fact that the transmission may rarely be received is not a reason for inaction.

There is a certain reasonableness, or even "logic", to the unitive understanding—up to a point. However, in the case of this uncommon understanding, there is a point beyond which logical progression will not take you. At that point, only an intuitive connection can be made. However, once the tumblers have fallen into place, it matters not that a hairpin replaced a key.

For the past fifteen years, I have conducted a considerable number of discussions (both individually and in groups) with persons who indicated their interest in resolving—and in recognizing that they had resolved—what has been called the perennial question. I have carefully observed the junctures at which their confusion compounded. I have also observed that for a few individuals there was no point at which their confusion was not surmounted, to their satisfaction.

The essence of the unitive understanding is that it is liberating; the marvel of the unitive understanding is that it is basically effortless. Its liberation is a consequence of the non-attachment it engenders. This is not a detaching of piece from piece, item by item. It is an across-the-board release of attachment, which even includes non-attachment to the continuity of one's life. This dispelling of attachment is, in the same moment, the dispelling of correlated fear—and that is dynamic liberation.

And, so, it is not that one first removes fear; removes attachments; and then the unitive revelation falls into place: it is that the latter is coincident with the former. This is the true marvel of the unitive realization, the effortlessness of the deconstruction.

Based on my observation, up to this moment, there is a cistern of confusion which bedevils nearly every discussion concerning the unitive realization. I will say what that is, and then I will explain the meaning: mis-identifying the relative as the absolute. Until this matter of relationship is clear to you, I predict that any further consideration will be fruitless. Conversely, when this matter is clear to you, it may be unnecessary to ponder further.

Relative, of course, means that which depends upon another for its identity or pertinence. Martha is your aunt because she is your mother's sister, and you are related to her because you are her nephew. The condition we call warm depends upon not being hot nor cold. You are you because, by definition, you are not I. The degree of light visible is relative to the degree of dark which might otherwise be visible.

So, the fact that Martha is your aunt is relative to the condition of you being her sister's son. Warm is relative—in unequal proportions—to hot and cold. You are *you* because you stand in relationships to what is defined as *I*. Light is merely a reference of relationship to dark. And so forth.

To view a particular thing in relationship to some other things—the price of steak today is high, compared to the price of hog maws—is our "normal", or at least typical, way in which we view everything. This is a mode, or framework, of perception which we have traditionally so taken for granted that it does not usually even occur to us to question it. But is relative perception the only perception that's available to us? Is there a perception available to us which does not depend upon a relative perspective? This might lead to another question: Is there anything which is not relative—which does not depend upon anything else for its identity or pertinence?

Apparently, we humans suspect that there is at least one thing which is not relative, because we universally have a word for it, which in English would be rendered as *absolute*. The very meaning of the word absolute is "not relative; not dependent upon anything else".

The importance of this preceding statement somehow seems to slip past our attention. *The absolute is not the opposite of the relative.* If the absolute were the opposite of anything, it would have to stand in a relationship to that thing. The absolute is *not relative to anything,* not dependent upon any thing for its identity or pertinence. If this were not so, it would—by definition—not be absolute, it would be *relative.*

To put it another way, the absolute is "beyond"—not *confined* to —any thing which is relative. (And since it is, by definition, non-relativity itself, all that is not "it" is, by definition, relative.)

And so, if it were possible to perceive in a non-relative way—to return to our previous question—we could (for lack of alternatives) say that it would be to perceive in an absolute way.

However, we are trained to, and habitually accustomed to, perceive in a relative way. The very activity of thought is to interpret that which the senses apprehend by dividing the sense impressions into relative elements (the better to leverage one against the other, for physical survival or continuity). A non-relative viewing is entirely foreign to our customary thought process: in fact, to the relative thought of our personal individuality, it is fatal. Therefore, the thought-processing mechanism (which we collectively call the mind) guards assiduously against such an "unnatural" perception.

You will recall that earlier in this discussion it was asserted that, at one point in the unitive revelation, "only an intuitive connection can be made". This intuitive connection, revealing the full dynamic of the absolute, is recognized by the reflective ego as the death knell for the presumption of individual personhood.

And the thought process is not entirely in error in arriving at such a conclusion. True unitive awareness—profound understanding of relationship regarding the absolute—cannot help but impact upon every idea of individuality or separability.

For, that which is not confined to the relative (and all that is not absolute is, by definition, relative) is not confined to relative limitation. Put another way, an explanatory meaning which man has given to the word *absolute* is "without limitation". This is usually defined (in more positive terms) as *infinite*, in reference to space or time: not finite, not an entity, therefore not in relationship to things. Specifically, the dictionary renders the word thus: "without limit or boundary, beyond measure or comprehension, without beginning or end". In short, beyond—or transcending—anything which could be considered relative. Not surprisingly, the Infinite is another name for God. Organized religions hasten to tell us that we are not that. So does our mind. Both have a vested interest in that conclusion.

We all have a choice at any given moment. We can continue to (as we each have been conditioned to do) perceive our self—and each and every thing which is "outside" of, or "around", our self—as a separate entity, standing in relation to all those things we define as not our self.

Or, we can recognize that our relative perspective obfuscates the possibility of a perspective which is "without limit or boundary", the perspective or perception of absolute inseparability. We are free, in other words, to remove the self-imposed limitation or boundary between our "self" and the "infinite" at any and every moment.

In fact, the removal of this boundary is what has traditionally come to be known as enlightenment. And the effortless removal of this boundary is effected in the sudden, certain realization that such a boundary has never actually existed.

You (and *only* you) can see for *yourself* that this is so. To do so, you need to be willing to—at least temporarily, while exploring the dynamic—suspend your relative habit of thinking. At some point, you need to discern where linear thinking has reached its limit, and free the psyche to move from what it knows to what it does not know.

This is one of the reasons why it is so important to understand what is *relative*, regarding the absolute. Anything which would be truly absolute (and, for the time being, we will assume that there is such a thing) could not be envisioned in comparative terms ("It's like …"; "It's not like …"). Therefore, obviously, there is no means of describing the absolute. All that can be accomplished, in discussing it, is to recognize the ways in which the relative (which we "know") is not the absolute (which we cannot, logically, know). As sages have said: to recognize the false as the false is to see the truth.

You may also appreciate the difficulty of discussing the non-relative within the confines of a language which is purely relative; our linear, rational thinking process is entirely dependent upon that very same language. Nevertheless, this has—some times—been the apparent means by which unitive awakening has been transmitted from one to another.

For the sake of continuing our discussion, we will assume that there is that which can be defined (which is, of course, a limitation) as the absolute: its nature, according to those who claim to have perceived that, is infinite, eternal, free of causation, and—given that it exists—actual.

For shorthand, let me refer to this as Q (since many other appellations—Tao, for example—are already "loaded" with inferences), in some of the monographs that follow.

If Q were infinite, it is not that it would be too vastly "long" to measure (conversationally, we might speak of the cosmos, say, as "infinitely wide"; that is a misuse of the word); it would be too ubiquitous to measure. That which is entirely unlimited and unbounded is uncontainable, thus unlocatable. Not restricted by anything, there could be no point at which it was not; permeating everything that was material or immaterial, no such thing as "space" would remain. There being no location at which it was not already fully present, "distance" would be irrelevant: *here* is *there*, without interface. Knowing no capability of isolation within itself, at any and every point of its occurrence it would all be entirely, 100% present. And having absolutely no borders, margins or perimeters, it could in no manner be regarded a separate entity. It is not an "infinite being", it is superlative to being. Not being any "thing" it is never present in "part"—it has no parts. Nor can anything possibly have been apart from it: it is absolute, which means whole, complete and entire—unfragmentable, and unavoidable.

Similarly, if Q were eternal, this does not mean "lasting forever in time"; it means time-less, utterly beyond relationship to time, either linear or comparative. Neither existence nor nonexistence are relevant to Q. Being *omnipresent,* there is no moment when it is not present; nor is it any more nor less present at any particular instant. In fact, with no capability of not being present, it is pointless to say that it is present: it was no more present in the "past", and will be no more present in the "future", than it is "now"; to it, past, future and now are meaningless. Being wholly free of temporal limitation, the entirety of eternity is in no way apart from this very moment. Anything which is, ever has been, or will be actual is not in the least removed from this actual instant.

Unlimited through space and time, having no center, no point of origin, no spatial or temporal continuum for "cause and effect", Q is spontaneously self-actualizing, without "internal" or "external" referencing. With no "other" in relationship to it, not anything is comparable to it. It is immanently present while, simultaneously, it transcends existence. Being in every place at all times, it has no separate or special identity. Having not even an opposite, there is no way in which it is incomplete.

This is the wholly non-relative, the absolute. Carefully consider it, for your own sake. If there were a possibility of anything which could be described as infinite, eternal, uncaused, and actual, what could possibly stand apart from—or in relation to—it? Except you, perhaps?

All of the things which man thinks of as relative to each other (such as "you" and "I") are simultaneously inseparable from this non-relative actuality. This presence (or anything which we would call absolute) could not be apart from anything, however relative it may *appear* to, or be *thought* to, be. We may, consciously or unconsciously, choose to perceive from a relative viewpoint. But that is not the sole perception that we are capable of.

From the so-called "cosmic", or non-dual, viewpoint, our chronic perception of things as relative to, and separate from, each other is false. To recognize that it is false is to open the mind to the potentiality of truth.

Where there is any possibility that the essential condition in this cosmos is the condition of an all-pervasive presence, please inform me how you could be apart from that. This is not to say that, from *the relative viewpoint*, some thing cannot be argued to exist apart from its "creator", or some such. But one must recognize, as I trust you do, that the nature of the absolute does not lend itself to finite distinctions. When you refer to "me" on one hand, and "God" on the other, you are not in a discussion of the non-relative. This, again, is one of the reasons why it is important to understand the indivisible essence of the absolute.

And it is this understanding—when it is so clear as to be startling—that is the substance of unitive realization. When it is indubitably recognized that your nature and the nature of the absolute are fundamentally the same, indivisible nature, this is the "recognition of one's true identity": the realization that any and all identity is eclipsed by an actuality which renders separative distinctions ultimately meaningless.

Such a realization, or non-dual perspective or awareness, cannot help but have a profound effect on one's consideration of "personal individuality". One cannot recognize that truth, of all-pervasive indivisibility, and continue to maintain the fiction of separate personification—of the "me" that was born and the "I" which dies.

This fruit of the realization—that the absolute essence of all being does not "come" from some place nor "go" anywhere—quenches our deepest, final fear, the fear of extinction. Then the liberated may, indeed, "take no thought for the morrow".

. . . .

Know Thy Self: an owner's manual

The teachings of nonduality ("advaita": not two), written in the Vedas, are evidently the world's oldest spiritual pronouncements. They were given freshened interest several centuries ago by the historic Indian sage Shankara.

Within our era, these teachings gained world-wide attention in the presence of Ramana Maharshi, who experienced spontaneous Self-realization while still in his teens—not having read the Vedas or Shankara. ("When I left home in my seventeenth year [already Self-realized] ... it was only years later that I came across the term 'Brahman', when I happened to look into some books on Vedanta which had been brought to me. I was amused, and said to myself: 'Is this [condition] known as 'Brahman'?")

Ramana, at seventeen, immersed himself in several years of the deepest meditation imaginable—death-like—as he sat silent and desireless in a mountain cave. For the balance of his life, while engaged in the role of a (reluctant) guru, he owned no personal property, had no romantic life and never traveled.

Basically, he had nothing to gain from anything he said. Yet, because he personally experienced the sweeping range of human religious discovery, his teachings make it unnecessary for spiritual seekers to reinvent the wheel. Like Buddha and Jesus before him, he speaks from the authority of first-hand realization. *Unlike* Buddha and Jesus, his teachings come to us unfiltered by historic doctrinal censors.

And thankfully, for the present-day seeker, his advice is brief and direct. Ramana is deservedly the fountainhead of nondual teachings in our time. From the standpoint of Self-realization, all that one needs to know can be found in a distilled form in such transcriptions as *Be as You Are: The Teachings of Sri Ramana Maharshi* (edited topically by David Godman, who lived in Ramana's ashram for years and edited its magazine, Mountain Path).

It is the Absolute (our "true nature") which gives rise to the ego (or sense of personal selfhood); it is this ego which identifies itself (I) with the body which it animates. "You" are not this impermanent body; you are not this transient ego; you are that which is the very ground of being, the eternal presence in which ephemeral occurrences appear.

Ramana refers to this essence as Self; that which is not the creation of (or affected by) thought: thought, like ego, is a creation of the Self. Anything which (separative) thought can identify, he refers to as non-Self. Also, the "I" which is the *real* I is the Absolute (or Self)—which he sometimes refers to as "I-I" (subject and object as one unit).

Aside from these conventions, one need only to discern when Ramana's teachings are given from the standpoint of the relative, and when instead they are given from the standpoint of the Absolute, in references in the monographs which follow.

Framing the Question

I arrive at the home of John L., whom I have been told by the Hospice staff is dying of cancer, and I go into his bedroom to meet him. As I shake his bony hand, he looks up at me from the dark wells of his eyes: "I've seen you before." His voice is high-pitched and nasal, and he seems to be toothless.

"Very possible", I say. "I've lived here for twenty years. How long have you been in the area?"

His eyes focus on his wife, who is standing by my side. "I can't remember. How long have we lived here?"

"Nine years."

"Yes, it's very possible that we've met", I repeat. He and I continue to scrutinize each other. Aside from the thin, long form under the quilt, all I can see is his head and one pale arm. Thin hair, sunken eyes, an aquiline nose, a bristly beard. No, he is not someone that I recall having seen before.

Over the next few days, in a couple of brief visits, I get to know him a little better. And on the third occasion, I am alone with him for a couple of hours while his wife catches up on some grocery shopping. I sit by his bed, hold his glass of Dr. Pepper so he can drink it through a straw, and let him know that I am there to listen to him if he wishes to talk. But he is mostly monosyllabic, and gruff in a covertly amiable way. Considering his physique, appearance, and mannerisms, I would cast him (if I were directing the play) as a crusty goldminer.

Prominently on the wall of his living room are displayed framed scale drawings of a Swedish-made sailboat with beautifully flowing lines; not just a photograph of it, mind you, but a scale drawing showing even its inward detail. Next to it is an expensive sheath knife with his name engraved on the blade, the kind of thing only a skipper could wear on his belt in earnest today.

"You sailed?" I ask.

"Every weekend."

"I've never sailed. I have no idea what it's like."

"Nearest thing to heaven you'll ever get, my boy!"

He dozes off. I make a cup of coffee in the microwave and wander around the living room. Toward a rear corner, on one wall, is a collection of about a dozen family snapshots which have been matted and framed. A few of the pictures are of his daughter at various ages, and his son. But there are about three pictures I find myself lingering over, returning again from one to another. They are pictures of him and his wife. The first one was taken at their wedding forty-one years ago; it was a second marriage for both, and she is wearing a corsage and he is in a suit; he looks like he is in his thirties, tall, lean, sensitive, like a businessman on his way up.

The latest picture is in color, and I recognize his wife, at his side, so instantly that I suspect this picture was taken only a few years ago. The man is much taller than his wife, wearing a sports shirt and an easy smile; he looks vigorous but relaxed. I can picture this man as the skipper of a sailboat, a casual hand on the rudder, squinting confidently into the sea breeze, the wind tousling his hair.

I can picture him inviting me into their comfortable dual-wide in this mobile-home retirement park, asking me if white wine is okay, and then sitting back cross-legged in the easy chair to tell me all the things I don't know about how finely the Germans craft steel blades, his voice deep but warm.

Later, while out for my evening walk, I am struck by the fact that if I had known that man as I sense him in the photograph, there is no connection I would have made with the man I know in the deathbed. They may be the same height but that is a different body in the deathbed; and my guess is that their personal ambiance is at least as different.

What became of the man in the photograph?: it is obvious to me that he is gone, has left this earth. We like to think in terms of continuity, that the other man somehow became this man. Could this man, even if he regained his health, ever again become the other man? No.

No, somewhere moment by moment the other man disappeared. The evidence we have that he existed is a photograph, a knife, a blueprint. The man in the bed, though still alive, has already let go —even if not consciously—of the man in the frame.

I think back to what I have known of myself. If there is any continuity, it is only in my memory. Can I let go—am I letting go —of the man who only exists in my own picture frames?

By their fruits shall ye know them. By the lives they lived, we know the saints of enlightenment. Standing out among these, in full stature, is Ramana Maharshi. Because he lived in recent times, we have the spiritual teachings in an accurately recorded form (as compared, for example, to those of Buddha). Also, living in India, Ramana's (Tamil) words have been translated directly into English (as compared, for example, with those of Jesus: from Aramaic to Greek to Latin to English).

Ramana represents the fountainhead of nondual enlightenment teachings, in their directness and succinct clarity. "If you had asked", as Jesus said, "I would have given you the water of life." In any one of the few books recording Ramana's commentary, the truth is there for the asking—authoritatively. "If it were not so", again as Jesus said, "I would not have told you."

However, as with spiritual texts in general, discernment is required if there is to be comprehension. Such texts are unavoidably paradoxical: what is said, at one time, from the relative standpoint, may be reiterated later from the standpoint of Absolute awareness. The irony is that this difference is best understood by the one who need not read any texts, the realized. Nevertheless, the subtle message can be comprehended by those who have the ears to hear.

The message of nondual actuality is not even dependent upon the word, as Ramana's own awakening demonstrated (and as did Buddha's). Albeit, this truth can be communicated with the aid of words, for those who are ready for it. The ones who are ready for it, have a single eye, and they prize what they see.

A recent book (*Padamalai*) is particularly useful (because of the way it is composed) for understanding the paradoxical teaching style of advaita: what you are taught at one point, you are later shown is an illusion ("There is no *you* to understand *anything*").

A questioner said to Ramana, "I do not know how to read. How can I realize?" Ramana said,

> "[A spiritual book] is like asking you to see yourself in a mirror. The mirror [book] reflects only what is on the face [in consciousness]. If you consult the mirror *after* washing your face [realizing Self-awareness], the face will be shown to be clean [free of confusion].
>
> "Otherwise, the mirror will indicate, 'There is dirt here [confusion]; come back after washing [clarity].'*
>
> "A book does the same thing. If you read the book *after* realizing the Self, everything will be easily understood. But if you read it before realizing the Self, it will say, 'First, set yourself right; and *then* see me.'
>
> "That is all. So: *first,* know the Self!"

The problem, which besets readers of spiritual texts which speak to the unrealized reader from the realized standpoint, is in comprehending when the response is given from the relative standpoint, in comparison to when it is given from the Absolute standpoint. This can be particularly perplexing when the response is intended to show that the limited (relative) can only appear within the unlimited (Absolute) and not otherwise.

Such is the source of the unrealized reader's confusion: From the Absolute standpoint, all that can be said is "There is no thing." Ultimately, that is, the formless Absolute cannot be regarded in relation to any entity or form or object. Yet, in order to speak of

---

* Bracketed comments are mine throughout the book.

this, we must speak of it as if it were something which can be identified, or objectified by the subjective hearer. Thus, it is referred to as That, or Absolute, or Formless, or God, or Self, etc.

But *this*, which necessitates being objectified in order that we can speak about it (the alternative being to remain silent, wordless), is *nothing*: no thing.

Where this becomes even more perplexing is that this *nothing* is existent in the form of—in the *appearance* of a form of—*every thing*.

To put this in context: Ramana (among others) refers to the formless Absolute as the Self—capital S. One of the (endless) forms which the Self appears *as*, is the individuated person: you; your "self". This self, being a form, is limited. Its appearance is within the Unlimited. (Even "within" is a misdirection, considering that the Formless is not an entity.)

The Unlimited being limitless, it comprises all things (which is how it can be said to appear as every thing). You appear within it. But it, being without limitation, appears in—so completely that it is *as*—you.

So, as the Unlimited appears *completely* as you, you do not have any reality as a *separate* entity (the formless Unlimited, having no point of beginning or ending, is *inseparable*). Therefore, it is said that "You do not exist."

It can be seen, by this, that it is critical to contemplate the teachings with a mind which can be fluidly open to the import of each pronouncement from both, or *either*, of the relative viewpoints (You [subject] are That [object]) *and* the Absolute perspective (there is no "You" and there is no "That"—only the unobjectifiable formless actuality).

Where the difficulty arises is that for the realized (Absolute awareness) to communicate these truths to the unrealized (with the limitation of only "relative" consciousness), the sage must, generally, speak in relative terms. But in order to show that what is being referred to is without limitations, the sage must also communicate the Absolute nature.

Where this is done effectively in a book, the bridge is there. But a bridge is inert; the explorer is responsible for the crossing.

The books that report Ramana's discussions, like other books of its kind, contains all that needs to be known by the seeker of enlightenment.

The Subject/Object Illusion

Your half dozen questions cover a lot of ground, so I'll have to be brief.

Because of our conditioned, dualistic thinking, the teachers ask you to divide reality into two categories, subject and object. Then they show you that our divisive thinking is a barrier to enlightenment.

In a sentence structure—"I see a tree"—I, the observer, is the subject of the sentence; tree, the observed, is the object. Such a sentence presupposes that I and the tree are separate entities.

We think (in our mind) in sentences. So we habitually separate our self—I—from every object we see. "I", the thinker, is the subject of every thought we have—what the importance of the thought relates to. The object in the thought can be any of the things in existence, whether material or immaterial.

We divide the world, in our thoughts: there is "me" (always the important subject) and there is all else in existence that is "not me" (the object of our thoughts).

In short, what the teachers are saying is that any object in the universe is—despite our giving it some separative name—a manifestation of the Absolute (or Source). They are also saying that *the subject* is not an exception to this truth: that *everything* in the universe is a manifestation of the same singular Source.

So, at the level of the most basic reality, the subject—I—and the object—tree—are the same thing: an aspect (although different in appearance) of the Absolute. This applies to every subject and every object: all are, at their essence, the same, one thing.

Thus, if we look beyond the separative names, there is only one universal thing, the Absolute. That is why it is said, "The Absolute alone is." There is not anything that is not it, in essence. A tree is That. You are That. And that is why they also say, "You are the Absolute."

If you are That *and* the tree is That, there is no "space" between you, in truth: even what we name as space between things *too* is That, a manifestation of the very same Source.

Time is also a manifestation of the one Source, so time too is That.

Therefore, time and space do not exist as anything other than additional "objects" (not-me) that we have named, and divided in our subject/object thinking.

The teachers are saying, "The observer (subject, which is That) *is* the observed (object—any not-me thing, whether formed or formless—which is also That)."

You (being as much the Absolute—100%—as anything else is the Absolute) and the tree (being the Absolute as much—100%—as anything else is the Absolute) are the same thing.

When you comprehend this, you realize that every subject and every object is That. Therefore, in truth, there is nothing *but* That.

The "I" and the "tree" names that we give everything are simply separate "subjects" and "objects" in the sentences that our minds create.

The teachers are saying that enlightenment is present when the seeker sees through these false labels—subject/object names— and realizes that every such name is just another name for the only thing which has true existence.

When you comprehend that (as they say) "All that is, is That", every one of your remaining questions will automatically be answered.

. . . .

Where I am Not

Mid-morning, after a light, early rainfall. It is cool, this late September day, but not at all cold. Surrounded, mostly by redwoods, sunlight scatters through in places on the ground. A few insects are on wing, in this clearing; one in particular, a moth or a butterfly in the distance, seems ecstatically happy. A sole pigeon is out of eyesight in a cascara tree, but the fluttering of wings can be heard as it browses among the thinning leaves for those favored cascara berries. A slight movement of the breeze shakes loose—from leaves and needles—those raindrops reluctant to join the earth; some of the yellowed leaves plunge, freeform, with them.

The clouds are an attraction. They were at first daubs of gray against the light blue background. They moved toward my left, nearly as slowly as the minute hand on a clock. And, throughout, they maintained their integrity, without changing forms as clouds seem usually to do. Beneath them, a slight film of wispy cloud moved, more quickly, in the contrary direction. Soon, this lower strata had disappeared. And, to my surprise, the daubs of clouds were moving now toward my right; they had become looser, cottony, and seemed to want to join with each other, as clouds so often do.

They are not under control, in any meaningful pattern as we would define it. Their movements are not to be predicted. In that, partially, is their beauty. They are not intent on any particular thing, changing their direction to meet changes in the circumstances around them.

World peace is here. I ask myself why it happens to be in this particular spot—but not, according to the newspapers, in the rest of the world. There's the same blue sky. The same stuff that all clouds are made of. Tall, silent trees doing exactly what trees do everywhere. The sounds of birds and bugs going about their daytime work as if it were their coffee break. There is the dampened brown earth, with some ants in sunlight, some not. There is a human, sitting quietly in a canvas chair in the clearing, watching a cloud that is moving in two directions, away from its center, in the same moment.

There is peace in this solitary spot on the globe because there is "no one" here. The human, who is merely part of the landscape, has no agenda, no ideas, no intent or motivation; he will not be rising from his chair in a moment to attempt to control something, to influence or change anything. Where could he begin to make any changes that would lastingly improve the situation?

Realization, Plain and Simple

Ramana Maharshi's teaching is that the Self (Absolute) alone is. There is not anything which that is not, therefore it is in no way *apart* from anything. Though this is so, we do not automatically recognize that our fundamental condition is that we are in essence none other than that.

As That (of which all that is, is manifest), among the manifestations are the human organism, its brain, its sense organs, the thoughts which arise, the mind which is comprised of these thoughts, *and* the ego by which the organism declares "I think."

It is this ego—self identification—which constructs the subject-object duality: me, and that which I do not perceive as me. Though this separative bias stands as an obstacle which seemingly causes us to view the subject I as dissociated from anything which is not recognized as the body-brain-mind-ego, it is in fact nothing more than another manifested product of the omnipresent Self. You—all elements and aspects of you, *including* the ego which posits otherwise—are only the Self.

When this is clearly realized, it is realized that there is no individual ego (*all* egos, as is everything else, are the same Self), and the subject-object bias *dis*integrates. There is then recognized to be but one thing—the Subject which sees no "other", separate object. This *Self*-realization has been the condition of the awakened throughout the ages, expressed at least 3,500 years ago as Tat Tvam Asi: That Thou Art. (*Whatever* "that" is.)

Ramana focuses on the self-awareness which each seeker has, of his/her own existence. That very existence is *essential* to the Self. Our true nature or identity can be summarized as "I am." Anything which follows, or is added onto that, is merely another extension or elaboration of the Self: e.g, "I am the doer"; the *Self* is the doer. "I am the thinker"; the *Self* is the thinker.

Ramana utilized particular ways in which to attempt to bring the seeker to recognize his/her underlying essence. (And on some rare occasions, the seed of realization was obviously planted, as evidenced by the listener confirming having gotten the point.)

For example, in our relative, human condition, it could be said that there are three different but connected levels of consciousness: what we consider to be our "normal" condition, when our eyes are open and we are wide awake and in relationship to the "real world"; when our eyes are closed and our body in repose, yet the thinking, imaginative mind is still functioning in support of our discriminatory ego, and we are acting in relationship to an acknowledged "dream world"; and when consciousness has sunk beneath the stage of thought and ego identification, and we are in a deep, death-like, "unconscious" sleep condition, dream-free and thought-free. The connecting thread in all of these varied, cyclical conditions is consciousness; if consciousness ceased to be present in any of these three conditions, the life cycle would end.

While consciousness is the underlying and connecting presence in all three conditions, it varies in its manifest form in each. In the awake state, it is the substratum on which the ego interacts with material elements and phenomenon considered to exist objectively in time and space. In the dreaming phase, it is the screen upon which the mind plays images and possibilities, free of the constraints of limiting time, space or cause-and-effect. In the period of deep sleep, consciousness exists free of the imposition of cognitive thought and interpreted sense impressions; purely subjective awareness with no "real" or "unreal" object envisioned. This aspect of unadulterated, unconditioned consciousness is our Absolute essence, the common and unitary presence at the core of each and *every one* of us.

Since this indiscriminate consciousness is our fundament at *every moment*, it is permanent and unchanging. It is our true Self, upon which our changing self—and its consequent thoughts, emotions, actions, etc.—are passing, inconsequent phenomena. No one can deny the presence of this abiding consciousness. No one, upon investigation, can deny the presence or existence of the Self as the self. The condition of the Absolute, being indiscriminate, neither denies nor affirms its existence. In deep sleep, we neither affirm nor deny our existence; we simply are—as (and what) we are—without any identification or I-centeredness. And also without any idea of objective phenomenon, either "real" or "unreal". The "world"—and every "other" thing—is nonexistent in the presence of our true Self. When we recognize our essence (in our waking state), the false identification as a separate I dissolves. This is Self-realization, plain and simple.

Message from Galilee

Concerning your question: "What is a person to make of the conflicting tales of the life of Jesus, as they are found in the four gospels?"

One need only review the Old Testament to recognize that by the time of Jesus' appearance historically, the "gatekeepers" of the Temple had embalmed God.

Jesus—if one follows the thread which run through the accounts of the New Testament—recognized and emphasized that "God" is a living presence; and Jesus' actions were a manifestation of this spirit. ("He [God] is not God of the dead, but of the living.")

The accounts indicate that while Jesus was concerned that his message be understood (even by the illiterate), it became increasingly prudent—after the beheading of John the Baptist—

for him to speak in metaphor (parable), to avoid being promptly constrained by the "authorities" (religious or political). The calculated risk, that nevertheless he would be understood, has proven over the centuries to have been overly optimistic.

Not even his chosen disciples managed to agree on the details of what they had heard—or, in many cases, on even what they had seen. (Which would probably be true of any typical group of people today, as well.)

He stressed that one has a *personal*, intimate, relationship to God, as a son has to a father; there is a "spiritual" presence in the universe which is as accessible as is one's own father to oneself.

That expression which has been *translated* as the "kingdom of God"—or alternately, the "kingdom of heaven"—could also be translated literally as the "presence of God". (See the Encyclopedia Britannica, and *Asimov's Guide to the Bible* by Isaac Asimov for details.) And such references as to the "end of the world" are, in consequence, references to an ending of all that is worldly.

Jesus insisted that his followers must forsake the worldly, and, while being in this world, not be of it. He urged the giving of all one has to those who need it, and clinging not even to a concern for where one's next meal is to come from, or where one is to lay one's head. When dispatching his apostles, he instructed them to take only the clothing they wore, and not even one coin of money.

His *message*, in his view, was what was important—not the status of the messenger. His message, by example, illustrated the accessibility of a "heavenly", tranquil presence...and, in its *perception*, the ending of fear—which is the release of the energy of selfless love. His message was that we are each an aspect of God —present in this presence.

His references to this presence, or kingdom of God, were from a first-hand perspective, having apparently been the culmination of a personal realization during forty days of solitude in the desert, prior to his appearance at the Sea of Galilee. This living spirit, to him, was closer than one's hand. ("The kingdom of God is in the midst of you.")

Anyone with the eyes to see and the ears to hear was implored by him to give every shred of their attention to the immediacy of this present spirit.

Even his disciples, however, to the very last, could not conceive of any godly presence except for a "Lord", nor any heavenly state except for the state of Israel. Two apostles, after his death, were still remarking ruefully, "We had hoped that he was the one to redeem Israel!"

But Jesus was pragmatic, not idealistic: he responded to the situations which existed before his very eyes. He was not concerned with whether the world would change, but whether there were any individuals who might immediately change. The appointed time, he reminded, is *now*; and the place to start is *here* —with your self. ("...Receive the kingdom of God like a child.")

We need not concern ourselves with the messenger, nor—once we have heard it—the message. You need only concern yourself with whether you are actively living the spirit of that which you perceive the message of truth to be. "Redemption" is not a product of the messenger or the message, but of personal action —the kind of personal action which involves the same insight which Jesus had...the insight that nothing separates you from this presence, but your "self".

Ramana's injunction to "ask yourself, 'who am I?' " is considered by many to be his most important teaching. It's importance is in inducing the questioner to investigate "what is the *source* of the presumed *entity* which is asking the question?" (or any question, for that matter). The immediate source of any question—of all speculation, in fact—is the thought, the idea, that there *is* an "I" to pose the question: the innocent question "who *am* I?" can open the door to the provocative question "*Is* there an I?" Or is the "I" simply another thought form, as are any questions in association with it?

Yet, another of Ramana's teachings is even more instructive. He reminds us that we spend about 25 years of the average lifetime in sleep. During a portion of these sleeping hours, we are aware (cognitively) of the fantasy images which we term dreams. But we are also, for the remainder of the time, in a non-aware condition of deep sleep. And thirdly, we spend a portion of our daytime hours in what is called the waking state.

Ramana points out that during the period of deep sleep, we are "dead to the world". Self-referenced imaging ceases: we are not aware of our self—or any self or non-self—nor any other thing, or any conceived relationship between things. Our vital condition, our immediate presence, is that of (what could be called) pure spirit. No thoughts arise, there being no conception of an entity to which to attach them. In this condition, the question "who am I?" is automatically self-resolved.

Yet, there is a being—or rather, beingness—present: were one to be shaken by another's hand, waking consciousness would reappear as certainly as if it had never been absent.

Thus, Ramana refers to the three states, or conditions, of presence (or beingness) which we all personally experience: the waking state: the dreaming state; and the state of deep, un-conscious sleep.

The latter is our unblemished, original condition of beingness—such as experienced in the womb, of which we have no cognitive memory. It is the condition upon which the "I"-oriented dream and waking states are superimposed.

Dreams yield to it, and the waking state gives way to it (as, for example, when we are anesthetized); it is the vital, underlying screen upon which our dream and waking images are enabled. Therefore, it can be said to be the source of our I-dominated perceptions, both in dreams and waking behavior.

What "you" truly are, then, in your primal form, is that which gives rise to—or creates—all that is known to the I, including its self. "You", in your purest beingness, are not "I"; you are the source of the I—and all else which ostensibly is perceived by that presumed entity.

Ramana would say that *this* "you" is a "permanent" condition, therefore ever-actual or "real". The "I" comes and goes, dying (daily) in its dream and waking states into its persistent dreamless condition; so the I is impermanent (being recreated daily) and is therefore *not* real, a phantasm.

In this sense (only), it is sometimes declared that there is Waking, Dream and Deep Sleep states, and the Fourth State; the latter being like a thread which supports the three (aforementioned) beads, and merely represents the beingness upon which the previous three states depend. Were this Fourth State to not be present (as in physical death), you would not experience waking, dreaming nor deep sleep. The underlying condition of all three is the vital, I-thought-free presence that is referred to as the Fourth State—your unceasing "true nature".

What makes this (deeper) understanding of Ramana's teaching so important is that it is an unerring graveyard for the stubborn I-thought. Whenever a perplexity arises to the cognitive "self", Ramana would advise reflecting: "Did this dilemma arise during deep sleep?" No. Therefore, it is a non-real, a phantasmic, dilemma.

Did the question "who am I?" arise in deep sleep? No. Therefore, if you understand "who" you are in deep sleep, you need not concern yourself about it—or any other thought-generated concern, for that matter.

So, even more fruitful than asking your "self" who-am-I?, is the one-pointed reflection "Did this thought occur in deep sleep?" This reflection will silence the I-generated conflicts.

The Bottom Line

What is the first and foremost conscious priority in your life? If it is not to recognize your inseparability with the absolute, then neither spiritual reading nor guidance is appropriate to your primary interest or pursuits.

But if that divine recognition is your urgent priority, then the essential aspects of your daily life are—or are obliged to be—organized around that sustained motif. Are they? If not, then conditions are not appropriate for proceeding (whether or not one reads, or is attracted to, spiritual guidance).

What are the appropriate conditions for recognizing inseparability with the absolute? A woman, whom I know, was suddenly hospitalized. A surgeon insisted upon an immediate operation. She declined. He remarked, "Are you prepared to die today?" How would you answer? Are you ready and willing to relinquish all, today? Are you positioned to live from moment to moment in that condition? If so, where was the point of "embarkment" on the spiritual journey?

To be willing to relinquish all, from moment to moment, is to abdicate the future. When you are no longer inclined or impelled toward some future moment, you have come to a standstill (in terms of temporal reckoning). This private standstill is indicative or representative of surrender of the personal will. It is out of this emptiness which a revived spirit embraces and possesses our being.

This voluntary standstill is not a logical or rational procedure; it is founded on intuitive trust, or instinct. It is, in a sense, a matter of surrendering to one's deepest intuition. It is a matter of abiding by what one knows in one's heart is sacred—despite the supposed cost to oneself.

The appropriate condition for recognizing inseparability with the absolute is to give all that one has and is—for that is all that lingers "outside". It is for each person to consider what he individually 'has' or 'is'.

This letting go is not a one-time event; it is a letting go as long as there is anything left to which one clings. For, anything to which we can cling is not our sacred self. This includes our ideas about the urgency of life itself. Inseparability makes no conclusive distinctions.

So, it is not reading or learning, it is the resolution of fear that we are engaging. This must be underwritten internally, without regard to anything ever read or learned. It is a solitary, glamorousless endeavor, and you will not know when or if it is ended.

Therefore, for one reason or another, people generally end their reading and pursuit. For some, the trust is present to let go of all, including assurance of knowing. Only when all is gone, is there only one thing which remains.

Is that what you want?

. . . .

Fabled Enlightenment

The late Alan Watts titled his autobiography *In My Own Way*, a double-entendre to indicate that, in the quest for enlightenment, he was his own worst enemy. And so it is for most of us.

Not only does the self have a stake in doubting one's own liberation, it has an equal stake in doubting the liberation of others.

But even for those who are at the point where they can see through the transparent concept of the self, and its inherent insecurity, there often remain concepts which stand as a barrier to full realization.

There is, after several millennia, a mystique which surrounds enlightenment... a folklore of mythology: for example, that there is a moment of ecstatic clarity invariably accompanied by an eerie brilliant light. Or that the person, so enlightened, will henceforth beam a sense of charismatic tranquility on all whom they encounter.

Such stereotypical generalizations lodge as images in the mind of the seeker—and actuality is then compared with these images (and thereby deemed deficient). An example of such a generalization is the oft-quoted comment, "Who knows, doesn't say. Who says, doesn't know." If this implies that anyone who says that he knows, does not know, then it also implies that anyone who does not say that he knows, *does* know. But the inference that is drawn from this is that anyone who admits to his true identity cannot be worthy of an unbiased hearing. Someone once replied to such a person, "But aren't you the carpenter's son?" (To which the carpenter's son commented, "A prophet is never recognized in his own homeland.")

Of those whom the seeker senses has abided in the place of realization, the seeker often asks direction—and that passerby may respond to the best of his ability. But when the seeker carries to the encounter an image of the passerby's mythical features ("the Son of David...King of the Jews"), he has no capacity to recognize the anonymous messenger.

When someone tells you that he knows, listen without judgmental thought or conditioned image. Suspend your concepts of what enlightenment is, or how the enlightened appear.

If such a person asks you for anything, question his motives. But if he is trying to give you something, ask him to tell you what he can about love.

Neti, Neti

Without focusing on any particular question, here are some general comments that might be helpful.

Bear in mind that such terms as *awakening* are not meant to suggest a movement from one "state" to another, such as to a "higher" state.

When you awaken from sleep in the morning, you are not moving to a "higher state": you are merely continuing your existent life in a different form; more actively. Thus, a "spiritual awakening" is a *continuation* of the *present* life—in a *different* form.

What is on the other side of the coin of awakening is not a "higher (*or* lower) state" but "a different way of living": living from the perspective where the ego self is no longer the center of the relational universe.

In a sense, this represents the abandonment of the illusionary world, as waking represents the discontinuation of a fascinating dream. In this way, it could be said to be the ending of self-deception, similar to the way that the dream self was an illusion. In this case, the waking self is realized to be similarly an illusion, and our "belief" in this self—as a "separate entity"—a deception.

That this awakening—the ending of "self"-centered deception— has occurred for some and not for others appears to be related to how deeply one aspires to abandon the saccharine dream for the glaring reality of "awakened" life. If realization of the true nature of the self is not at the *top* of one's list of priorities, the egoic self "fulfillment" will *ever* take *precedence*.

But for awakening to be the number one priority, it must be acknowledged that the pilgrim will have to be willing to confront fears of "annihilation" of the self-created person-ality, the personal image. It is this fear of the disappearance of "self" identity which stands as a barrier, *even* for those for whom awakening *is* their fundamental priority.

What is discovered is that there *is* no "individual" self to *be* annihilated, neither in life nor in death. The self that "dies" is nothing more than an illusion that dissipates. With the dissolution of the self, goes the dis-appearance of the self's fears —including the fear of "nothingness" or "the void". To the question, "Why is this fearful (*or* blissful) experience occurring (or *not* occurring) for me?", the answer is finally evident: "It's not." Are the experiences that "occur" for the imagined figure, in a dream, real or imaginary? In deep sleep, when the imagined figures and their activities are *absent*, what can be said to be the *present* condition—*except* for nothingness, or the void?

We cannot even say what this nothingness or void is "like", as an experience. If we could come away from this condition as a knowledgeable "experiencer", it would not truly be the condition of *nothing*ness. So we need not fear the condition of nothingness, because there is no *identifiable* experiencer of it. If there is any residue—any *thing* at all—in (or as a part of) the "void", it's not the *void*.

Thus, all we can say about it is that there can't be more than *one* actuality that could be represented as *nothingness*. And because it is the one thing of which there can be no "parts" or fragments, it is that which has been characterized as "oneness", the all-encompassing essence, or Absolute.

From this nothingness, or void, arises the dream; and from the dream, awakening. And if we trace anything—whether waking occurrences or dream occurrences—back to the source, we inevitably arrive at the actuality, or presence, of the one, ineffable formlessness.

So, it is from this formless source that consciousness arises, and thus self-consciousness, or the "I-thought". And it is *to* this insubstantial "I" to which all "other" *appears*; the embodied "seer" and the "seen" world and universe, manifestations of the same, one source—the formless, through form, seeing "its self"; embracing itself, as the all-embracing.

The formless, *as* the *all*-embracing actuality, knows nothing of exclusion. All manifested forms, whether material or immaterial, arise from—rather, *as*—the same essential presence. You are that, and anything that you would rid yourself of—*or* become—is that.

You are *already* that which any "higher state"—which any conceivable form—could possibly *be*.

So, realization is not about going from one form or condition to another—both already being a manifestation of the same, one thing. It is not about moving from one form ("me" as the body) to another form of the formless (me as "pure consciousness"). Therefore, realization is not what most people think it is.

It is not about having some particular experience.

It is not about getting to be a "better" person.

It is not about making *anything* (such as the world) better.

It is not about maintaining a spiritual "practice".

It is not about an entity ("me") becoming some other entity (Buddha).

It is not about something that can be objectified, since it is formless, and thus inseparable, in essence.

It is not about something which appears (or is present) in a particular time or place, since time and space are dependent manifestations *of* this source.

It is not about something of which there is any subject apart from it (such as "me"), since the formless essence cannot be fragmented.

It is not about something that can be associated with any special experience, state or phenomenon, since *all* conditions are equally in its embrace.

What is referred to as awakening is the realization that there is no actual *I* apart from the formless essence; it is about the dissolution of self identification; the egoic mind's relinquishment of the hold on its projected image; the conscious erasure of the line between "observer" and "observed". *And* it's about living life from the continual reference point of this profound realization. As the sages have assured us, it *is* possible to live a fulfilling life without the persistent condition of a self image.

For everyone, there is at least the occasional experience, during the day, when one does not exist as a separate entity—to one's own consciousness; when one is so deeply engrossed, in what one's attention is focused on, that there is no sense of "self"-awareness. And yet we do not cease to function bodily, even though we are free of the image of our identity, in these moments.

To be spiritually "re-born" is thus to again abstain from self image, as if we were a baby: to *be*, without the brackets of "was" or "will be", without "did" or "will do"; the individual that would "be something" or "do something" gone, with only that which is aware and present remaining. This is the relaxation of tension, so that one is in attendance to "what is"—just *as* it *is*.

If one were to coin a phrase for the awakened perspective, it might be "proscient awareness": that is, a "knowing before" in the sense of an operative intelligence which continually directs one's behavior. It is merely a generally unrecognized aspect of the Absolute, of the source of even our superficial, egoic consciousness—the source, in essence, of all that is done. All that everyone says, does or thinks originates with this ever-present source. So, this essence is the only identity which any of us can rightfully claim. Recognize that this formless essence is your fundamental condition; and *that* proscient awareness will dictate the direction of your every act—without a "self-ish" perspective to be concerned about any outcome.

This extension of your present existence, into freedom, is "awakening"—just a different form, an inclusive form, of living.

So, while it's not about "doing good deeds", as a means to a desired end, being of dedicated service to others is an uncontrived consequence when *personal* self fulfillment has disappeared from the agenda.

Mind
(from the Greek "menos"; spirit, force)

"Mind" is a key element, from the standpoint of enlightened awareness. The spiritual seeker is asked to trace back (in contemplation) the *source* of the presence that we commonly refer to as mind. The usual initial response is that "I am the source of my mind." The seeker is then urged to "find the I"; trace back the *source* of the I-thought: where does the sense of being "me" originate? Where can the mind be located? Being itself immaterial, can it be a product of the brain—which is material? Where is the sense of "being present" *centered;* is it within the body? Find it!

Is it possible (and you can discover this first-hand, if you will) that your self-identification is nothing more than a projection of the mind; and that *mind* is merely an extension of the self? Since they are each fundamentally a reflection of the other, what is *their* originating source?

What is your *body's* originating source? Is it not, ultimately, the same as the source of all material manifestation in the universe, animate or inanimate? What is the source of animation that we refer to as life? Your awareness of being alive is not something which you created. That which is the source of your sense of presence is the source of your sense of being a unique "person" (the root of the word means 'a mask'), an individual; and your sense of being a person is the source of your reference to "my mind".

But whose mind is it? Who is responsible for the creation of its thoughts?...You?...

"You" as a physical being (no matter how full "your mind" is with "thoughts") are powerless to effect the course of nature in the universe. What is the power responsible for your (and the universe) being "present"? Is that not the origin from which your body, your sense of self, your thoughts and your very mind arise?

So, whose mind is it? Whose thoughts are these? Who is the self that is animate in all "selves" and says "I exist" in *all* consciousness? When you've discovered the source of your *real* identity, you've discovered the source of "your mind" and "its thoughts"—the source of "everyone's" mind and "everyone's" thoughts.

In Buddhism, they refer to this omnipresence as Buddha Mind, or just Mind: "Buddha Mind" because Buddha discovered that it was this singularity which was the root of his "true nature", and that all beings share this nature in common. In Eastern spiritual literature, the question is asked (for contemplation): Who is the doer? Are there countless "individual sources"—"minds" which have no connection with one another—which are responsible for the natural unfolding of events? Or is the very unfolding of events the extension of the presence which represents life from its very beginning?

So who, ultimately, is the doer? You; or that origination of which you are a collective representative? Whose mind is at work in "your mind"? What is the origin of all minds? Is there such a thing as an individual "mind"?

If you go to the airport to catch a flight to California and the departure board says to go to gate 8, you will miss the flight if you go to gate 10 instead. No matter how many times you persist in returning to gate 10, you will continually miss the flight that is listed to leave from gate 8.

The questions you ask about external "realities" will not get you where you want to go.

The solution to the dilemma of spiritual confusion cannot be found in propositions of logic. "If A=B and B=C, then C must equal A" makes sense from the standpoint of the material world. But what you are seeking—every teacher has said—is beyond the confines of time, distance or causation: in other words, not limited to a question-and-answer paradigm.

All of the teachers tell you to look for what you are seeking *within*, not outward in terms of conceptual forms.

More specifically, the teachers tell you to discover the *source* of the questions, instead of pursuing answers to questions.

Questions are gate 10. The source is gate 8. Don't ignore the departure board: "Go to gate 8. You will waste your life if you go to gate 10."

To take just three teachers alone, Buddha, Ramana and Krishnamurti taught for a combined total of more than 150 years. None of the three retired before they died, so evidently none "finished the job early" of transmitting the Truth. That is because the Truth contains a tough message.

The tough message is that when you close your eyes for the final time, the "you" who you maintain that you are—and everyone of its questions and answers—will entirely disappear, completely evaporate. So, of what value are these things? Ultimately, *none*.

The only thing that is of any value to you during this lifetime is to perceive the true nature of what it is that is dreaming this dream.

The "you", and all that you think is important, is a dream. What is real? This is the *only* question that you need to concern yourself with.

Could it be that there is That which is beyond time, which therefore is so permanent that there is no "arrival" and no "departure" for it? We know that every thing in the material, external realm "comes" and "goes". What is more "real": that which is impermanent, or That which persists when everything else has come and gone?

If the latter, is it possible that this timeless actuality is the "background" for all of the transience that is as un-real as a dream? If so, is this the source, the fountainhead, from which all that we perceive makes its "appearance?"

If this *is* the source of all that is *im*permanent, is it not the source from which "you" emerge? And, by extension, isn't it the source from which your thoughts and questions arise?

So, what is more important, contemplating the answers to an endless stream of (ultimately useless) questions, or contemplating your innate source? The teachers urge, "Look within." Isn't that a clue? If they said, "Keep your attention busy with asking endless questions" that would be a different kind of clue, wouldn't it?

That's why the teachers find the teachings to be a tough sell. When we look within, we discover that we are not who we thought we were. And this might just change our lives, and our lifestyles. It's possible that we may not "like" what we find behind gate 8. Buddhists, for example, call it the Void. "Void" means "nothing": 0.

That's where the answers to all the questions lead: ultimately no where; to the source that has no specific location, no material "reality". It's the One who has no questions to ask.

Find this One. That's the answer to all questions. Head toward the proper gate: *self-realization.*

Substantive Enlightenment

What is the *meaning* of enlightenment? The literal meaning of the word *enlighten* is "to give the light of fact to; reveal truths; to free from ignorance; to make clear the nature of something: illuminate".

And so we speak of an "enlightened scientist", such as Galileo. Until only about 400 years ago, it was rational (reasonable) to suppose that the sun revolved around the earth, since it is *apparent* that the sun "rises" in the east and "sets" in the west. However, when it is clearly understood that the earth is a globe (which became obvious once navigators were able to sail around it), it is evident that the sun never actually "rises" from anywhere; it is, instead, the surfaces of the earth—in the globe's revolution—which rise to meet the illumination of the sun.

Now every rational person is an "enlightened scientist" (science means "to know") today, because of Galileo; he was "enlightened" (free from ignorance) because he was aware of what the vast majority of people were not yet aware.

By the same token, there are other enlightened scientists (who are actually "investigators") today. Although the *form* of light has always appeared to be that of a ray or beam, Einstein's theories predicted that light could be observed in the form of particles ("discrete packets" of energy dubbed *quanta).* Because Einstein's other theories had generally proven true (he had demonstrated his capacity to "reveal truths"), research scientists set about to determine whether this could possibly be true—however irrational it sounded. And, indeed, Einstein's enlightenment has been transmitted.

Subsequent experiments have even surpassed Einstein's intuition. Experimental physicists have discovered that if you set up an experiment to monitor light in its particulate form, it will appear as particles. But if you set up your experiment to observe light in its radiant form, it will appear as a vibratory wave. Such experiments have been replicated so many times that physicists now accept—and operate on—the fact that light does not only take the form of waves, *or* just particles, but *both,* depending upon the circumstances of observation.

Therefore, when we speak about light "waves" or light "particles", we are speaking about the *same* thing. Prior to the enlightenment of science on this matter, no rational person would have maintained that a wave and a particle were interchangeably the same thing: merely different names, or description, for the fundamentally same phenomenon.

Another source of illumination for man's science has been the discovery of a level of radiant heat in the galactic universe which indicates a primeval combustion or "explosion". It suggests that there is a point to which all matter in the universe can be traced back to its original or common origin (so-called "Big Bang"). Out of the material of the stars, all substances we know on earth today —including our fleshy bodies—were formed. We could as well call every tree "stardust", refer to every rock as "stardust", and give every bird the generic name of "stardust".

If a scientist these days were to make a comment that, "Everything is the same: it's all stardust", another scientist would acknowledge the basic truth of his statement. But that statement, a hundred years ago, would not have been commonly accepted.

If we were to make a similarly unorthodox statement and say, "The observer is the observed", this would not appear to be so. Our currently common (due to our training or conditioning) way of appraising this proposition would be to say, "If I am the observer, and I observe a tree, I am not the tree!" But if the proposition were phrased, "The stardust is the stardust", the deeper meaning of the equation would be clearer; and by examining the content of this paraphrase, one can see that it points to the same conclusion as saying, "There is only stardust; everything is the same."

If I were to take a wide bowl, full of water, and dip a spoon into it, then ask a science student, "What is this?", she would logically reply, "A spoonful of liquid." That would be the label or name for the exhibit—just as "a human being" is the label for what you are. If I were to take another teaspoon, dip out a second portion and hold it alongside the first, its label would be "a different spoonful of liquid", or, alternately, a "separate spoonful". I might even switch to a tablespoon and dip out a bigger spoonful. If I were to name the first one "Me", and the second one "You", we could call this third one (by way of illustration) "God".

But what is the underlying common characteristic of all these spoonfuls of liquid? It is water. When these "separate" spoonfuls are released back into their common source of origination, the bowl, what was their condition prior to being labeled? They were all one—and the same—thing: undifferentiated water. In this reservoir, there could be no such distinguishing entities as "observer" and "observed". If there were any "observing" at all going on within the water, it would have to be one portion of the water observing itself as an associated portion of the water.

Therefore, the full implication of the proposal that "the observer is the observed" is that the observer which is observing "that" is none other than "that" in another (or different) form, observing itself.

The intuitive recognition, or realization, of the fundamental rightness of this cosmic, or universal, relationship (or, more rightly, principle) "frees from ignorance" and "makes clear the nature" of the truth of our actuality. It is "enlightenment".

However, we might say, enlightenment is as enlightenment does. Although Galileo's illumination changed him in no way except for his newly-aware perception, if he had ignored the importance of his insight, or realization, he would not have expressed himself as an enlightened scientist. If Einstein had said, "These intuitions cannot be true, because they are not entirely logical or indisputably rational", an unknown German would one day have retired from the patent office.

Although it still *appears* that the sun revolves around the earth, once you have recognized that this is simply ignorance, you do not persist in referring to the earth as "the center of God's universe". And once enlightened to the significance of the deep meaning of "the observer is the observed", you do not revert to the myopic question, "Then why do I seem to be separate from the tree?"

Where there has been penetrating clarity, such a question will not be seriously entertained. Any "me" which has the capacity to wonder about the universe is recognized to be nothing other than an aspect and expression of the universe.

Your consciousness which asserts that it is "conscious" of "consciousness" is nothing more than absolute consciousness in awareness of its very own presence. The stardust which this consciousness identifies as "you", standing in awe at the stardust of the galaxy, is the ineffable—embracing itself in its varied forms.

Even if we were to simply state that "You are that", it would merely compound the matter. When you acknowledge that *all* is that, every sense of division is recognized to be merely misperception.

That which is, is; it has no obligation to follow man's notion of what is rational. To comprehend that the observer is the observed is to witness the disappearance of the "observer", the "observed", and the "observing". That which remains is our own true nature. The "making clear" of our nature is enlightenment—"that which is" in comprehension of itself.

Once this comprehension is present, the false appearances fall away (are seen through) and thus the proposition is self-evident, similar to the way that a mathematical equation is self-proving.

Starting a Revolution

The most important single thing you can recognize about the human condition is this: for whatever reasons, we each "normally" evolve from childhood with the sense of being a separate individual, a particular "person", an autonomous "self".

It is obvious that, under this circumstance, we develop "self-interest": *primary* concern for the welfare of one human being before all others. It is evident that a self-*centered* focus inevitably results in selfish *behavior*. In a world in which each person's *priority* is to advance one's own interests, it is unavoidable that *conflict* will result.

A world in conflict is not a stable or secure environment in which to live: it is difficult to make practical plans for the future, where unpredictable disruption is virtually certain. Therefore—even though our own selfish behavior may be contributing to the potential for destructive developments—we recognize that it is in our own self interest to encourage cooperation.

The consequence of this contradictory dilemma, for most everyone, is a form of externalizing. We look out upon the world of self-important persons, or collective groups of such persons, and conclude that "they" are at the root of the problem. In our own self-concern, we ponder how we can encourage them to cooperate rather than compete.

The contrary option requires us to embark *ourselves* upon the course we advocate: to dispense with self-interest as *our* primary concern. It is a consequence of internalizing, of "looking within" and acknowledging that we have not yet relinquished self-centeredness *ourself*.

Where, do you suppose, we have the greatest prospect in convincing a person to eradicate selfish behavior: ourself, who comprehends its necessity; or another person, who may or may not be thoroughly convinced?

There is only one way in which you have definite assurance that selfishness will be reduced in the world. Once you have accomplished that, for yourself, you will be best qualified to instruct others in how it can be done.

There is a clear and continuing need for such instructors. Indeed, if there were such a thing as a social duty, it would be to labor in the vineyard uprooting selfishness. Your first obligation, then, would appear to be to discontinue externalizing and—with intensified focus—internally eradicate the self who persistently operates in a vacuum.

But how can the self eradicate the self—rationally, a contradiction? Could it be possible that our earliest assumption, that we even *exist* as a separate self, is fundamentally a misapprehension? Some aver that our earliest condition of consciousness—before we *considered* our "self"—was without any perception of self or not-self. It is, further, alleged this primal consciousness is the platform upon which our subsequent sense of self arises. In the same manner in which that sense of self has arisen, it can again subside. In other words, they say, the assumption of self existence is not entirely necessary to the function of operative consciousness.

If this is so, if our consciousness can operate without the perception of a "self" or non-self ("other"), this could have a profound effect on our self-conscious behavior, couldn't it?

To discover for oneself whether or not such an operative form of consciousness is a practical possibility, as some of sound mind have claimed, would seem to merit more of our attention than that directed toward fruitless externalizing.

Were we to discover for ourselves such a possibility, perhaps we might *then* have some effect on the "me" against "them" mindset among our neighbors.

Who Is God?

Due to our divisive (subject-object) habit of thought, the average person tends to envision God in two particular ways: as an entity unto itself; and, as standing apart from oneself. Thus, the traditional depiction of God as Jehovah, "up there" somewhere, to whom one raises one's eyes in supplication like a teenager asking dad for the car keys. Contemporary references to God as "Goddess" are the same kind of thinking, merely modified.

"Who sees not God everywhere", as Meister Eckhart said, "sees God nowhere." If the Almighty is indeed everywhere, that must include where you are standing. In other words, one who recognizes the nature of the Absolute recognizes that God is one's own personage. But it is not to say that the Absolute is confined to any particular personage. The shrub outside of your window is no less God. The realization is not that you are God alone, but that you are—along with all else that is—*God*. To suppose that you were God alone would be to suppose that God is a singular entity, with the capacity to stand apart from other entities. Such is a notion which many orthodox religionists hold, which prohibits them from recognizing, and acknowledging, their own identity as God.

No one is more—or less—Godly than you.

Science as Spirituality

If it could be proven that there is an intelligence operating in the universe that is superhuman (the dictionary defines this word as "divine"), it ought to put to rest the question which heretofore has been resolved only by faith. If scientific proof could be cited, would this not affect the very behavior of the man-in-the-street? No: not if such evidence was indifferently noted and casually ignored.

But the evidence has not gone away; nor is it being ignored by those who recognize its significance.

Superhuman intelligence, by its definition, is not limited by human standards. Humans are constrained by such relative considerations as, for example, time and space; humans are not accorded such exalted descriptions as omniscient, omnipresent or omnipotent. But some scientists have long suspected that there is an intelligent hand-print on the canvas of reality which is other than—and far surpasses—the human alone.

Physicists speak of "locality" and "nonlocality". A *locus* is a place: it has a particular relationship to space; and a location can change with time. Cause and effect, too, are related to time and space: a cue ball, which is *here*, "now" strikes a billiard ball, which is *there*, "then" deflecting it into a side pocket. The cue ball is said to be the *cause* of an *effect* on the billiard ball: a "local" event has transpired.

The best way in which to translate "nonlocality" is to say that events in this category are not confined to a relationship in time or space. Put another way, nonlocality is transcendent of locality, similar to the way that the omnipotent would have to be transcendent of cause-and-effect.

Physicist David Bohm, as a consequence of his quantum research, began to sense a nonlocal reality at the base of our physical universe. A development in physics had made it clear that an observer (experimenter) cannot be considered to be objectively isolated from the observed (experiment): in other words, an experiment is not unaffected by the experimenter. Indeed, physics had gone so far as to conclude, as a result of laboratory experiments, that the outcome of an experiment can depend upon the intent of the physicist's investigation. If the cause (physicist's intent) cannot be conclusively separated from the effect (experimental outcome), what are the broader implications for assumptions based on "locality"?

In 1959, David Bohm read his first book authored by the sage Krishnamurti. This initiated a series of dialogues between him and Krishnamurti (such as that published as *The Ending of Time*). By 1974, Bohm had (co-)authored a paper entitled "On the Intuitive Understanding of Nonlocality as Implied by Quantum Theory".

"Parts", said the theoretical physicist, "are seen to be in immediate connection...extending ultimately and in principle to the entire universe. Thus one is led to a new notion of *unbroken wholeness* which denies the classical idea of analyzability of the world into separately and independently-existent parts..."

Bohm's earlier writings along these lines inspired another physicist, John Bell, the author of Bell's Theorem. Bell initially set out to disprove the principle of nonlocality, but his mathematical conclusions actually supported Bohm's premise. However, though proof, it was merely on paper.

The mechanics of the calculations in Bell's Theorem lent themselves to laboratory experiments—most notably one in 1982 performed by physicists in Paris.

Because the description of such experiments can become so technical as to be opaque, the following will be so oversimplified that it may contain some omissive errors. However, various scientific reports of this material are available for you to verify at your local library (such as the article I will later quote).

Suppose that you simultaneously fired off, in different directions, "paired" photons. By paired, we mean that one of them, say, was negatively charged, while its twin was positively charged. Let us say that, mid-flight, the polarity of one of the photons was mechanically switched. This change should not affect the other photon, causally, since both are racing away in entirely different directions.

And, yet, the remaining photon will simultaneously react to the identity switch of its twin—by instantly reversing its own polarity.

Such a supernatural occurrence—as that demonstrated to be physical actuality just twenty-seven years ago—can have only one reasonable explanation, in terms of "locality" or normal causality:

somehow the first photon communicated its change of state to the second photon.

However, in our known portion of the universe, anything which moves (or is transmissible)—within the confines of relative time and space—is limited to an upward speed. Not anything, in the natural world, can be "propagated" at faster than the speed of light, according to a fundament of physics. Therefore, any earthly message which is transmitted between subatomic particles could be communicated, over a distance, at no more than 186,000 miles per second.

Twelve years ago (May 1997), the experiment was repeated, this time outside of a laboratory. Given the minuscule size of a subatomic particle, any interactions over a mile or so apart are akin to "universal" distances. The experiment was conducted by a physics team at the University of Geneva, who effected the phenomenon at a distance of approximately seven miles.

"Measurements at the two sites", says the Encyclopedia Britannica Online (Year in Review: 1997), "showed that each photon 'knew' its partner's state in less time than a signal traveling at light speed could have conveyed the information—a vindication of the [nonlocality] theory of quantum mechanics (but a problem, for some, for theories of causation)."

Without speculating about an omnipresent field of omniscience that is transcendent of cause-and-effect, it can at least be said that it has been proven to be a fact of life that an unearthly intelligence is present in our physical sphere.

How many people do you know (you, of course, excepted) who are aware of this scientific—not "merely" spiritual—truth? By its very nature, such information will be sequestered to the science page of the Daily Times: the copy editor is saving the 34-point red italics for the Second Coming of Christ.

There is another reason—aside from its obscuration in technical jargon—that the man-in-the-street will not be aware of paranormal discoveries (this, and more yet to come). Such powerful information is co-opted by the military. As I write this, physicists in government research facilities, of the major powers, are siphoning this research into a system for the transmission of codes (negative and positive photons can represent the zeros and ones of binary encoding, and changes in their polarity can signal a message).

But there is an even more critical reason why such information will be overlooked or dismissed, even though it can no longer be categorized as mere conjecture. If there is indeed a supernatural force or intelligence, it is not unreasonable to suppose that it forms "an immediate connection" between every particle (and antiparticle) throughout the realm of space and time, "nonlocally": "extending", as Bohm put it, "ultimately and in principle to the entire universe". It would connect the observer (me) and the observed (you) in an "unbroken wholeness which denies the classical idea…of…separately and independently-existent parts".

Do we live that way, with a recognition and acknowledgement—unequivocally—that this is the actual, physical condition of our biosphere ? Or do we ignore this truth, even when it is proven?

The Beat Goes On

These little brown ants have finished their siesta of some one and a half hours, which began about noon. It's shadier and cooler now. The tentacle has reached out again from the handful of mounded sand that surrounds the entry to their earthen village, and it stretches north to south along the path's edge. They follow one fallen stalk of grass after another, on a microcosmic single-lane freeway. At any given moment, there are about six moving bodies per inch of route, and the route stretches for five or six feet before you lose sight of it from your chair. Given their tiny, relative size this must be a foot journey of many miles in each direction. They are travelling fast enough that it is difficult to follow any particular individual by eye, and so each ant presumably travels many roundtrips per day; none of them appear, from here, to be overweight. You cannot discern that they are carrying any cargo in either direction; these hundreds of commuters are continually encountering one another head on, along a wire-thin stalk of grass, sometimes climbing over each other; given their speed, we humans would doubtless find this cursingly stressful.

You cannot help but wonder what is the source of the direction for their ordered, cooperative and coordinated behavior. Their communal energy is directed to, and from, the cool and dark subterranean mecca, and you would like to be able to look down in there and try to possibly make sense of what is going on. But you could not, even with delicate scientific instruments, unearth and cross-section this community and expect that its organic mysterium would meanwhile remain intact. Unfortunately, when man observes, man inevitably affects that which is observed.

There is, in truth, no observer which can be apart or disconnected from that which is observed. For as long as we view the mystery of existence as a question which can be posed and answered by the questioner, as subject to object, we cannot be one with, or wholly involved in, the question. Asking "Who am I?" is to irreparably sever the "I" from the "Who". There is no "I", there is no "Who", there is only being. The "Who" does not issue forth the "I", and the "I" does not return to the "Who". That consciousness which we know as a fragment—the personal self—can never know the consciousness which is wholly unfragmented, or "universal"...the consciousness which transcends individuated intelligence and is your true self and that of the ant.

Who Says 'That Thou Art'?

The teachings of nondualism have been with us at least as long as perhaps the earliest written language.   The Vedas (of India), recorded before 1500 B.C., were an oral tradition before then. ("Veda" is Sanskrit for "to know", Truth being the implied knowledge.)   The celebrated Upanishads ("secret doctrine" or teachings) were one part of the Vedic literature.

The subject of these writings is the ultimate, universal and single underlying reality which is termed Absolute.   Such wisdom teachings are referred to as Vedanta, which means "the end of knowledge"; that is, complete ultimate clarity regarding the nature of the Absolute. The Sanskrit word used to convey this sense, or "knowledge", of the presence ("always already here") is *advaita*, which means "not two": non-dual.

The earliest teacher of advaita, of pronounced historical importance, was Shankara (788-820 A.D.). His yoga ("yoke", or way) was *jnana*, "self-knowledge" or Self-awareness: being aware of one's true nature, or identity.   (An enlightened person is known, in Sanskrit, as *jnani*: an unawakened person as *ajnani*—a being "not".) Shankara's teaching (in Sanskrit) was "tat tvam asi": That thou art.

The Vedanta advaita teachings of Shankara were basically not different than those of Siddhartha Gautama (563-483 B.C.), the Buddha (Sanskrit for "the awakened"). After six years of ascetic disciplines, the former prince surrendered to "not knowing" and was enlightened at 35, without recourse to a teacher (guru: "who points the way").

Meanwhile, the teachings of the Tao ("way", or path) were exemplified in the *Tao Te Ching*, reputedly written by Lao-Tsu, whose birth is given as around 600 B.C.   Taoist emphasis on surrender to "what is" is relevant to the non-separative enlightenment of advaita. China's teaching successor to Lao-Tsu was considered to be Chuang-Tzu.

When Bodhidharma brought Buddha's teachings to China in the 5th century A.D., it wedded with the Tao as what we know today as Zen. A major figure in Chinese Zen was Hui-neng (638-713 A.D.), an illiterate woodcutter. He was followed by a lineage of Zen masters, as Zen migrated to Japan in the 14th Century, such as Hakuin. The writings of D.T. Suzuki and Alan Watts have been primary in introducing Zen to the West.

Padmasambhava was the patriarch of Buddhism in Tibet, in the 8th Century. The nondual teachings of Tibetan Buddhism are embodied as Dzochen (zo-*chen*); also spelled Dzogchen.

Meanwhile, the most enigmatic of Eastern teachers of the nondual presence (who may have been influenced by the earlier, historic teachings), Jesus lived and died. His perspective was at least understood by the German monk Meister Eckhart (1260-1327 A.D.), whose sermons have rarely been translated accurately. The Church regards him as a "mystic"—enlightenment being a forbidden term.

In Islam, the nondual teachings are most readily found in the poetry of Rumi and Hafiz (Persia: 1207-73 A.D. and 1325-90 A.D.); and are categorized as Sufi (rather than Muslim).

The late 1800's saw the birth of several sages of nondualism of whose words (and existence) we can be confident; such has even been preserved in film and on tape.

Krishnamurti may be the most perplexing of these, but probably none has ever reached a wider audience.

Shankara's true successor has been Ramana Maharshi. He is primarily the fountainhead of today's panel of teachers in the West. He is also probably the most direct, due to the profound depth of his awakening.

Among his "lineage" are H.W.L. Poonja, who died in India recently; his American "disciple", the woman known as Gangaji; and her follower here in Ojai, John Sherman.

A contemporary of Ramana, Nisargadatta lived in India; his primary disciple has been Ramesh Balsekar (also of India).

Today, there are a number of teachers here in the U.S. which are sharing a common message of nonduality, such as: Francis Lucille, Satyam Nadeen, Steven Harrison, Eckhart Tolle, Adyashanti, and Toni Packer (and in England, Tony Parsons)—to name a few.

The sources—old and new—are readily available… plentifully!

Tiger By The Tail

Our world, of reality, appears to be an organism which symbiotically integrates myriad disparate, yet quintessential, parts. We each normally think of ourself as one of these inter-dependent parts, somewhat like an atom in a cosmos that we liken to a vast molecule. Viewing ourself to be a "part" of the cosmos, we are ineluctably condemned to be "apart" from the very cosmos that we determine that we are "in", in the same way that we consider an electron to be "apart" from the atom that it is "in". (Such typical "logic" is in disregard of the fact that when an electron is truly apart from an atom, it ceases to have existence.)

We hold the idea that while the cosmos is entirely necessary for the presence of my particular being, my particular being is not entirely necessary for the presence of the cosmos. In other words: the cosmos is limitless, I am not. Put another way, the deep feeling is that the cosmos is one thing, I am something else.

The consideration that you are a non-essential part of a quintessential whole is bound to present a psychic quandary, however unconsciously. Because of a subliminal sense of being organically incomplete, our sensitivities often lead us to seek a "union with god"; that is, to experience what is poetically referred to as "cosmic consciousness".

And, indeed, serious contemplation of the meaning of wholeness —indivisibility—makes it evidently clear that any sense of separateness which we harbor is a contradiction of truth, if there is any universal truth in wholeness. (Which even the word *universe* attests to.) In other words, in a cosmos which manifests consciousness, a supposed absence of "cosmic consciousness" is an absence of complete (whole) consciousness. And so, vaguely aware that our personal feelings of separateness are a contradiction to the truth which apparently abounds in the whole universe, we are naturally motivated toward ending this disturbing contradiction.

However, that humans find themselves generally divorced from the actuality of Truth—"cosmic consciousness" not notably common—is not likely by chance. Truth is undeniable; it is hard. Its unequivocal message is hard for man to "hear"; it is even harder to acknowledge, to assent or acquiesce to. To be "unconscious" (or "unawake") is more common, in the same way that it is common for man to normally seek comfort.

And, yet, we find discomfort in our separation, our isolation and the feeling of loneliness which it engenders.

However, while one may reasonably be motivated to seek that radical shift in perspective, or "consciousness", which affirms that one's true identity is "universal oneness", there are considerations which may tend to temper that motivation. These are considerations which are not often addressed in "spiritual literature".

Basically, the radical departure in consciousness, which is traditionally referred to as "enlightenment", is a profound realization of the "non-dual" nature of actuality. It is, in other words, a thorough-going ending of the personally-held notion of separateness; conversely, it is an irrefutable recognition of the indivisibility of all that exists.

In essence, enlightenment is a way of seeing—that is, of experiencing and relating—to which we had previously been unaccustomed. To be more specific, it is to comprehend as false the conventional view that one is a subject in a world surrounded by dissociated objects.

To truly see the false as false is revelation of the ineffable truth. However, we cannot over-emphasize, here, what is meant by *see*. It does not mean (as one sense of the word is defined) "to obtain a mental impression of". *See* shares the root of *say* ("to express, declare"), and is synonymous with *perceive* (Latin: "Take hold of"), which shares its root with *have*. To perceive is "To be *sensibly* aware of; to sense, as to *feel.*"

In other words, it could be stated that this is a seeing which "takes hold" and expresses, or declares, a presence perceived by the senses—a seeing that is *felt* in the gut (or, if you will, in the heart). It is not merely an *impression* which is registered in the mind.

The consequence of this authentic perception of actuality is a shattering of the ego—not temporarily, as in the *reforming* of the ego, but persistently, in that it is the dissolution of the ego.

Put another way, the genuine realization of nonduality as fact triggers an undeniable shift in perspective, "a change in consciousness". Such a change in perspective, or consciousness, mandates a consequent change in behavior: in the same way that one previously acted in relation to how one saw the world fragmentarily, one now acts out of one's perception of universal indivisibility.

Obviously, an unprecedented change in one's view of the cosmos, and the subsequent effect on one's moment-by-moment behavior, will generally percuss on the way one has been living one's life—in terms of such things as lifestyle, relationships, goals, activities, patterns, etc.

This is not to say that foreshadowed changes will be either negative or positive, but it is to say that there will likely be resounding changes.

And not every person, it must be acknowledged, is necessarily receptive to the prospect of provocative changes in their customary life. This possibility needs to be contemplated, therefore, by each spiritual seeker. For if there is not the implicit willingness to follow wherever the lamp of revelation may lead, there will not be a capacity for surrender of attachment that is the very essence of assimilation in "oneness".

You're Not Responsible

Comprehend that you are still living with a pre-Copernicus mindset.

A clergyman in a cathedral, in 1543 Copernicus published a treatise postulating that the sun does not appear to rise and set as a consequence of it revolving around the earth (the latter of which the Church presumed to be the center of the universe); to the contrary, he asserted, the earth revolves around the sun, which is stationary, and it is the earth's axial rotation which provides the appearance of a rising and setting sun.

Nearly ninety years passed before *Galileo's* interest in physics and telescopes resulted in publication (in 1632) of experimental verification of Copernicus' revelation (followed by Galileo's trial before Rome's inquisition the following year).

Like the pre-Copernicans who were without doubt that the earth graced the hub of the universe, most people today still suppose that "cause and effect" is such a truism that it is a physical fact.

This was disproved, now more than 40 years ago!

Most people today would recognize the name of Alexander Graham Bell of the telephone, but not the name of Irish physicist John Stewart Bell. But the latter, in 1964, did for physics as much as Copernicus did for astronomy. And, as recently as 2004, Swiss physicist Nicholas Gisin established the revelation of Bell, as firmly as did Galileo that of Copernicus.

In sum, to quote physicist Nick Herbert:

> "Bell's Theorem* states, in effect, that after two [subatomic] particles interact in a conventional way, then move apart outside the range of the interaction, the particles continue to influence each other *instantaneously* via a real connection, which joins them together with undiminished strength no matter how far apart they may roam....

---

* A theorem is not a theory; it's been experimentally proven.

"Bell's Theorem says not merely that superluminal connections are *possible*, but that they are *necessary* to make our kind of universe work...."

"Bell's Theorem shows that...things are hooked together by an invisible, underlying network of superluminal connections."

Another scientist, Steve Hagen, adds:

"Though we conceive of a 'here' and a 'there', such conception is not supported...by experimental results. The 'two' are intimately related, and a change in 'one' *immediately* creates a change in the 'other'...of the very fabric of time and space itself."

Physics professor Lee Smolin:

"This means that the entangled nature of the quantum state reflects something *essential* in the world.... This makes it one of those rare cases in which an experiment [such as Gisin demonstrated over 31 miles, likened—given the relative size of particles—to 31 light-years across space] can be interpreted as a test of a philosophical principal [viz., nonduality]....

"We—who live in the universe, and aspire to understand it—are then inextricably part of the *same* entangled system."

Physicist Shimon Malin:

"Such a connection takes place because both events [the cosmic interaction by two—or more—particles] form a *single* creative act, a single '*actual entity*,' arising out of a common field of potentialities."

And Henry Stapp:

> "The important thing about Bell's Theorem is that it puts the dilemma posed by quantum phenomena *clearly* into the realm of *macroscopic* ["visible"] phenomena… [showing] that our ordinary ideas about the world are somehow profoundly deficient *even* at the macroscopic level."

Gary Zukov:

> "Bell's Theorem tells us that there is no such thing as 'separate parts'. All of the 'parts' of the universe are connected in an intimate and immediate way… 'Commonsense' ideas are inadequate even to describe macroscopic *events*—events of the *everyday* world!" [e.g., cause and effect]

Renowned physicist David Bohm:

> "We can say that *inseparable* quantum *interconnectedness* of the whole universe is the *fundamental* reality… any attempt to assert the *independent* existence of a 'part' would deny this unbroken wholeness… This form of description cannot be closed on the large scale, any more than on the small scale…. This means that our *notions* of space and time will have to *change* in a fundamental way….

> "Notion of the constitution of the world out of separately-existent parts is turned upside down…. There are *indivisible* links of action between each object, and its environment."

This, then, is the physical *reality*, the actual *fact* of the universe that *we* live in.

There is no such *actuality*—throughout time and space, as we know it—as cause that is apart from effect.

Most people today are basing their assumptions on pre-Bell doctrine; just as most people, before 1543, based their assumptions on pre-Copernicus doctrine.

But in terms of how you live your life, based on the assumptions you are making, the former is more important than the latter.

Will ninety years pass before you incorporate the supportive scientific evidence of what the sages have maintained for some 3,500 years: "You are *not* the doer"?

The Needle's Eye

In investigating a matter, we typically consider its "history"—that is, what can evidently be known of it, up to this moment. In considering the phenomenon of human spiritual realization, most everyone becomes acquainted, in some manner, with the legendary exemplary activities (some, possibly, more legend than truth) of various spiritual "masters" or (presumably) inspired "religious" teachers. Few of us, in other words, have not been touched or enthused by the biographies of exceptional, sagacious forefathers.

His first sight of a holy man disturbed the insulated prince, Siddhartha Gautama. Jesus was impressed with Isaiah, Elijah, the baptist John and others. Ramana Maharshi was inflamed, as a youth, by a written account of the lives of saints. Krishnamurti made occasional, admiring references to the Buddha and Jesus; et cetera.

Those whom we each refer to as "holy" were exceedingly uncommon people; that is *why* few people do not know at least a few details of who St. Francis was or who Mother Teresa was. It is striking, to anyone who diligently reviews the reports, not only how uncommonly these religious figures acted, but how similar their uncommon behavior has been. In other words, one need not investigate these biographical cameos very far before one senses a common "message" (but not even, necessarily, in their *message*)— in the way they lived their *lives*.

The most apparent message, which first stands out (whether verbally "preached" or nonverbally demonstrated), is that a profound spiritual awakening radically changes one's "normal" behavior. Gautama left his fief, never again to resume it. Jesus left his home, never again to have another. Maharshi left *everything* behind him, except the loin cloth he frequently wore. Krishnamurti renounced his imposed, appointed position. And so on, through biographies which line many shelves.

The dramatic message seems abundantly clear: exposure to profound illumination is exposure to definite risk of radical transformation of one's material existence or security. The willingness to risk is not separate from the openness to awakening. One who is not willing to take this risk—of possessions, career, family, security, stature, future and past—has encountered the first barrier, the eye of the needle.

The primary barrier to spiritual discovery is fear. Where it cannot be dissolved, it will be impassable. This is elemental.

Specifically, the fear which dominates is that of the future (or, conversely, the fear of not maintaining a future). Fear and any idea of future time are unmistakably wedded. This irremediable relationship has likely been the immediate insight of every saint who has come to the confrontation with risk. Fear is insurmountable, as long as the future gapes around it.

This pivotal recognition propels the adventurer into a seminal contemplation of the alleged property of time. The only prospect for surpassing the limitations of fear is to somehow transcend the bondage of time. And this is precisely what each spiritual discoverer has indicated. Fear does not die *in* the future, it dies *with* the future—as the future is laid to rest.

To pierce the heart of the dragon of time is the real function of "sitting quietly, doing nothing". Stillness, utter stillness, is the antidote to the compulsion of volition, to the bondage of chronic activity. It is to permit one's future to wither and die of neglect, as alarming as that may seem. A sudden unanticipated (even unintended) lurch, and the chain falls aside. Buddha arises from under the Bo tree, Jesus arrives on the shores of Galilee, Maharshi sits outside the temple, Krishnamurti lights his parting bonfire at the Order of the Star.

Not everyone finds themselves prepared to turn their face toward the immaterial and their back on the material. We each do what we do. But the dissolution of conflict is to see choice through to its *ending*, to be unequivocally consistent in one's interpretation of truth. It is only in this way that truth *can* be interpreted. And only the firmament of truth is worthy of our exploration. In this, too, our mentors concur.

The Truth Shall Set *You* Free

The pandemic disease that afflicts the seeker of spiritual truth is inconsistency.

If one affirms that "God is all there is", and that is a truth, then one embodies this truth or else lives in untruth. To those who are *sincere*, such is more than a rhetorical statement: "All is One."

If *That* is *all* that *is*, That is all that is *real*; anything perceived "other" than That is unreal—therefore, not *truth*.

If That *is* all there is, there are not two things: there is *only* That. Therefore, That is an *indivisible* whole. An indivisible whole is not subject to partition: *all* is That.

There is, therefore, no God (or That, for that matter) that can *stand apart* from anything else. *This* is all That (or God).

There is no "part" of it that is "greater" than any "other" part; there is no *separate* Entity.

To deny this obvious implication of "God is all there is" is to live in untruth, *inconsistency*.

The One of which you speak is a one without a two. This Oneness neither "knows" nor "cares", as a remote knower or carer. There is no *separate* place in Oneness in which oneness has taken up a distinct location from which to know, care, intervene, intercede, instruct or any other privately definable action. Being in no way relative, it does not stand out somewhere in relationship to the human condition, nor any human in particular.

To affirm truth on one hand and live untruth on the other hand can only lead to confusion and (perceived) suffering.

To live the truth *consistently* is an end to confusion and suffering.

If God *is* all that is, "you" are God. If *this* is *not* true, God is *not* all that is.

Which shall you affirm? Which shall you *live* as the *truth*?

As recently as 1914, the last "wild" Indian was taken into captivity, a Yana from central northern California. His parents, circa 1850, were without any general exposure to the following:

They had no refrigeration, no stoves, no matches (though they knew how to start a fire). They had no frozen, canned, packaged or "convenience" foods. No garden vegetables or orchard fruit, no livestock or poultry, no milk or dairy products, no candy, pastry or soft drinks. When available, they had fish and game (broiled, boiled, smoked or dried), herbs, tubers, nuts, seeds, berries, acorn bread, herb tea, water and sometimes salt.

They had no alcohol, no stimulants (coffee, tea, cocoa, etc.), no recreational drugs; occasionally tobacco, when bartered from the far south.

No books, magazines, newspapers, comics, novels, videos or movies; few toys, games and amusements; occasional "music", song, dance or storytelling. Possibly a dog; no cat, canary, goldfish, etc. Little chit-chat, gossip, debate and witticism. No notepads, signs, instruction manuals or maps. No school, church, hospital, post office or bank. No stores, markets or pharmacies.

No horse, wheeled vehicle, skateboard or pavement. No tent, canteen, compass, hatchet or bear-free campsite. No metal tools, no hardware. No gun, fishhook or steel trap.

No electric light, no flashlight, no electric blanket, answer phone, clock or calendar.

No organized sciences, technologies, professions, industries, commerce, institutions, judicial system or political parties.

And with all of that which they didn't have, these were not a restless, disturbed, aggressive, disease-ridden people.

Five-Word Key

These five words of yours are the key: "there cannot be any separation".

As Krishnamurti put it, "Where there is division, there is conflict." (Sometimes he also said it this way: "Where there is conflict, there is division.")

At the time that I read this, I was examining the conflict in my life. Everywhere that I could identify conflict, I could see that some sort of divisiveness was involved.

Conversely, by being aware of the divisive nature of the thought process itself ("This is good. *This* is *not* good."), I could see where conflict arose ("I am a good person. You are a bad person.").

It became obvious to me that if I was to end conflict in my life, division (divisiveness) must end. I began to ask myself (almost as an on-going meditation), "What would it mean if there was *no division*?"; that is, if in fact the *actuality* of our *existence* was that there was no such *condition* as division.

I could see how the thought process created duality. The thought that "I exist"—as a "me", a self as a separate entity—is inevitably followed by the thought that "All else, that exists in the world, is *not* me." "You", for example, are not me. So, there is "me" as opposed to "you"; there is *my* self and *your* self—a latent premise for eventual conflict.

So, if the separative dualistic notion is the basis of conflict, how could the separative perspective be transcended? According to the "spiritual" material that I was reading at the time, by *non* duality.

What I thought this meant, at the time, was "union", or unity. If I think of "you" and "I" as "one" (or "God" and "I" as "One"), doesn't this end separation? No; because it's divisible. 1+1=2; but 2 is merely a "union" of 1+1: 2 is *always* convertible back to the separation of 1+1.

The Sanskrit word for nondual, I learned, is advaita (dating back 3,500 years to the Vedas): its literal meaning, "not two". In fact, the Vedas go on to explain that the deepest teaching of nonduality is: "not two; not one". In other words, the 2 here is not a *reality*; *nor* is the 1+1 that comprise the 2.

Pondering the message of Vedanta, it became apparent that "union" (two) is not the intended condition to be *realized*: *not* two; *not* "unity".

What, then? "One"? No: "not one". Where there is a one, a separate entity (such as "me"), there is always the implication that something exists *beside* (or, *outside* of) that one (such as "you"; or, "*not* me").

The teaching is saying that *not one* exists as a reality (therefore, 'two' neither; because there are no 'ones' to comprise the 'two'). The pointer "*not* two, *not* one" is saying that there is not any thing which exists—at all—*as a separate, independent* entity!

Wow, I realized, this is what "no division" *really* means: not that there is no separation between "you" and "me", but that "you" *and* "me" are merely separative *distinctions*; "you" and "me" do not *exist* except as definitional ideas.

Therefore, "unity" plays no part in the enlightened realization of the truth of nonduality; there is—where division is not presumed from the beginning—not a one and another one, to be connected as a two.

It also became clear that "not one" means that there is not even some thing or entity or form that *replaces* "you" and "me"; that would simply be a subtle substitution. For example, if we say that "you" and "me" are the "Father", we are merely establishing another "independent" *one*.

Where there is *no* division, no *thing* exists; form-less-ness. What is formless is clearly indivisible.   I came to understand what Buddhists refer to as the Void; nothing-ness.

It is out of this nothingness ("not even one") that the *appearance* of "separate" entities—ones—arise. Though these "ones" appear, they appear from (rather, in) the condition of no division, nonduality.   Having their origination in the nondual, they never were separate, or apart, from their beginning. Thus, they need not be artificially "unified".

What is the consequence of the realization of the actuality called nonduality? It is the disappearance of the idea of being a separate "self"; or, more yet, their being *any* separate "selves"—"yours" or "mine".

So, the key is now held: "there cannot be any separation". Any!

Contemplate what this *means*. The teachings (all) tell us that the actuality of our existence is that there is *no division* whatsoever any where at any time. And that the awakening to the significance of this truth is the long-sought ending of conflict and confusion.

It is also the ending of seeming identity of a "you" and a "me" (or any "others"). Therefore, it is also the *end* of the *search* for "unity", since there is no *dis*unity in the formless actuality, to begin with.

While you are reading this, a galactic bombardment of subatomic particles—the virtually massless neutrino—is passing through your body. Not just through your body, but through the core of the earth, out the other *side* and on through any other material it encounters. Though unseen, unfelt, unbeknown and unexperienced, this invasional radiation is your continual lifetime reality.

This can be an analogous metaphor for the penetration, of all that exists, by the infinite presence of being.

Suppose a neutrino were to cease its relentless journey, stop dead in the middle of your living room, and expand to the perimeter of the living room—and beyond. Walking into the living room, you are completely permeated by the presence of the neutrino, Ned. In fact, by its undeterrable nature, there is not anything in the living room which is not similarly inundated. In other words, not only everything within the room's space, but the space between things, as well, is totally and fully occupied, engulfed, by Ned.

The outline of your body, your skin, "contains" Ned, on the inside; and is "contained" by Ned, on the outside: there is no filament between you and the neutrino, that is not also saturated by Ned. In fact, except for being a superimposition on Ned, there is nothing at all to set you apart from Ned.

And everything else in the room is likewise merely a form in something which—unrestrained by any obstacles—is unconfined to form. The lamp and Ned are no more apart than the lamp is separated from the space surrounding it. When you reach over to turn the lamp on, Ned's "arm" moves through Ned's "space" to connect with Ned's "lamp". When Ned's "light" appears, it dispels Ned's "darkness".

But whether you connect with the lamp by touch, or not, you are already unknowingly connected to the lamp—and to everything else in the room.

In fact, unaware in the meanwhile that Ned has expanded beyond the unrestraining confines of the room and has completely filled the visible universe, you are insensibly connected with the furtherest galaxy.

But Ned, with its infinite capacity, has diffused beyond even the *visible* universe, to that expanse which we can but conclude disappears into infinity. So, as it happens, your own Nedness is in no way disconnected even from that which stretches eternally into the Unknown.

Now, no matter where you go, what you do, or your interconnections with other Nednesses, Ned is inescapable. You don't have to go prospecting for Ned; Ned would be the prospector, the prospecting and the embodiment of the discovered. Your mother-in-law, coming to visit you, would be Ned passing through Ned to arrive at Ned for an indefinite stay with Ned. When your friend asks you, "What occurred while your wife's mother visited", you can say, "Nothing really! But remind me, sometime, to tell you about Ned."

Your friend will be surprised (perhaps startled) to learn that *she* is no different from your mother-in-law (or your lamp) than the form of an ice cube is, in water. Be tactful; and don't be surprised if your friend doubts it. But then, that's Ned, doing what Ned does.

Forever Yours, Ned

P.S. You are not a neutrino ("neutral"), because a neutrino is *also* Ned. Ned is what has been characterized as the omnipresent

God; or the universal Essence of Being—or other more-or-less confusing names; self/Self, for example: or "you" and "me".

<hr />

In a Rut

There is a fundamental *idea* which you cling to. When you *cling* to anything, you cannot be "free".

You have a notion that freedom (or realization) has something to do with "betterment". That when you "improve" to some imagined standard, that you will have reached the peak, the zenith that you imagine represents the "highest point". This supposed improvement can represent an increase in knowledge, or "wisdom". Or an improvement in one's character or behavior or "outlook on life", one's attitude—such as learning to be kinder, trying to be more understanding, controlling impatience, etc., etc. You suppose that such improvements in one's person is what elevates one to that zenith.

If this "ever upward" bias was merely an idea, it could cause little harm. But it is an idea, a fixation, which you cling to—and insist it must be part of "realization". You have been told that this notion is false, but you will not abandon it.

Because you presume that realization is a process in time, an evolutionary or accretionary process which takes time, you envision this as a "path" along which you continue your improvement until the improvements pay off in realization. Perhaps you have puzzled over Krishnamurti's statement: Truth is a pathless land. Path-*less*. No path. No progression.

You have heard and read that it is purely a matter of subtraction, *not addition*; not accumulation—of merit, knowledge, time, momentum or any other thing.

You have heard and read that what is being sought is *here* (no path) *now* (no accumulation in time is involved).

You have heard and read that what is being sought—the "zenith"—is a condition in which the separate "person" ceases to be where one's identity resides. So, of what value is accumulation of merit, wisdom, etc., to a *non-existent* person?

You are telling me that you perceive an obstacle on the path. Your idea of a path is itself the obstacle. If the One is omni*present, your* path of improvement—which takes your focus *out* of the present —is leading you *away* from what can (in *this* moment) be seen!

....

Mother Teresa's Devil

The difference between true spirituality and religion is embodied in the difference between the Absolute perspective and the relative perspective. And also emphasized in the difference between first-hand, personal revelation and collective, institutionalized observance and ritual.

The root of the word *religion* is the same as the root of "refer": to associate in thought or meaning; that is, an abstract relationship. There must be—for a religious gathering to have cohesion—a generally agreed-upon common standard, belief or image. From this arises an external dictate, which must be able to appeal to the lowest common denominator among the adherents. The external dictation is through the form, in general, of an idol which is recognized by all, and given a name which humans can relate to as a person-ality (such as Jehovah). To anthropomorphize *God* (that's a title—like "it"—not a name) is to make it ("Him") seem to be less abstract, more approachable.

When this God-figure is given characteristics like humans (including a relative form), such a God is presumed or expected to have a human-like behavior: willfulness, jealousy, anger, forgiveness, etc. Among this God's attributes, such as desire, might then suppose to be a desire for human "welfare", as akin to a fatherly concern for his progeny. From this arises dictates of "appropriate behavior"; the promulgation of which—through fables such as the Garden of Eden—render religion as little more than moralistic mythology.

Built into this abject deification is a contradiction for which a doctrine of unsupportable belief is required. Since the purpose of this God is to reign superior, as the icon of the religious institution, He must also maintain *super*human attributes, such as miraculous power, infallibility, etc. As the idealized figure of a human-like being but transcendent of human weaknesses and sinfulness, an impossible standard is established toward which the parishioner is exhorted to aspire. However, no one can actually ever be "God-like", under the imposed circumstances—such as adhering to the God's dictums of perfect behavior. All that one can do is to contritely "worship" this almighty being and beg its forgiveness for one's *assumed* shortcomings. This is what one observes practically everyone else doing, and so it seems that the proper and correct thing to do is to have "faith" that this represents "righteousness". For those who do otherwise, there is a contradistinctive image of God to which that heathen can relate, the Devil. One can be assured of the Devil's instructive relevance, it can be assumed, for he would have had to have been a *creation* of the *Almighty*.

A conflicting God and Devil, a perfect superhuman and an imperfect superhuman, and the (opposing) destinations to their kingdoms in Heaven and Hell: such a divisive and fanciful construct requires an elaborate and dogmatic theology to provide assurance to bewildered followers.

Could such a *problematic* construct provide effective guidance in any meaningful arena of human activity? To one who discovers its falsity, at some point, could there be any reaction but painful dis-illusion-ment?

True spirituality is not second-hand convention: it is directly-experienced illumination. It is a revelation of the non-dual nature of our existent actuality, in the recognition of what is intimated in the word *omnipresent*. That which could be described as omnipresent would have to be every where, at once. Therefore, it would permeate all forms; and must then transcend "forms", and itself be beyond form; or "formless". It could in no way be a separate *entity*; its presence would be present in every of the forms, saturating even every *human*—saint and sinner alike. No one could possibly be apart from this omnipresent "God", this transcendent *and* imminent Being.

Yet, I have heard a college Professor of the Philosophy of Religion (and a Christian) offhandedly define omnipresence by saying that, "This just means that God can be wherever He wants to be, whenever He wants to be." No: *this* is a description of an anthropomorphized Deity who decides He wants to pop into one location as opposed to another, because—as God—he desires to be there to attend to his duties. No, the Omnipresent Reality is not some entity which supposes that it is some character called "God" who needs to be somewhere in particular to assure that it maintains control, in its role-playing.

Is it any wonder—with this remote, paternal Jehovah-like image —that even the most devout sense themselves estranged from their God seated far away in Heaven? Even Mother Teresa, it has now been revealed by her private writings, lamented, "Where is my faith? There is none. "

> "So many unanswered questions live within me; afraid to uncover them, because of the 'blasphemy'. … Did I make a mistake in surrendering blindly to the (church)? … .

"I am told God loves me.... If there be no God, there can be no 'soul'; if there is no soul, then Jesus, you also are not true....

"I (often) spoke as if my very heart was in love with God...you would have said, 'what hypocrisy.'

"Such deep *longing* for God, and...no faith...(Saving) souls holds no attraction. Heaven means nothing....

"I don't have Him."

Newsweek further reported, "Toward the end of her days...her troubled and sleepless condition gave rise to such concern that she was subjected to an exorcism."

Ironically, the *Devil* had no doubt of the personification of the Christian God.

- -

Three-Word Solution

Once again, when we say that "mind, thoughts or consciousness exists" we must bear in mind that every named thing "exists" only from the point of view of the *relative*.

Let us take, for example, as one of the "named things" (something which a word has been devised for): cold. The very naming of "cold"—as an existent, separate property—suggests that there is something *other* than cold, something which is *not* cold. *This* we conceive of, we posit to be "hot".

So, from a dualistic, *relative*, standpoint we think in terms of "cold/not cold" (or, "hot"). "Hotness", then, is merely an abstract idea: its meaning is in *relationship* to—*dependent on*—"coldness". And vice versa. Similarly, with all of the other (abstract) "named things"—such as the presumed conditions that we identify as "mind", "thought", "consciousness", etc. If we say these "exist", it supposes that there is another, relative condition: "no mind", "no thought", etc. To establish the "existence" of *any* thing, is to simultaneously establish its *non*-existence.

Where Absolute awareness is present—*non*-dual realization—such polarized designations disappear. Simply put, for the sage there is but one (indivisible) actuality: "Everything that *is*, is *That* (One infinite presence)."

So, "cold" is just a name for That, in one of its endless forms. "Hot" is just another name for That, in one of its endless manifestations.

Therefore, "cold" (as a *separate* reality) does not "exist", in actuality. *Nor* does "hot". All that (ever) exists is That—in its countless, different, ephemeral appearances.

Similarly, "mind"; "thought"; "consciousness"; and so on, through the list of *every* (designated, or conceived) thing.

Now: a person comes to the sage. All that this person is aware of is the *relative* reality. In order for the sage to speak with this person, she must resort to speaking in *relative* terms.

Thus, the sage says, "Your *mind* stands in the way of your enlightenment." From the *sage's* point of view, the mind does not even *exist* (as reality). In fact, the sage may proceed to say, "Realize that your mind does not exist: not any thing actually exists, except for one—the Absolute" (or Self, Brahman, God, etc.)

If you *understand* this, then you must ask, "Do *I* (the supposed possessor of the mind) exist?"

No; not from the perspective of Absolute awareness (enlightenment): not any thing is *actual* except the One ever-present "isness".

So, with awakening, the idea of being a separate "self" ceases as a *reality* (even though it may continue to be useful, practical, as a *relative* designation).

The seeker raises all of these questions (as above) because he believes that he is an "individual". When he recognizes that this is nothing more than an *appearance* (just as his "individual self" is, *in a dream*), these questions cease to arise! Peace results.

Tat tvam asi. *That. Thou. Art.* How much more simply could it be expressed? Does not every awakened master say just that? What *more* needs to be comprehended?

There is no "you" to whom mind, thought, consciousness could possibly *belong.* There is *only* That. And *That* is the true identity of all named things. "All" *includes* you!

False Leads

Evidently, you have spent many years investigating many various aspects of "spiritual" teachings. Like many who have done so, this appears to be with the desire to be in "direct contact" with the presence out of which our seeming existence unfolds—the "who am I, and why am I here?" question.

My investigation, like yours, included several well-known disciplines. All proved to be false leads—until (now) about 20 years ago.

The other teaching's brought "experiences" of "closeness" to that Absolute presence. All such experiences or "encounters" disappeared with time. As of the time I mentioned, I came to understand why these other teachings could not bring permanent samadhi, or clarity.

Without permanent samadhi, not only our searching continues, but our dissatisfaction continues (in fact, increases). As long as we continue to be "confused", all that we *do* is a product of that state of confusion. Our *first* responsibility to our self is to arrive at a state of spiritual clarity—permanent, self-evident and unequivocally beyond doubt.

A person who has this clarity will do his/her best to communicate it to you, to (likewise) release you from "bondage". The attempt to communicate it is all that this person can do. If the "teaching" falls on "ears that can hear", that is up to the hearer.

Your point of view, at this time, is that "something unique is out there, connected to us". Many of the disciplines you have studied have put it this way—erroneously.

This "something" (I generally use the word Absolute) is not "out there" anywhere, nor "in here" as its locus. It is ever present, every where, at every moment.

A teaching, or point of view, which establishes any kind of *distance*, for the ever-present actuality, must be false.

Krishnamurti once said, in effect: to find the truth, first see the false as the false.

The realization that is called self-realization is that you (as the self) are not now in any way (and never have been) *dis*connected from what you are seeking, the Absolute. Any teaching or viewpoint which indicates otherwise will not lead to the clarity called self-realization. Hence: since the seeker *is* what it is that is being sought—the immediate presence that is omnipresent—*any* rituals, rites, ceremonies, etc., are pointless activities.

The purpose of such activities is to ostensibly draw the Infinite nearer to the self. The Infinite cannot possibly *be* any nearer to the supplicant than it is at any and every moment already.

Such activities are, therefore, a *dis*traction. They will not lead to an "encounter" with this actuality which you cannot, for one moment, *escape*.

To see the false as the false, you need to lay aside all the search-oriented teachings, and focus on (contemplate) the reality that your presence and the Absolute presence cannot be other than the *same* presence.

This realization, this permanent clarity, is available to you, but not if what you want to do is to cling to your past schoolings.

This is not a matter of speculation or conjecture for me. If you want to investigate more deeply into this matter, I will try to be of assistance.

Doing Our Homework

A careful perusal of the vast amount of material available—from all spiritual traditions—reveals general patterns that appear rather consistently in the process of individual awakening. While these signposts do not present a pat formula to be prescriptively followed, they provide sufficient pointers that one need not attempt to reinvent the wheel.

The following is a mere skeletal outline of some, or all, of the developments which are often involved in accounts by individuals of their realization of their infinite nature. These processes are not "practices", whereby one attempts to "repeat this procedure exactly as instructed, or else you will fail to advance". (Notions that one will accrue merit with "practice" are invariably dismissed by those who have clearly awakened.) Instead, these processes are more akin to a form of contemplation in which consciousness is attentively, but passively, watchful.

Neither is it a "practice" in the sense that, with time, one "achieves higher levels of mastery". Rather than a cumulative, constructive process, it is a matter of *de*construction. For this reason, it need not be a lengthy development: for some, it has been a startling (if not explosive) awakening, occurring as an unheralded surprise in time, place or intensity.

Clearly, a "process of deconstruction" (as some of the realized have described it) is a matter of letting go, "surrender". When novices in Buddhism consider "severing attachments", they often initially assume that this means abandoning one's attachment to personal, material property. What truly is meant is releasing one's attachment to everything—material and immaterial, physical or mental—even up to and including the overweening desire for the extension of life itself: entirely releasing our white-knuckled grip on "the wheel of life and death".

It is in emptying out the vessel, which the psyche has filled, that the Void and the vessel are one. Frequently, the final dregs which we release are those of spiritual ambition and its accumulated ideas, practices, knowledge, attainments and expectations. When one is as open as a blank page, unfettered, that which cannot be invited can be perceived to be *present* as eternal, illimitable consciousness.

The external panoply is not the *source* of our attachments and desires, but rather the *object* of them. The construction of our mental/emotional panorama, though subject to influence from external sources, is fundamentally an "inside job". In observing the mechanics of our psychic constructions, it is possible to deflate them. The process is somewhat similar to the relinquishing of "mindstuff" which occasions the death of a terminal patient: minute-by-minute, what is recognized to no longer be essential to existence is quietly released from the mind.

This does not suggest a conscious effort to "control", repress, or "stop" thinking. Even if you were able to acquire the ability to "think no thoughts", it would likely be counterproductive. It is not thought itself which is problematic; thought can serve an indispensable function. There is *thought,* and there are *thoughts.* Some forms of our thoughts, if not the vast majority of them, are the substance of the veil which obscures our perception of the Omnipresent.

The first of the forms of thought which one might consciously, but passively, observe (as they appear upon the screen of one's waking awareness) are those relating to one's historic past and those projecting one's anticipated future. (Again, a whole chapter could be written to spell out in detail what is being suggested now, but exploratory contemplation on the reader's part ought to make apparent the implications here.) Clinging to associations with our memorable past—good, bad or indifferent—is one of the attachments we would wisely relinquish. The conception of a personable "self" which trajects from a past into a future is one of the basic misperceptions which enlightened sages decry repeatedly. The past is dead; the future is unborn. Enlightened awareness is *present* awareness. Referencing what *has been* is not necessary; concerning oneself with what may *come to be* is inconclusive conjecture. Dissatisfaction with one's past, linked to ambitions for one's future, is the motivation which prompts the seeker to project unrealistic expectations—which in Buddhism are called "gaining ideas"—into the pursuit of realization. The sages would point out that it is not a "self-ish" satisfaction which is encountered in "self-less" awareness.

Secondly, one can meditatively observe the form of thought which relates to *evaluations*: notice, upon their arising, the multiplicity of opinions, beliefs, ideas, assumptions, comparisons, and so on. These are the lattice upon which the self entwines. Here is the primary source of the thoughts which stimulate our self-protective emotions, such as pride, anger, jealously. Notice the plethora of ideas concerning the way things *should* or *shouldn't* be—in disregard of how they actually *are*. It is such ideas—particularly those socially agreed upon—which are the pedestal of our "ideal": what something *could* or *ought* to be (but, by contradistinction, is not). These are the un-real-istic ideas which get us into the most trouble, individually and collectively—particularly when compounded with emotional "values". In many cases, it is idealization (e.g, "romance") which is at the root of our destabilizing emotions.

By now, you will likely have begun to look closely—through simple attentive awareness—at the very nature of thought itself. The *function* of thought is to separate the particular from the whole. Thoughts normally appear to us in the form of words unspoken, words that could be—and frequently are—enunciated. Thought breaks the "objects", in our field of awareness, down into bite-size pieces, so that we can string these conceived items together into a form that can be manipulated—either physically or mentally. Each separate item, or link, in our thoughts can generally be—and usually is—represented by a word. Each word defines a separate, particular item. The word in our language which gives all others their relevant value is "I". Thought has separated, out of the field of actuality, a perceiver ("me") and all else that is perceived ("it"). It is due to the nature of thought that we think we know who we are. The enlightened assert that this is a sadly mistaken presumption.

It is through the mechanics of thought that the conviction of a separate "self" is established and maintained. And yet thought, in its reasoning capacities, makes the organism's day-to-day survival practical—as it does for even the profoundly enlightened sage. However, recognizing the (self) limitation of thoughts—and relinquishing those which foster and support a false identity—is a gateway to awakening. When it is clearly perceived that it is only by the divisive nature of thought that the absolute whole is fractured into individually-labeled "parts", the potential exists for you to shift your attentive awareness from the individually identifiable to that which has no identity, being wholly *all* that is.

Anything which we identify, even the Unknowable, is limited by its definition; thus the sages point out that the Illimitable cannot be reduced to words. Labels such as "self", "mind", "future", "enlightenment", etc, are ideas *about* something; they are concepts (which means: something which the intellect has conceived). While such conceptual words might have a practical use for the purpose of communication (such as this), they obscure the perception that they are merely particular references to apparent aspects of an actuality which surpasses, and completes, all identities. As the Gita suggests, no matter how many named objects we manufacture from gold, they originally were, and continue to be, the same substance at their core.

"You" are "That" which you seek. "The seeker is the sought" is not intended by the sages to be a clever, but hollow, phrase. When the impression of self identification has disappeared, the line is erased between "you" and the "Unknowable". Buddha is alleged to have wryly said, "You will not necessarily be aware of your own enlightenment." When the idea of a separate "you" dissolves, the idea of any actuality which you are apart from *also* evaporates. Your identity then is simply Presence In This Moment, which is the sacred or "Divine Presence".

That *is* your true identity at this very moment, but reliance on thought's separative, analytical power proposes otherwise. Once awakened to your true identity, there will be a recognition that perceived thoughts are not really *your* thoughts. For lack of a better way of putting it, they are the thoughts of the Doer of that which is done. In that light, you will witness, in choiceless awareness, the appearance and disappearance of thought, taking no personal responsibility for That which is Present. Thought will cease to define and instead will inform, a continually-open window to the true presence of the actuality which surrounds, permeates and activates all that is.

Within Oneness as Oneness Within

Awakening to the truth of Absolute actuality cannot be a "second-hand" experience—or it is not *awakening*.

For this truth to be a *first-hand* experience, the seeker must take it upon herself to realize a *shift* in perspective. All that the sages can do is to point out the direction in which the seeker needs to turn attention.

The gist of this realization is called "non-dual" for a critical reason. The nature of the shift in perspective is to attune one's awareness to the absolute unicity of the actuality which is being sought.

One cannot stand *outside* of this actuality and look for its *Absolute* unicity! *Because* of its absolute limitlessness, the seeker is—by definition—*within* the very thing which is being sought.

You have an idea (the idea of the unawakened) that you are a sugar cube sitting outside of a cup of tea *hoping* to "become One". The sages are telling you to move from this "me-it" position. In *abandonment*, jump into this *all*-encompassing cup of tea: you will merge with what it is that you now sense yourself separate from. "Merge: Sanskrit *majjati*, to sink in; to lose identity by being absorbed; to unite."

86

You do not "unite" with this truth by holding your self outside of it and looking for it. You unite with it by becoming *lost in it*, disappearing into it so that there is no longer a "seeker of truth" *apart* from truth. Then "you" are a *sugar cube* no longer. You and the tea are the same, One thing: Non dual. *Not two.*

There no longer is the sugar-without-tea ("me"), nor tea-without-sugar: there is just One.

So, what becomes of the sugar cube that was previously dreaming up questions about "how to become One" with the tea?

The sages keep repeating to you, "You *are* what it is that you are asking questions about." The questioner is simply another *form* of (or "within") the Absolute. You do not have to try to figure out how to merge. Wake up to that! *That* is what awakening is. "Oh, I get it. I am That. I *am* That! That and I are not two, separate things. There is *only* Oneness!" (*Otherwise*, it wouldn't be "oneness".)

Since "there is only Oneness", Oneness is *all things*—in different forms or appearances.

Evaporate sea water, and sea salt appears. All of the "named things" are merely different grains of the same all-encompassing liquid substance.

Your body and that tree are grains of different shapes. Both will eventually lose these forms; other forms will appear in their place. The Absolute actuality will remain unchanged throughout.

You manifest *as* That, from within it.

Once this is clear to you, you do not ponder questions about "me" and "That": we are talking about the *same* thing. Nisargadatta: *I Am That*. Not two. *Non*-dual.

When you wake up to the actuality that there are not two things, what then is "mind"? What is "consciousness"? What is "life"? What is "a human"? What is "self"?

The Absolute, being *all* things, non-dual, it is not *only* these material appearances, but the *immaterial* appearances as well. So, what is "destiny"? What is "experience"? What is "freedom"?

This, then, is the answer to (not just your, but) all questions. *All that is, is That.*

Go over each of these questions you've asked *from the standpoint of the non-dual*—which is what the sages teach. "If all that is, is That—*all* is—then what is the answer to the question?"

But don't do this if you *don't* want to find your "self" (what is it?) "merging" (what is it?) with "the truth" (what is it?). You risk melting into the actuality that you are contemplating. And once you "lose identity by being absorbed", there will be no "me" to continue the seeking.

The Oneness will be *inescapable*—which it really is right now.

. . . .

I.D.ea

One of man's separative notions has to do with the "holy"—a word which, ironically, shares its root with "whole".

It is the typical dualistic viewpoint which sets the Divine in opposition to mankind: God, the puppeteer, remotely above; man, his isolated "subject", below. According to this configuration, those who are "closer to God", such as the agents of a worshipful religion, are holier than others. Godliness and worldliness are not viewed as merely different descriptive aspects of a cosmic, inseparable whole—but as *counter*posed—by this faction.

On the other hand, when a sage such as Krishnamurti speaks of the "sacred", he is referring in a conventional way to that Absolute which has no opposition, no apogee or "farther" point: it represents a whole without division (whole means "constituting the entire, not divided up"), thus devoid of "parts". To such a seer, there cannot be anything which is *not* sacred; the Absolute, being omnipresent, nothing could be closer to God than anything else.

Krishnamurti, as did Ramana Maharishi and others, tried to make it categorically clear that no human being could be considered more holy, or even valuable, than another. The water in the temple is not more holy than the water in the sea; the temple made of marble is not holier than the shepherd's hut; the spot upon which the marble temple sits is not more sacred than the rain forest; the infidel is not less close to God than the priest who lights a bonfire beneath his feet. "All is one, one is all"; nothing could be more whole.

The idea of holiness and sanctity spills over into the notion of rightness and righteousness. ("Sanctimonious" means "pretense of holiness; to affect righteousness, as in religious hypocrisy".) "Godliness", when thought to be an acquired quality, is a "higher virtue", "morally correct". Therefore, those who *think* themselves most holy consider it their duty to enforce their pious zeal upon the "unholy". Since their mission is "divinely right", they presume themselves justified to utilize any means to accommodate their ends. This may range from the practice of instilling superstitious fear in children (or in adults with childish mentality), to the murdering of adherents of "erroneous beliefs".

Therefore, attachment to the sense of holiness and righteousness has been eschewed by nondualist teachers. "He has about him", comments the Ten Ox Herding Pictures, "no smell of saintliness", no odor of unctuousness. Further, right and wrong, moral and immoral, are seen as interdependent fragments of a limiting ideal, and means and end are viewed in a balanced way.

These perceptions can be found in the sutra by Seng Tsan *("As long as you remain in one extreme or the other, you will never know Oneness.")*, and the reported comment of Jesus that "figs don't grow on thorns".

Identifying one's self with a holy doctrine leads to exclusivity and divisiveness; divisiveness results in conflict, internally *and* externally. Attachment to an identification of any kind is attachment to a mere definition, an idea. It has nothing to do with the limitless actuality which no word can harness.

What the sages refer to as sacred cannot be worn on a sleeve. Our true identity is that which has no separate identity.

Unquestionable Purpose

If there was a "purpose in life", would it (yours) not have to be part of a *larger* plan (*inter*dependent with that of others)?

If there were a plan involving the purpose of each of us, would it not (of necessity) need be devised by something superhuman—beyond the humans that the plan involves?

And considering that mankind is an element in the universe, would this planner not be engaged in a development which involves the entire universe?

Under those circumstances, would the entity behind this purpose not need (of necessity) to know of all the related things that are going on in all parts of the universe—including this world—at all times?

If so, wouldn't the designer of the entire purpose *know* precisely what it is that you need to be doing in order to fulfill that magnificent plan?

If it knows what it is that you need (of necessity) to be doing in order to fulfill its purpose—which *is* your purpose—would it have you do anything in, or with, your life that is not in perfect *harmony* with that overall purpose?

Surely, then, everything that everyone is doing with their entire life *has to be* an orchestration of that supernatural planner's purpose. You could not *have* a purpose that would not be *its* purpose.

So, what is "your purpose in life"? To do exactly what you *are* doing.

If what you're doing right now doesn't seem a *grand* enough purpose for you, consider how little you know of how vitally important it is in the overall, coordinated plan.

If there is a purpose to our lives, there is a planner behind the purpose. In that case, why not trust the planner? If you *needed* to know the "purpose", don't you suppose you would somehow be informed? Unless you are instructed otherwise, why don't you assume that you *must be* fulfilling your purpose? If you're *not*, then evidently it is your purpose to be an exception.

Who Is the Dier?

Life unfolds, moment by moment—unpredictably. Why try to suppose beforehand how one will respond?

However, there is one outcome of life which concludes with certainty: physical death. And we can determine, from the experience of others, that our death may be so sudden that the event may not even be cognized; or, there may be an indeterminate window of time—from seconds, to minutes, to hours—when the event may be recognized to be impending; or,

91

even, there may be a developmental process—over a period of days, weeks or months—when we can expect that its resolution might end with our demise.

The fact, that the one certainty in life is death, gives every person an opportunity to contemplate their possible response to the event, assuming the varying circumstances which could be involved. If any question is central to spirituality, it is probably the question, "How am I to relate to death?" It is a central question because, to the extent that one consciously responds to the matter, it can affect the rest of one's entire life. As a friend of mine once put it, "The *central* fact of *my* life is my death"; as a consequence of this awareness, this person focused his attention on each present moment.

The question of one's relationship to death is the "bottom line" of nondual realization. When the sense of separative individuality is ended, the line between "me" and "death" is erased; it is what is meant when the sages speak of "dying while yet living". Resolved, in nondual realization, are the questions "Who am I?"; "What can death be said to be?"; "What is my relationship to death?" For one for whom such concerns have been resolved, fear of death is dissipated.

To the extent that the fear of death has been consciously resolved, one's responses—in the face of death—will be dictated by that. But there is no ideal scenario for one to rely on following, under any circumstance. One can only consider, at the time: "Why resist, or attempt to evade, what is not only inevitable but natural?" For one who lives each day as if it were the last, why cling to another day, or days?

Is it possible to live without an attachment to the idea of a continuation of one's life? The sages make it clear that it is not only possible but the most practical way to live. We can only investigate for ourselves whether this is so. This may not answer your question, Tad, as it was specifically asked, but it is as indicative of an answer as can be given without the decisive moment being present.   And how more assuredly can we *determine* our response *without* that moment being *present*?

NB: You might find suggestive, along these lines, the reported accounts of the facing of death by (for example) Buddha, Jesus, Ramana, Nisargadatta or Krishnamurti—among others.

The Black Period

Poet Robert Bly has promulgated an instructive analogy. Three colors predominate most universally in primitive cultures, he observed, both in ornamentation and allusive description: white, black and red.

White seems typically to be associated with purity, innocence and youth (e.g., Snow White).

Red has been archetypal of passion; excitement, vigor, lust—the hottest of the colors, the color of blood.

Black is commonly associated with death, the void, the silence of the night, the priestly robes.

Their order in the natural course of life—allegorically in fable, poem or song—has suggested a "white period" from birth to adulthood, a "red period" of family and career activity through midlife, and a period of blackening, banked embers as the heat of physical life subsides.

However, given the relativity of what we refer to as time, there is not in every life an identical chronology. Nor are the distinctions so conveniently, as we say, black and white; while these colorations are different, they are—as are all things—in no way separate: all are forms of the same colorful energy. And, of course, no color has a higher ranking, or is consistently more appropriate, than the others.

Given this analogy, one may plunge from one period, or color, into another in an instant: from virgin to expectant mother; from high school graduate to bridegroom; and so on.

One may transit, by an unexpected divorce, from the red period of family responsibilities and business pursuits, to the black period of freedom from obligations and to introspection in spiritual inquiry.

One may also cross the black threshold through the sudden death of the self; the profound recognition that the separate self is an illusion; and that there is but the impenetrable void in which all, and nothing, are the same.

The questions which surface in the mind, during its black phase— the questions that revolve around "Who am I?"—are often present in the red or white phase, but as fruit yet to drop from the tree: the conditions, the order in a person's life, are not conducive to resolution. The black period is characterized by an end to personal ambition, to the psychological absence of a future, to an ending of time and all that it implies. This can occur at any instant in one's life, simultaneous with the realization of one's true identity.

Walking Through It

Q. I intuit that there is special significance in phrases like "all that is, is That" or "there's nowhere that It is not".

I was walking today and—to keep it simple—I was aware of the walking body, the pavement, the trees that were passed, and the air between all this. I kept trying to sense how to bring That—the transcendent actuality—into the picture.

A. You needn't bring anything into the picture. Not anything is missing.

For the moment, consider a tree. Every single branch originates from the one trunk: each branch is not considered a "tree" itself; the tree is the trunk *and* the branches that spring from it.

At no point is the trunk separate from the branches; if it were not for the life in the trunk, there would be no life in the branches. While the trunk is the source, or origin, of life for the branches, this source is not unconnected to the furtherest tip of the tree.

The elements in your picture spring from a common source, but have taken different forms—just as on a branch there are leaves, buds, flowers and fruit. The source did not "create" these forms and—once the formation was completed—sever itself: the prana, or force or energy, of the source is what sustains, like power, the ever-changing continuation or existence of these forms. There is no discontinuation between the source and what springs from it; *springs*, not "sprang", past tense.

You need not "bring" this source into the picture. No picture could exist without it.

Q. If we say that all originates with one source, wouldn't there be a source for the source?

A. If the source were merely another form—there is *me*, this form; and there is the *source*, that form—then we could retrogressively look "behind" the form of the source, for what formed the form. But, ultimately, all forms that "come from" somewhere must have as *their* source a pre-form condition; that is, unformed.

This is the ultimate source of all that is, of all that is formed— body, pavement, tree, air, and their intangibles; thoughts, change, growth, space. The source is not an originating *form*. It is not something in another category from the formed. Being unformed—form-less—this source is not containable within the creations that it forms, nor can it be designated outside of the forms of its creation. Because the source is not separately identifiable from the creations—tangible or intangible—that it is the source of, we cannot say that there is a "me" *and* the "source".

In other words, you do not have to bring That into the picture. "That" *comprises* the entire picture.

Q. Which is why it is said that it is That which "is looking through these eyes"...

A. From the standpoint of what was just discussed, the eyes themselves are That. From the recognition that "nowhere is It not", thus "all that is, is That", there is not something separate —such as the "source"—which is doing the looking. The source permeates the looker, the looking (an intangible activity) and the looked at. The source in no way can exist as a distinguishable entity: it's identification is "All that is." It is the one who ponders how That can fit into the picture; it is the pondering; and it is the picture.

When this is clear, the pondering will be followed by some other form of the source's presence—even just deep silence, or awareness of body, pavement, trees and air, with nothing more needing to be added.

The nondual teachings are unbelievably simple. Enlightenment means the removal of confusion. Confusion results because of misapprehending appearances. The appearance is that there is an entity which we call the self. All nondual teachings emphasize that the image of a self is a false appearance. Recognizing the false as the false ends confusion.

When one actually recognizes that there is no self, then there is no "mind" and there are no "thoughts". Where there is no mind and no thoughts, there cannot be confusion.

So enlightenment is the permanent awareness that such entities that are referred to as self, mind and thought are false appearances.

Yet, there is a consciousness—universal among beings—in which appearances appear. This consciousness is present when a person is in deep dreamless sleep, when even appearances cease to appear. *And* this consciousness is present in waking activity in which self image—and its mind and thoughts—appear.

Consciousness, then, is present in the form of a self when images appear, and is present as the absence of a self when no images appear. The self is obviously an appearance in consciousness, and clearly is merely an impermanent appearance since it is not always present to consciousness. Where there is no permanent entity as the self, there is not the permanent entity that we refer to as a mind or its thoughts.

Universal consciousness is the source of the self. Universal consciousness, through its form of self image, is the source of the mind. Universal consciousness, through its form as the mind of the self, is the source of thoughts. Thoughts appear to describe, relate and refer to entities. Clearly, in this comprehension then, consciousness is the source of entities; more precisely, the appearance of entities. It is thought which even suggests the entity which we refer to as "consciousness". In deep sleep, there is not even the appearance of an image that is thought to be consciousness. The source of the appearance of consciousness, through thought, is consciousness itself. There is, in this comprehension, not even a separate entity such as consciousness.

Enlightenment, then, is the permanent awareness that *all* entities are a false appearance. Even enlightenment, permanence and awareness are entirely without meaning. Where there is no self, even "meaning" is meaningless.

Aside from false appearances, there is nothing. That is the substance of nondual teachings—and the end of confusion.

Who Has Ears to Hear

We hear a persistent, ethereal sound. What is its significance, its deeper significance?

One aspect of its significance is that it reminds us that there are some phenomena, which appear, that are beyond the pale of understanding in the context of linear rationality.

But once aware of such ephemeral phenomenon, how are we to relate to its presence? What message does it suggest?

What is the connection between the hearer and the heard? Can there be something "heard" *without* a "hearer"? Can there be a "hearer" without something "heard"?

Is there a "connection"? Or are both merely (polarized) appearances of the same fundamental phenomenon, or manifestation? In other words, is there a hearer which stands apart from what is heard: or are both essentially the same inseparable actuality—*indivisible*, though to the selective process of linear *thought* "different" forms?

What ultimately is the source of that which appears to be heard? What ultimately is the source of that which appears to be hearing? What is the source, that is, of the awareness in which both the appearance of the heard *and* the hearer are present?

Are you, the "individual" hearer and the identified heard, *apart* from this awareness? What is this *awareness* apart from; is it *apart* from *any thing* of which you are aware?

As this awareness, of which *no thing* is apart, are "you" apart from anything?

Aside from awareness, do you—as a distinct "individual"—*exist*? If not, is there anything which exists prior to, or independent of, awareness? Can awareness be self-aware?

What is it that you, as awareness, are aware of when you are aware of "your" awareness? Are you the subject of awareness; or the object of awareness? Both? Neither?

So, the deepest significance of the sound that is heard is the question which this—and *all* "experience"—raises: what is the real nature of that which *identifies itself* as the "hearer" of the "sound"? What—beyond thought—*is* the hearer? What is the sound? What truly exists "beyond" self-awareness? Can you, as a "separate individual" know this?

You *can* find out!

What's Happening?

The average human being has difficulty in considering his own demise; so it is not surprising that he should have difficulty in considering the mortality of his entire species. Yet, all things in the cosmos (and likely the cosmos itself) have a finite life. The cosmic cycle, indeed, is nothing other than repetitive birth, maturation and death.

It seems reasonable to view the human species in the context of its birth, maturation and death. In terms of the "white, red and black" paradigm for the individual human life (white representing the period from birth, to the red period of family and career life; and black representing the quiet years of retirement and senescence), the species can be said to be in its "productive" red phase. In fact, if the red trajectory were plotted as a bell curve (as it could, in most human lives), there is formidable evidence that the species *homo sapiens* is embarking on the downward slope.

In the individual human experience, the transition (from the innocent white to the vibrant red and subsequently to the sober black period) is bracketed by birth at one extreme, and death at the other. In the final days (and certainly minutes) of natural death, the individual relinquishes his attachment—increasingly—to everything in life: the material, the cerebral, the factional, the personal. At the moment of returning to the "Ground", nature has whittled our attention down to the awareness of "Am/Am not".

It seems reasonable to suppose, in other words, that the human species will move inadvertently toward its collective black phase. As the demise of the species becomes unavoidably inevitable, personal advancement, factional concern, intellectual pursuits and material attachments will increasingly fall away as attention is unerringly focused on the obvious denouement. As a body, mankind will be required to surrender its attachment to every so-called value in life—including life itself.

This may be (as it *is* for some individuals) mankind's finest and most Christ-like hour. Such a time as this, in Jesus' reputed life, was followed shortly by his death. And, some say, he is our intended example.

There will be some individuals who will mature and pass through this phase earlier than others (and some, perhaps, not until the eleventh hour).

Like Jesus, the surest sign of their foresight and their readiness for their noblest hour will be the surrender of their attachment to even life itself.

Nine Contemplative Stanzas

One sees Reality in the present, or doesn't see Reality at all.

The many worldly "things" are unreal. There is but one Reality—ever present.

Reality is like a rope, in its actuality; when it is mistaken for a snake, that is the "many things".

The world being a creation of the mind, those who perceive themselves as *in* the world are imprisoned in the mind.

When conscious attention is on the manifestations, the Source of conscious attention lies obscured.

Reality presents itself as consciousness, and thus is hidden from itself.

The one standing in front of a mirror is projecting an image —and is the one perceiving the image projected.

In a dream, the same mind is the Source of everything that everyone says and does; why so difficult to comprehend that neither thy nor I are doers of what's being done?

Since Reality itself is the cause and the effect of all actions, nothing is really being done.

The Soul of Humanity

You have asked, "Does the aware individual concern herself with the future 'fate of mankind' in general?"

The evolution of humanity has, at times, been considered to be analogous to the development of an individual human. That is, the human *species*—like a human individual—is considered to have been "born" at a discernible transact (however approximate) in temporal time and place. And given the relative "maturity" of the human race, based on contemporary social interaction, it has been suggested that humanity has crawled barely beyond that period of infantile development which mothers refer to as the Terrible Twos. At the most charitable, one might estimate that humans, generally, have attained a maturity that is approximately equivalent to that of a five-year-old: we are amenable to sharing some of our toys some of the time.

Like the human individual, which manifested from nothingness, the human race appears to have bloomed at a noticeable point— in the endless cycle of creative destruction and destructive creation—during which a seed dies into the realization of its fruit. From the seed of animate life, after millions of years of gestative cell proliferation, a bipedal primate *Homo erectus* evolved, through nature's parturition, as another distinctive flower to be found among the forests and fields.

As with a baby, man's original mind, so far as has been determined, was as simple as that of any other animal; while this creature could now wiggle its thumbs, its unsophisticated brain was merely another unbidden inheritance from its animal forebears before it, as was its teeth and hair. This animal exhibited the consciousness which all animals share—consciousness without self-consciousness—with an additional modifying distinction, the prospective capability for orderliness.

At a point in the creature's development, vocal sounds were ascribed common meaning which could be recalled by other humans, so that utterances like "father", "thirsty", and "this", began to define particular, recognizable entities or processes. Likely the first such identity was that of "Me".

Having acquired a sense of self as distinct from, and relative to, all else, man—collectively and individually—has unwittingly cut himself off from those other entities and separated himself out of all those processes which are, were and will be his true nature.

He has, through his limiting and limited concepts such as time and space, "become" the world's only, self-recognized, isolated phenomenon; he thinks in terms of separate units which can be manipulated to ensure the security of one particular unit— principally, the self-centered ego of this self-centered species.

Through the habitual speculation of his own thought, he has allowed himself to be persuaded that his unusual ability to "order" can be employed as a means to resist the discomfort of change; he believes that he can use the reality of order to control the order of reality.

In the same way that it is *possible* for an individual, mankind collectively has the *potential* to awaken to the realization that the wholeness of truth is not to be found in the divisiveness of thought.

There is a tendency today to *assume* that such an awakening or enlightenment on the part of mankind would be "salvation" for the human species, as a whole. This is the same type of thinking which presumes that personal enlightenment would be the salvation of the individual seeker.

Can it be that, for the human race as for the individual, there is no perfection for either the enlightened or the unenlightened? Can it be that this species of humans can, at best, anticipate old age, sickness and death—the same fate of the enlightened as well as the unenlightened?

Were that to be the case—a species which dies a natural death, as an individual dies a natural death—ought we not to face our implied collective mortality in the same way in which an individual must contemplate his personal impermanency? Do we not need to die to the notion of the potential divinity of the human race?

Put another way, for the same reason in which improvement of the transient self can be seen to be futile, an effort toward the lasting improvement of the collective spirit of humanity is also futile.

Can we give up our evangelism toward the wayward "soul" of humanity, in the same way that we recognize the sensibility of abandoning the idea of salvation for our individual soul?

A common word in virtually every spiritual tradition is *surrender*. The meaning of this word is "to give up, yield, abandon; to let go, relinquish control".

This word is often associated with another word, *sacrifice*, which shares its root with *sacred*: "a giving up, forgoing; specifically, a life offering".

And these words are often associated, in context, with another word, having to do with attachment (whose root means "a stake, or post"): *non-attachment*; a freeing abandonment.

The frequency with which these words are seen in spiritual writings is an index to their importance. Ultimately, what is invariably abandoned (in the arising of Self-realization) is "me", "my" and "mine"—all that the self identifies with. This self-abandonment is sometimes referred to as "the death of the self". It is the yielding, the relinquishing of control, that is similar to that which generally precedes physical death.

That which survives this "life offering" is the eternal Self. Not anything is necessary to *establish* the presence of this omnipresent Self; all that is necessary is to allow to die the illusory sense of self which is *superimposed* on this inherent presence.

Erasing the Lines

Lines (boundaries) are the means of fragmentation. Fragmentation is the source of human conflict. Conflict is primarily "opposition"; lines (borders) create opposites.

We inherit the lines that our parents, and peers, draw…the oppositional assumptions (dualities). Heaven and Hell are of man's making; "gain" versus "loss"; success as opposed to failure; progress/stagnation; the past compared to the future; positive contrasted to negative; happiness poles apart from unhappiness. Etc. There is only, at most, "multiplicity"; the values assigned are by us.

By taking the opposing object seriously (assigning positive or negative value), we attempt to eradicate (or assuage) the "bad" half, or "part". We try to "accentuate the positive and eliminate the negative", as the song says. Our energy is directed to either coercion or resistance; we are engaged in a do-or-die battle: conflict. Socially, we do not question the proposition that "It's me or you, baby!" This translates as, "If I can subdue you, my troubles are over".

But your troubles are lodged in your way of thinking: there's no end to perceivable differences—so, conflict is perpetual. (i.e., the Indians rallied to rout the dreaded British; then the Hindus and Muslims turned upon each other. Would we say that there was "progress" for the Indian people?) Think of *any* conflict in the world: is *division* at the bottom of it, somewhere—ideological, economic, cultural, etc.?

The poles appear to exist (*ex-ist*: "to stand out") as separate entities: but hot is only in relationship to cold; pleasure would have no virtue were it not for *dis*pleasure. If we cannot understand the basic simplicity of mutual interdependence, our divisive thinking has doomed the species. Do you see that conflict will not end until our tendency to focus on *fragmentation* ends? If you feel that this is so, let us proceed.

Lao Tzu: "Must you fear what others fear?" Must we pass along the "sins of our fathers"? Or can "the buck stop here"? Can we view reality in its wholeness, rather than focusing on fragments?

Dare we look away from the spider, so that we may enjoy the beauty of the web? Or shall we be transfixed with the spider, and miss the web for our lifetime?

The web is not separate from its space and its time, and the same space (stretching to infinity) and time (traversing eternity) are not separate from anything else—including each other.

"You" and "I" are in time and space, and connected with all that is.

The second important point, after mutual interdependence, is that all things are impermanent, changing, insubstantial. At most, we can identify ("different") *events,* not "things". And none of these events has an arbitrary starting point nor ending point. Did your origin begin when you left the womb? When sperm met ovum? When father met mother? When grandfather survived typhus? All events are always in a continuous unity, at the very least—with no "point" more essential than any other point...like a web.

But a continuum of motion has no significance unless we point to arrested events by contrast; however, isolated events (birth, death) have no more *significance,* or meaning, in the overall web, than has the spider: the web is useless without the spider, and vice versa. Your life would have no "value", were it not temporary, destined to end.

No matter how much you "succeed" or "fail" in this event of life, any single event ultimately has no significance. Fragmentation is to concentrate on "my success", my ambition, to the exclusion of other, wider considerations. Hence, conflict: "dog eat dog".

At the ultimate bottom of inseparability and impermanence is an apparent actuality: the infinite and timeless quality, or nature, of the cosmic web. Put another way, aside from man's ideas about "things" ("events"), not anything in the cosmos is significantly in conflict; cosmically speaking, there are no such realities as "fragments" or parts. There is no whole without the perfect fit of the parts; there are no parts that are not a perfect expression, or reflection, of the whole. Where there are observable "lines" in nature (such as a fissure in a rock), they are a "meeting" or "joining" place—not a point of contention or disharmony.

The third important thing, that one must recognize, is that there are phenomena which we may characterize as "different" (such as the mountain and the stream), but they are not *separate*, in any independent way. "Manyness", or plurality, represents differences; but the many are *unified*, in that they are simply a manifestation of the singular cosmos. Were the cosmos not a manifestation of more than one thing, there would not be a cosmos; and were the multiplicity not ultimately one thing, the flowing cohesion of existence would not pertain. From the cosmic point of view, though, "manyness" is purely an idea in the mind of man (and, likewise, "oneness", or unity).

In short, thought—distinction, definition—creates dualism, such as our ideas of "permanence", and concepts of "separateness". It is, therefore, human thought patterns which are at the bottom of fragmentation, and which results in the "conflict" that the human species (alone) endures.

To abandon the normal pattern of thought is effectively to abandon ego-centered ("me" versus "you") activity. Generally speaking, such a shift in perspective has its most profound consequence at the deepest root of our discord—where our basest fears reside; a person's tendency toward control/resistance, on every level, will likely be affected. One's personal "values" will change, in other words, as one's patterns change.

In a unified vision, there is clarity; whereas, in bifurcation, there has been confusion. One now can operate, or act, from a cohesive point of clarity, intelligence. "Clarity" does not necessarily translate as "bliss".

There is a difference between *reaction,* which is concerned with outcome, and *action,* which is not concerned with outcome. Action which is not concerned with outcome is action that is ultimately not *limited.* But this action will be based, from the outset, on the comprehension that—in this cosmos—not anything is significantly amiss. Put another way, it can be said that "all imperfect things are perfect in themselves". Or: not anything is more indispensable than any other thing. This is the essence of inseparability, of choicelessness.

For most of us, to *live* such a principle (choiceless awareness) means *capitulation:* trans-form-ation. Deeply. This is the "price" which one pays to end fragmentation and conflict: complete, resigned "union".

Concern for outcome is concern for outcome *in the future.* Action *without* concern for outcome is not practical where there is concern for the future. Generally, our concerns for the future revolve around one issue: security—specifically, *personal* security. To abnegate concern for one's personal future security is apparently possible only where there is absence of fear. And the quelling of fear may be possible only where there is a realization —and complete trust in that realization—that "where all things are one, there can be nothing to fear".

Seen another way, from the cosmic viewpoint, there is but one, timeless moment of existence; merely an invention of the mind of man is the "past, present and future". Where there is truly no future, what could possibly be feared? Said differently, where there are no two "separate" *things, who* is there to fear *what*?

The fourth, and most important, point is that rather than "oneself" there is One Self. However, this perception does not entail clarity if it is not one's own (visceral) *experience;* it will not sustain, when merely a slogan.

The fifth, and pivotal, point is that "no experience is necessary" prior to this realization: there is no relationship to time, as duration. Since there is actually naught but oneness, all that we need to "realize" is that this is the fact.

Thus, the sixth, and cardinal, point: having realized that fact, to live our life factually—that is, as truth.

This means living—and acting—in the awareness that "personal self" is a fiction. *Living* this truth is, at once, the means and the end: "the first and the last step".

This does entail, in our society today, a measure of risk; it means to be honestly uncommon, anomalous. This means to be still, in a world of commotion. At the very least, it means to radically experiment: it is to live in a moment that is without normal reference to past nor future. It is a realization—and complete trust in the realization—that time is without meaning. Not intended figuratively was this: "Take ye therefore no thought for the morrow", and "give us *this* day our *daily* bread", and "store up not treasures where moth and rust doth corrupt, nor thieves break in and steal".

There is no other time, in actuality, than this *present* time. There are no critical choices to be made, concerning past or future. Relinquishing our identification—which *is* the past and future— is the crux, the crossing point.

Point number seven: we will discard our self-image at death—or, we may do so *before*. The latter is our option, to be born anew... and this rebirth can be from moment to moment to moment.

To be conscious of true identity is to be without bondage, limitless; it is to be uncommon, unconditioned, unconventional.

In short, we are speaking of "a wholly different"—but not separate —"way of living". It is a way to which no one can bring you: it can only be experienced, and expressed, in whole measures: it is *sine qua non* of priorities.

Awaken.

Most Vital Principle

Your question is unclear, but these comments might be pertinent.

If it was said that the body is an object, the intent may have been to point out that "you" (as "subject") look down and view your "body"—as an object: there is "me" (subject) and my "body" (object).

Are whatever it is that you are identifying as "me" (or I)—"my self", or "my mind", or "my awareness", etc.—in *any way apart* from "my body"? No. The "subject" and the "object" are *one*. The *idea* that there is a "me" (on the one hand) and my "body" (on the other hand) is *dualistic* thinking. Recognizing that in actuality there is *no separation* (no such *reality* as "subject" and "object") is to be aware of the non-dual ("*not* two").

So, saying that a "body is an object" may have been intended to cause you to inquire: is there a *subject* apart from this object—or, is subject/object thinking at the root of a general failure to *recognize* the nondual?

You have linked this reference to a second question. In *this* case, here's what might be meant: the seeker supposes that the body is "real". Some teachers point out that the body itself is merely "inert": a piece of meat. A dead body has no qualities that we associate with being "vital". So, what is it that *animates* this chunk of meat, that *makes* it vital? The teacher would call it "the vital principle" or life-force. It is in the *absence* of this that the body is inert.

If there is such a thing as life-force, does it evaporate when the body dies? No. This "vital principle" is present in the very movement of the cosmos: evidently, it is universal and eternal.

So, the teacher would ask: what, then, can we consider *real*; a piece of flesh which decays and returns to the earth, or the force which is eternally *present*?

Without the presence of this universal force, the body *does not* "see and hear". We cannot rightly say, then, that the *body* "sees and hears".

That which is seeing and hearing right now is not the body—it is the vital Principle. "You" are *that*.

Next, space and time are *ideas*. Space is what we think of as being between two (or more) non-space (usually material) items. Time is what we think of as a measure (minutes, or days, or years, etc.) in moving between point A and point B (even such point A as birth, and point B as death). Both are abstracts: they point to nothing tangible; so, *as such*, both are the same—merely abstract *ideas*.

The sage would, further, say that neither exists. When you die (or even tonight, in deep sleep) will time or space have any reality for you? No. Time and space exist in your mind.

In fact, scientists maintain that at the moment of the Big Bang even *measurable* time was *nonexistent*; space *too*! We tend to think of the cosmos as *in* space and time; but cosmos, space and time are all simply different names for *expressions* of the vital Principle. Their "reality" *depends* on That. As does *yours* (another expression of That). So, "you", "time", "space", "universe"—all of these are *abstract* concepts, ideas…and, in that sense, *unreal*. Only one thing is real: the originating, vital Principle—*beyond* time, space or universe. "You" are *that*.

Awareness: No *Real* Difference

There is no real difference between you and me, except for our perspective, our "view of things". You are (as I *was*) standing apart from what you see, or (more generally) standing apart from all things. *I* view my "self" as all that is: there is no "me" apart from what this organism is aware of.

This general description of the latter perspective requires a note of explanation. In my awareness, there is this dream that we call "life", living. In this dream, there is a dream figure—"me", Robert Wolfe—who interacts with other "individual" dream figures. In this dream, these "individual" figures—"me", and those "not me"—are in *relationship* to one another. This "dream world" is therefore called the *relative* world.

But I am fully aware that when I close my eyes in death, this dream world—me, as a "person", and all else that is not-me—will totally vanish. It—this world—is completely impermanent. In fact, when I fall into deep sleep each night, I *experience* this impermanence: "I" no longer exist as a form; the world (including *you*) no longer exists as a form. The *relative* world, then, is as much an illusion as is a mirage which evaporates on an overcast day.

But my *experience* tells me that though this relative world disappears entirely, *something remains*. Even in the deepest sleep —when "I" am absent—awareness persists undiminished. Yell "fire!" (or pinch me) and I will sit upright and say "What's happening?!"

This non-relative awareness, in deep sleep, is non-separative: *All there is* is awareness, not even awareness of any "individual" thing (including my "self"). This is not a "relative" condition, since there are no two (or more) things in relation to "each other".

When I said (in the first paragraph) "there is no 'me' apart from what this organism is aware of", this perspective of "mine" (using relative terms) is the same as the non-illusional, non-dream, non-relative, non-separative awareness described in the paragraph above.

We could say that you have *one* perspective: that of the relative, illusional, separative world in which "you" and "other things" exist.

It could be said that I have an *additional* (expanded) perspective. First, I have the same perspective that you have: the relative. Like you, that's the only perspective that I was raised (conditioned) to experience. One *has* to have that perspective in order to function as a flesh-and-blood embodiment in the physical world.

But it has become clear to me (as it may for you) that this relative, functional perspective is applicable only to the *impermanent* aspect of the ultimate reality.

Therefore (in that clarification) it has also become clear that my underlying awareness (experienced regularly in deep sleep) is not dependent upon—does not disappear with the disappearance of —the relative perspective.

So, the paragraph above represents the difference between you and I. We both are capable of operating in the day-to-day world, where "you" and "I" interact.

But I am aware that there is more to my reality than just my capacity to function as an "individual being". For me, there is an additional awareness (rather, an extension or expansion of our "normal" awareness) that at my core—when *all-else is removed*, as it is in deep sleep—there is nothing more than pure awareness.

Since, in this pure awareness, there is no "me"—no *self* conscious thoughts—nor any "thing" outside of or apart from me, this additional aspect of awareness (often referred to as "ultimate" or "absolute") has no practical value in the day-to-day world.

Its only value is to serve as a constant reminder that the relative world is "false", in that it is no more lasting than my waking acknowledgement of it.

The "me"—the relative figure who acts as if it is in relation to "other things"—is recognized consciously to be a dream figure: close my eyes in deep sleep, or death, and it vanishes.

With the realization that, in truth, there is no me or other, there remains only awareness of what is. And there being no separative "this" and "that", this awareness is *not apart from* anything which it could be aware of. In my deepest sleep, nothing exists but awareness; and *yet* this organism is still "alive". So I, in my "ultimate" perspective, identify my "self" with *that*: pure awareness.

That is the only difference between us. You identify yourself, consciously, as a "separate being". I identify myself (to the extent possible under the circumstances) as that which is aware of all that it can be aware of—and with no *separation between* what is aware and what it is aware of. In other words (as said at the beginning), my view is of a self that is in no way disconnected from *all that is*.

That means that I am not disconnected from you.

And, obviously because your deepest awareness is not different from my deepest awareness (there is no "me" nor "you" in either of us, in this condition), you are in no way disconnected from me.

That is my realization. It can be your realization as well.

Hear Now

Because that, which every spiritual seeker searches for, is not an entity, it cannot be found in the way that a (limited) object can be found.

It is in the recognizing of one's utter inability to find the non-entity that is the discovery which is characterized as enlightenment!

The nature of this non-entity, the sages concur, is that it is everywhere. Being ubiquitous, it cannot be "lost". Since it is impossible to lose that which is omnipresent, it is futile to attempt to "find it".

Its condition being that it is everywhere, without exception, it is right *here*, right *now*. It is ever present in every moment; fully present in this very instant. Therefore, the sages invariably refer to it as time*less*, dimension*less*: total presence, without beginning or end, in the universally-seamless moment.

Since the seeker is unfailingly *in* this moment, the seeker and what is sought are already, automatically, united! The comprehension that the foregoing sentence is clearly the truth is to "realize".

Neither time nor distance are a factor in an undeniable unity which already is in place. This is a union which is unconditional: one cannot evade momentary presence by moving away, either in time or place. Your present awareness and this present moment are an inseparable actuality.

Even if you were to suppose that you are unaware in this moment, the awareness of *that* is in this moment. Like the moment, your awareness is not a finite entity. To be aware *of* some "thing" has its limitations; but awareness as a mere characteristic of presence is what makes this moment an actuality.

Momentary awareness and momentary presence are inter-dependent aspects of a singular actuality.

The real you that you are, without affective modification, is Present Awareness. (Change the initials on your luggage.)

There is not anything in particular that you need to acquire, experience or even comprehend in order to express your true nature as Present Awareness. *Everything* that you experience is as awareness in the moment.

Whatever you are aware of in the present moment is a presence equal to your awareness in the moment. Whatever you are aware of is not separable from your awareness of it.

So, you won't find the actuality you're looking for by looking outside of this present, unlimited moment.

You are *now* "here", even when you wish you were "there".

You cannot escape the Presence which is the common denominator of all that exists.

You are the Presence that is presently aware, even when you are not aware *of* that particular reality.

The consequence of this realization is that you stop looking elsewhere and elsewhen for the dimensionless Presence which you inevitably re-present. That complete, satisfying cessation of seeking is the sign of the effortless discovery; the peace and quietude, the bliss of *self*-discovery.

Were you to pick up the Gita now, you would recognize that the Truth must always be "Ever-present". All your inclinations to look away from this present actuality were leading you away from that sought. Not anything needs to be added to this moment—and you can be aware *of* that anytime you desire!

Suffering: A Practical Response

In spiritual writings, it's not uncommon to see the word intelligence (lower case) in reference to a human capacity, and Intelligence (upper case) used to refer to a capacity beyond the limitation of humans. By intelligence, we plant trees. Only Intelligence can create a tree (or earth, or cosmos).

The root of intelligence (small i) means "to choose among", to discern or understand. The Intelligence evoked by the capitalized word (albeit a misnomer) has no need to choose, discern or understand.

No doubt there are some, on whom the intended subtlety is lost, who will ascribe the former tendencies to the latter. And then, of course, the image is of a "God" (nee "Intelligence") who chooses, decides and determines. This is, as an extension of the image, a "God" whose "mind" is busily at work (like ours). And, of course, being a kind and just God, acting persistently on the side of the positive, the "righteous"; the Governor who, inexplicably, has done such a poor job initially that all sorts of affirmative activities are now necessary.

We discerning mortals, you may have noticed, find it difficult to conjugate Intelligence with *chaos*; the word, as far back as the Greeks, designates *space*, in the sense of void: "the apparent disorder of formless matter and infinite space; order that exists within disorder, such as the irregularities of a coastline".

So this is a "God" of irregularities (we could ascribe the name Disorder instead of Intelligence) without which there would be no regularities. While man does not get credit for creating a tree, man does not merit blame for the eruption of a volcano.

To Chaos goes the blame for natural disasters. Mankind reserves for itself the credit for alleviating the wanton suffering.

One might suppose that a rational species would keep itself busy enough responding to the natural disasters, without contributing man-made suffering; but "choosing among", we manage to generate *regular* disorder and conflict. *Needless* suffering.

Have Love, Will Travel

What actually, is the seeker seeking?

Freedom.

Freedom from what?

Freedom from fear.

The most basic fear, actually, is fear of suffering: primarily, fear of the unknown, in terms of potential pain, injury, discomfiture or the undeterminable or indefinite.

The antidote to fear, most people suppose, is security and its certainty. Security depends upon being in control. For most people, their contentment or happiness is precariously based upon these elements.

At the center of these concerns, like a hub of the spokes, is the person who would be protected, the person who has—at least for the moment—reduced the perimeter of fear.

But the seeker invariably has another, a deeper, more subtle desire. Not freedom *from*, but freedom *for*. Freedom in order to actualize one's fullest human potential, the only freedom which makes life truly worth living: the freedom to love.

Not to love in a possessive, restrictive or limited manner, or a reciprocal or physical way in which allure or attachment are present. But a love which goes beyond self interest and gratification. What is sometimes spoken of as sublime love, or selfless love.

The word *selfless* is usually regarded as an antonym to the word *selfish*. We tend to think of selfish-ness as a contradistinction to generosity: as not being willing to share our goods or possessions. But selfishness is actually a term for self-centeredness, one's self being the hub upon which all relationships and activities pivot.

What is a self? "The identity of one's person, as separate from all others." And a person is "a bodily form or appearance, having a personality or individual pattern of behavior". So a self, basically, is a form which appears to be separate from all others, each differing in its behavior. How do we differ in our behavior? Primarily by acting out of our self-centered concern.

Mostly verbs, my dictionary lists 34 inches of small-type definitive words in which self comes first, from "self-absorption" to "self worth".)

Clearly, self-less love indicates the absence of self-ishness, *self*centeredness: in essence, the absence of "the identity of one's person as separate from all others". As long as identification with one's self-image remains at the hub of one's relationships and activities—one's person-ality—self-less love can be nothing more than an abstraction, a concept or ideal. "Love", Krishnamurti succinctly put it, "is the total absence of the separate 'I', ego or self."

While all of the above is obvious, why is it generally so rarely recognized in a manner which places us in an uncompromising position to express selfless love?

Because of our fear of loss—of the "person".

The *paradox* is that when our self-centeredness is relinquished, a consequence is freedom from fear. The latter is unequivocally dependent upon the former. When self-attachment is surrendered, fear of loss disappears with it. Every true model of selfless love, in every time, has demonstrated the truth of these observations. And typically we know this, and have no doubt about it. The absence of the self as the center of behavioral expression is the condition of the freedom to love.

And this is our most subtle, compelling desire, more resonant with our intuition and wisdom than our hope for freedom *from*. Freedom *for* the actualization of our most dynamic potential, the freedom which permits our life to be truly whole and fulfilling. And all that is required is the surrender of our self-identity—which all the while has been at the root of our fears and suffering.

No Thought for the ...

What do we mean when we speak of "living in the moment"? Is this purely a common ideal, an intriguing concept, an impractical idea?

When we hear such a phrase as "take no thought for the morrow", our reaction is: "Oh, I could do *that*. But the day after tomorrow, and the day after that... well, I don't *know*...!"

If we truly take no thought for the morrow, can there *be* a day after that?

But that may seem too philosophical; what we're concerned with is the *practical:* What would I eat? How would I pay my bills? What if I got sick?

It is commonly presumed that living in the moment, heedless of the future, implies: 1) loafing, 2) debauchery, 3) irresponsibility and/or 4) foolhardiness—in general, a wastage of time and human potential. There seems to be something vaguely "spiritual" about attending fully to the present, but perhaps only because various sages have spoken of it. And spirituality is, disturbingly, associated in our mind with material insecurity.

Ah, isn't that the rub, though? Living in the moment seems to us to be a voluntary form—almost a masochistic form—of insecurity. Yet there are thousands, if not hundreds of thousands, of people living today—in just this one country—who could live tomorrow, and an adequate number of days-after-tomorrow, with no particular need for concern about financial security.

The place we come to, ultimately, when we think about living in the moment, is a confrontation with risk. We, practical beings, are concerned not only about material security, but about security in general (with a capital S); for example, "What would my family think/do, if I had absolutely no plan for the future?…Even if I were responsible to/for myself, mightn't I be considered irresponsible toward them?…Surely, living one day at a time no longer is feasible!"

The real risk is that living for the present implies major changes in our current style of life, unsettling changes, disturbing to our comfort and to the psychological comfort of others. Even so, one might seriously contemplate such changes—if the rewards for doing so were large enough. But when one lives in the moment, one is not concerned about material rewards—and material rewards generally do not come to those who do not seek, or worry about, them.

And what of the immaterial rewards? Yes, there certainly must be some reciprocity when one's attention is on the immediate; one cannot be fully engaged in the moment, for instance, and be worried about the future (or past) at the same time. This apparently is what the sages have been saying, in recommending this change from our usual way of life. But is there any *certainty* these beneficent realities will be present for those who take the risks? And are these immaterial "benefits" worth the upheaval in one's life, when one is open to them?

No, there is no certainty; that's what the risk is all about!

No one ever said, "take no thought for the morrow, and it shall be guaranteed to thee that security shall follow thee all the days of thy life". It is much more *reasonable* to be concerned about the future, anxious about security (even though one generally might be financially secure at present), untrusting of the natural wisdom in the moment. Those who trust their lives to the wholeness of the day are not reasonable people. Is it possible that each day or night contains within it reason enough?

Relative Beads, Absolute Thread

What the so-called enlightened teachers invariably point out is that we are enculturated, conditioned, into a dualistic society, each of us from the time we are infants. This is a world in which the average, "normal" person takes it for granted that there are separate items—material or immaterial—which stand in relationship to one another: such as "you" and "I".

These teachers each say that their personal discovery has been that the true actuality is one of non-duality: You and I are, *in essence,* one and the same. They give various names to this essence, but they emphasize that it is not only the essence of "you" and "I"—merely a couple of its myriad manifestations—but it is the essence of all that is, whether regarded as material or immaterial. Choose the name which you feel most comfortable with, to represent that which embodies the common denominator of all that can be named (or not named) : God, Brahman, Tao, Void, Self, Consciousness, Buddha-nature, et al. I personally prefer the term Absolute.

The realization of each of the renowned spiritual teachers has been that the Absolute (or whatever "referential" choice they've made) is all that is—in the most fundamental (ultimate) sense. They generally posit this by suggesting that every phenomenon we have named—or could possibly name—arises from that Absolute actuality, and returns to that Absolute actuality. In other words, when the impermanent nature (appearance) of every named thing—whether material or immaterial, formed or formless—is stripped away, what it re-presents is the Absolute in merely one of its innumerable forms. *Because* the fundamental essence of every thing is the Absolute (including the Absolute itself), there are not—anywhere, under any circumstances—two *separately identifiable* things (*non:* not; *dual:* two). The message of these enlightened masters uniformly is—whether you agree with it or not—all that is, is That. Not anything (that your mind can conceive of) is *not* That.

When one has had a personal realization that this must indeed be the true actuality of our (and all) existence, there no longer is an identifiable *relationship* between any "two" or more "things"—as considered from the recognition of the truth of non-duality. "You" are, in essence, That. "I" am, in truth, That. *That* and *That* are not relatives of each other: "they" are one, inseparable constant.

Every enlightened teacher has had the profound realization that the basic truth of "our" existence is that *all* that is *is* That. This realization—for whatever reason—does not appear to be a common occurrence; evidence indicates that the majority of human beings live an entire lifetime and die while still engaging the perspective of duality: on their deathbed, the perspective is that "I die"; not "Leave you?! Where could I *go*?" (Ramana)

Therefore, while an enlightened teacher's realized perspective is that of Absolute actuality, he or she is not *un*aware of the dualistic perspective we all have (at least initially) been immersed in. When necessary or appropriate—*particularly* when relating to someone who does *not* share the Absolute perspective—the awakened being will respond to any given situation from the *dualistic* standpoint.

In other words, to this person the Absolute perspective and the dualistic perspective are always simultaneously available as an option through which to relate to "others".

There is a critically important element in this situation, however. To the person to whom the Absolute perspective is thoroughly clear, any particular thing can be viewed in its relative context, without ever losing sight of the fact that all that we consider to be relative is *in truth* the Absolute: that which we can name is always none other than the Absolute, in one of its endless appearances or forms.

In the most practical terms, this means that if you ask "who am *I*", the answer could be given, "the Formless."

"What is mind?"	"The Formless."
"What is thought?"	"The Formless."
"What is action?"	"The Formless."
"What is suffering?"	"The Formless."
"What is liberation?"	"The Formless."
"What is God?"	"The Formless."
"What is form?"	"The Formless."
"And the Formlessness?"	"The Formless."

Relative categories, on the one hand; awareness of the Absolute on the other. The dualist looks at column A and column B and sees two different things. The non-dualist sees—or at least has the capacity, when needed, to see—that all is ultimately only one thing ("without a second"), no matter what is viewed or conceived; column A *and/or* column B.

The point is that, from the standpoint of the *Absolute* perspective, there is no such separate, identifiable entity as "me"; "my mind"; "my thoughts"; "my (*or your*) actions"; "problems"; "solutions"; "needs"; "imperfections"; "betterment"; "world"; "life"; "death"; "suffering"; etc. All that is, *in essence*, is That—in its myriad manifestations.

However, that is not the "experience" which most people, say *they* have had. In such a case, where someone is limited to the *relative* perspective, the teacher will respond to "your" question about "suffering" and the "action" to "surmount" it. *Meanwhile,* awakened teachers invariably point toward the fact that a shift in perspective is evidently a possibility for anyone who can relinquish their conditioned, separable identifications.

Manifestation Is "Appearance"

The sages speak of the "ultimate ground of being" as consciousness; you have pondered: if this is so, then how does this consciousness manifest as the material?

This is a typical example of the value of recognizing the relative nature of our conceptions. A Zen roshi might say, as a means of indicating the ephemeral and impermanent quality of matter, "The 'ten thousand things' are a manifestation of the void." Considering that our language posits a subject which is eventually linked to an object by an active verb—"the void manifests all things"—our conception is that there is a void which pre-exists, *out of* which matter is manifested. Thus, by *this* construction, the immaterial void (or illimitable consciousness) exists *prior to*— and independent of—material ephemera, with the phenomenon of manifestation (or "occurring") bringing the two categories together.

This is similar to the way in which some scientists think of the creation of the world: there is vast space, an empty energy field, out of which our ball of earth was manifested—as if the earth is somehow now actually independent of the field which surrounds it and in which it is evolving. The earth has not evolved *out of*, or away from, its cosmic atmosphere: it is entirely *composed* of this cosmic atmosphere; only in *form apparent* can it be said to be *different* from its supportive field. In this sense, it can as well be stated that were it not for the earth, the *cosmos* could not be manifest—since both are fundamentally the same, and neither can thus be considered to be independently prior.

So, when we consider "How does consciousness manifest the material?" we must recognize that consciousness is not a state or condition *out of which* the material is ejected: that which is material has never in any way been apart from the immaterial. Put another way, consciousness has not been, and is not now, separable from that which appears to us to have taken form. "Form is formlessness (void)", says a Sanskrit sutra, "formlessness is form." (Some translations say "emptiness" for formlessness.)

Consciousness is a *relative* term: it suggests that there is something which is *not* conscious. Material is a relative term: its opposite is immaterial. And manifest is a relative term: it depends upon some other thing out of which to emerge. A concept, by its nature, is limited (thus relative); our concept is that there is a discrete phenomenon which we call consciousness, and that there is also (distantly) a category which we call matter. The dissolution of these (conditioned) concepts results in the realization that separative constructions are illusory.

Freedom Now

There is no separate self. If this is not so, generations of spiritual teachers have been lying to us. They tell us that what is present is only a false idea of a separate self.

It is this self-idea which is at the root of the formulation of such presumed phenomena as "creation" and "destruction"—and *all* other named forms of things, in their supposed arising and disappearance in time.

Since the self is not really true, any of its creations are not really true. With the vanishing of the personal-self idea when one's lifetime has run its course, all of the named forms of things evaporate along with it: no world remains, no universe is seen—

only emptiness, void. All principles perish, values, virtues and actions too. Gaté, Gaté... gone, gone, all gone!

Since the things created by the self-idea are no more real than the false idea at their root, why concern ourselves with them now? The concerns of a false self can be only false concerns.

In deep sleep, the false self also dissolves, and all created concerns with it. This nightly occurrence is a reminder that the absence of the false self is possible even before the body ceases its animation. This, the spiritual teachers tell us, is what it means to perceive emptiness, the non-arising of the self-created world illusion and consequent concern for its empty forms.

No Creation, No Destruction

The ostensible connection between suffering and enlightenment, in your question, is that (as Buddha put it) all who are unenlightened are suffering. How? Because unenlightenment can be described as the condition of dualistic perception. Where one envisions two, or more, things, there is then always the potential for conflict: incompatibility, contradiction, opposition, etc. Enlightenment can be defined as the condition of nondual perception. And where there are no two (or more) things, there is not the arising of conflict.

So, to be unenlightened (according to Buddha's framework) is to be subject to suffering—as a matter of *fact*. This suffering is usually expressed in terms of anxiety, or anguish. The very feeling of being an "individual"—by definition, *apart* from all that is "not me"—gives rise to a subtle, discomforting sense of alienation. And it takes more obvious forms, such as apprehension of death ("I" will be separated—permanently—from the "world"; a classic dualistic anxiety).

It is this suffering, however, that generally prods one to seek an end to suffering. And as one considers possible means to this end, one sometimes discovers the message of nonduality—and may then discover the reality of "enlightenment."

And, yes, it might be said that the greater the extent of "suffering" which one experiences, the greater the motivation to move toward this practical "ending" of it.

But that is *not* to say that there is an actual relationship between suffering (in whatever degree) and enlightenment. Why? Because from the "enlightened" perspective, there is no such separate condition as "suffering". *Nor* is there any such *separate* condition as "enlightenment". The discovery of the nondual perspective dissolves all such separative, subjective *suppositions*.

This, likewise, applies to your question concerning whether the physical status of the seeker's body has any relationship to enlightenment. Bear in mind that, from the standpoint of nondual perception, there is no such separate condition as "enlightenment". *Nor* is there any such separate entity as a "body" which exists *independent* of the Absolute actuality which "is all that is".

Any mind which has the potential of conceiving of definitive entities, such as "enlightenment" or "body", has the potential of perceiving the deceptive nature of the dualistic bias; and, in consequence, perceiving the nondual actuality—thus ending all such confusing questions.

What is often referred to as the "source" is another name for the Absolute: *that* which is all (indivisibly) that *is*: the nondual actuality. Since this *is* all that is, everything which *appears* to be (individually) existent is merely an aspect (a "reflection") of this one, inseparable actuality.

Hence, it is said that all that "arises" has its origin in this "source". The "all" would include *every thing*, material or immaterial: such as the so-called "body" and its so-called "ego". These "things" are, if you understand what's being said, nothing more than selective "names" for the one all-encompassing Absolute.

As the sages point out, all of these apparent manifestations (such as body and ego) "come and go"; are impermanent. The source from which the appearances arise, however, is unchanging; thus, by contrast, permanent.

So, it could be said (and has been) that the source of the ego is the Absolute. But that, of course, would be putting the conception in dualistic terms: the Absolute "up here" (for example) and the ego "down there"; two "things", identifiable as separate from each other.

From the sage's point of view (nondual awareness), only in relative terms could one speak of the Absolute and the ego in such a construction. There is no Absolute as a *separate*, identifiable entity: it must be said to be (if anything) all that is. Therefore, it *is* the ego (in another of its "appearances"). It cannot be said, then, even to be the "source" of ego. Ego, in this sense, does not "come from" or "return to" the Absolute: it was never anything *other* than the Absolute, except in *appearance*. Superman was *never* anything *other* than actor Reeves, except in appearance.

So, there is no *separate* Absolute; therefore it cannot accurately be viewed as the *source* of ego: it *is* the ego—*and all else*.

Just as it's inaccurate to think of the Absolute as the "source" of anything—rather than realizing that it *is* these things—so, too, is it deceiving to speak in terms of "creation"—as a noun, an entity. There was not a "creation" and then whatever follows, or "comes after", such a creation. Creation can only be supposed in terms of a verb: manifestation is an ongoing process, the balance of which is destruction. One would not think of destruction as an already-completed process: *nor* is creation.

The cycle of creation/destruction is not inert: it is very much alive and acting this very moment. Therefore, the entire cosmic drama —including this world and its people—is a by-product of this living process.

But the real question is not whether the drama is alive (in that it is gestating at this very moment) but whether it is *real*.

The cosmos (and *all* that's *in* it) *began* in some sense, scientists infer: and indications are that it is subject to *end*, in some sense. And, as is said, anything which can evolve and devolve is not "permanent". What *is* permanent is the (back)ground upon which it plays out its development. This "eternal" presence is what is signified by the Absolute.

So, the sages would compare the temporality of our world and its biology to a dream—which similarly "comes and goes". This *apparent* living "reality" is *unreal*, in the ultimate context—as *compared* to the absolute, ultimate Reality.

If the universe is subject to "coming" (being created) and is subject to "going" (being destroyed), creation/destruction are also "unreal"—simply impermanent manifestations or conditions of that which *is* Real.

Both "creation" and "destruction" are (our) *ideas* about Reality; take away all the minds that generate these conceptual ideas and what is left of such definitive designations?

All of the above is exemplary of how "confusing" questions are dissolved when one shifts the focus from duality to nondual awareness.

One could write a (stimulating) book on the comparable ways that "a sage knows how it is that he/she *knows*" (enlightenment). The common thread would evidently be that, at some moment, the falsity of the dualistic bias is recognized ("seen through") and the obviousness of the nondual actuality is simultaneously realized. I have heard people exclaim (in wonder), at this moment, "My God! How could it be *otherwise*?!": meaning that the obviousness of complete and utter unity of "all that is", as being "none other than That" (Absolute, Self, Brahman—or whatever term), is as profoundly clear as the *seeming* "reality" of separation appeared to be previously.

Beyond this "realization" (usually sudden), there are no "experiences" that are necessarily attendant with it. One simply is aware that one now recognizes the actuality of our existence, which had not clearly been recognized in its entirety before. I have sometimes just heard, "Ah...*Aha*!" from someone's lips.

But these are *all* matters that you need to come to know *yourself*. Examine the dualistic bias of your subjective thoughts. Consider the full implications of what is meant by "*all* that is, *is* That": no separation exists—except in the (unreal) mind!

....

Feeling the Way

X. My life feels meaningless, repetitious and full of conflict, even after all the years of spiritual search.

Y. Perhaps it's because of the years of spiritual search.

X. What do you mean?

Y. On the most basic level, any search for anything is bound to create conflict. Where there is the desire to find something, there will always be a lingering dissatisfaction as long as it is not found. Dissatisfaction with the existing condition is the hallmark of what Buddha called "suffering"; the anguish or agony—or conflict—of not being where we'd prefer to be.

X. I've been engaged in the spiritual search precisely to put an end to my suffering—to all forms of conflicted feelings or emotions.

Y. A search presumes that the searcher is apart from—separate from—what is being searched for. In general terms, the idea of the spiritual search is that the seeker will one day become unified with the universal consciousness that is being sought. To put it another way, *you* are "here"; and universal *consciousness* is someplace "other" than here: that is a supposition which creates conflict from its very beginning!

As a spiritual seeker, is that which you are seeking eternally present?

X. Eternal? Yes.

Y. Then It is present this very moment, isn't it?

X. It exists always. But my heart-felt connection to it doesn't exist yet.

Y. Is this, which you seek, truly universal; or discovered only in certain places?

X. It's boundless: cosmic consciousness.

Y. If something is always present and everywhere present, when or where can it be hiding that someone needs to seek it? Would it not be *here*, right *now*?

X. But I don't feel that.

Y. There are things that cannot be experienced as apart from the experiencer, because there is no separation from the start! Your eye cannot directly experience seeing itself. What it would see, is that which is doing the experiencing. Because you suppose that you need to search for something which is right here, right now, you are artificially creating a separation between your presence—right here and right now—and the eternally universal, which has to be right here, right now.

X. So I'm here, and that's here; but I don't feel the connection.

Y. You will never feel the connection, to that which you have never been disconnected from in the first place! Your search for some connection in the future negates the connection that is so immediate that it can never be experienced in the past, as a recognized feeling.

X. But some say they felt *that*; and that ended the search.

Y. What you are feeling this very moment is universal consciousness. It's what *all feel*, at *all* times. It's universal and eternal, is it not? It is not to be found *somewhere*—because it cannot be escaped right *here and now*. When it is recognized that this must be so, the search is ended!

X. Hmmm....

Z. We're closing now. Can I take these dishes?

Of the spiritual teachers who are said to have had the capability of relieving, or curing, physical ills, it's worth noting how little of it was done. Why? Because the priority of interest, by the spiritual teachers, is on that which is permanent and unchanging rather than on the impermanent and temporal.

The suffering which is associated with physical ailments is predominately rooted in the psyche, rather than in the sensate flesh. All true spiritual teachers are essentially directing their attention to this root "cause", whatever their outward activities may appear to be: the mind that is the producer of the "sufferer".

This mind is the projector of individuated experience, such as the experience regarded as happiness, or that regarded as unhappiness. Unhappiness is experienced as suffering; the *disappearance* of happiness is also experienced as suffering (un- happiness). So Buddha emphasized suffering as the net outcome of individuated experience (the primary of the four "truths" he postulated).

He went on to say, basically, that our mindset, our perspective, can be recognized to be the axis of our suffering. And, thirdly, from his own experience, it is possible for that troublesome— separative—mindset to dissolve.

The fourth, and final, point was that what this mindset must dissolve into is "emptiness": not a different, or better, mindset, but the absence of the separative perspective—the discrimination between such things as happiness versus unhappiness; "suffering" as contrasted to "not suffering", etc.

The core of the entire teaching (his 45 years of it) is summarized in that one word: emptiness; empty of all comparative elements.

Not just the apparent "this" as opposed to "that" (e.g., happiness/ unhappiness), but *every* "this" and "not this". Me/you. Us/God. Divine/profane. Life/death. Yes: *even* existence/non-existence. No-thing remaining. *Emptiness*. "Void".

"Ah, yes," the tenacious mind would reply, "I see what you mean. There is this world of suffering, which we call Samsara. But there is salvation: the bliss that is called Nirvana."

"No. You didn't get the point", Buddha likely sighed. "Emptiness. No-thingness. What you are conceiving is one condition, or state, superseding or replacing another condition or state. Samsara and Nirvana are the same thing, in your mind: an *experience* by the individual, over a period of time. No individual. No experience. No time. No two things. No-thing."

"Hmm", the listener replies, "I have a hard time picturing emptiness in my mind."

"In emptiness, there is no 'I', there is no 'mind'. Where there is an I and its mind, suffering will result."

"That's what I wanted to ask you: how can I end my suffering?"

Thy Will or Mine?

You say that your mother used to comment on every event, "It's God's will", and you ask how this differs from what is being referred to as 'what is'.

The implication of the expression "God's will" is that there is a supernal personality somewhere which consciously directs every miniscule detail of the events in the cosmos. If that were so, is there anything which would *not* be God's will?

To speak of the *what is* is to refer to that reality, that truth, which is the essence of this eternal moment—the only moment which has ever existed or will ever exist. It is, being what it is, *all* that there *is*. It has no need of a will, because there is nothing which is in opposition to it, nor is there anything which it lacks and therefore needs to "accomplish" or acquire.

Because this reality *is* what *is*, there is not anything which one can do to affect it: it will not, under any circumstances, be anything *other* than what it is. It will do you no good, in other words, to either accept it or resist it, to pray to it or to curse it.

When that is fundamentally understood, it can be seen that "man's will" is as superficial as is the notion of "God's will".

Even if the universe were created by a perfect god, we could assume that that which was created was perfect. Why would either god or man then will to change, or alter or affect, a single thing?

When we can go beyond the idea of a Walt-Disney-like consciousness which is behind the scenes, creating human Pinocchios, we can appreciate a reality which is far more *astounding* than any scenario that the mortal mind—or its Supernormal Ego—can "create".

. . . .

Eightfold Checklist

Consider the moment-to-moment activities of your life, and the extent to which they revolve around these eight, common concerns.

1.

Seeking pleasure. All of the following activities share this, to some extent: it is perhaps our most general motivation. Though we may

138

not always be seeking pleasure directly, much of the time we are alternatively engaged in seeking avoidance of pain, boredom, futility; an inordinate amount of our energies are typically expended in entertainment, hedonism, or romantic involvements.

2.

Seeking experience. In addition to pursuing experiences as a form of excitement, we seek the memorable or cumulative experiences which reinforce our sense of self-worth.

3.

Seeking reputation. Many of the experiences we cultivate are aimed toward the substantiation of our reputation, and a remarkable number of our ancillary activities are directed toward the establishment of our personal image or projected identity.

4.

Seeking improvement. This major focus is involved with the notion of "better/worse", gain versus loss, and our insistence that there is a reliable mechanism by which cause inexorably produces effect. This is at the root of our endless pursuit of the ideal—the ideal of the future betterment of the self, or of others, or of the world.

5.

Seeking knowledge. Central to the desire for improvement is the accumulation of knowledge, technique ("knowledge is power"). We hypothesize that knowledge will automatically provide understanding (as another development of cause and effect). We assume that with a proper explanation we will proceed unerringly.

6.

Seeking control. Knowledge is a springboard for control. A considerable amount of our energies are expended in the effort to control.

Seeking security. Virtually all of our activities are dedicated to the objective of attempting to establish dependable security in an utterly insecure world. We long for certainty.

Seeking escape. In this world of uncertainty, we seek an alternative...escape. Through pleasure; through experience; through our idea of the isolated self; the ideal; knowing; through control; we hope to find the security through which we can escape uncertainty, a way to pass through the unknown with assurance that we will not err.

. . . .

Mandate

The only possible point there could be in enlightenment would be to sever the bonds of our selfishness. Though symbolically we speak of *wholeness* and *fragmentation*, fragmentation means nothing other than selfishness. When Krishnamurti said, in dedication of his remaining life, that he would only be present to "set men absolutely, unconditionally free", what could he have meant except free from selfishness and its accompanying fears and turmoil?

The only question is this: can we live without selfishness? If so, what does that specifically entail in our actual moment-by-moment behavior or presence?

The dictionary says that selfishness is "having such regard for one's own interest and advantage that the happiness and welfare of others becomes of less concern..." Not *equal* (as implied in "whole"), but *less* (as implied in "fragment").

There is only one item of substance for you to decide, and it is this: can you be a non-conformist, in a world conforming to selfishness? And not merely a nonconformist in *thinking*, but in *action*—moment by moment, day by day?

Selfishness is based on fear, insecurity. Fear is berthed in a warped perspective of reality, that tunnel vision which precludes the panoramic view. When this cataract is removed, there will be realization.

All One Can Hope For

Your vision seems to be coming clearer. Your analysis of the relative reality, of our world, is accurate (to this observer of it for seven decades).

The pendulum swings: sometimes the world's (locally or globally) condition seems better, sometimes it seems worse. But, either way, ultimately it is "sound and fury, signifying nothing".

We live in a universe so vast that our peering into it ends in an edge of darkness, all around: we can only muse at how *immense* it *must* be. The universe is crowded with galaxies (*galaxies*—each may average 100 million *stars*, suns like ours), like our night sky is peppered with stars. We humans are not even *dust* here! Our *short-lived* species may evaporate in a cosmic twinkling. From this standpoint of cosmic perspective, hope*less*ness for the "human condition" is nothing more than sensible, realistic.

Selfishness is mankind's most fundamental characteristic. Institutionalized selfishness is summarized as "The ends justify the means." Carried to its logical extreme, the consequence is fascism.

The only historically-demonstrated antidote to selfishness is spiritual rebirth. This can *only* occur *voluntarily* within the heart of *each* individual. So, the only practical cure for selfishness/fascism is to first remove the mote from one's *own* eye, through individual voluntary spiritual rebirth. Then one is in a position to serve as a guiding light for others.

But, even then, ultimately the prognosis for our species is extinction. In fact, the ultimate prognosis for each individual is "hopeless": extinction. At death, whether you are selfish or selfless, the entire universe disappears.

This hopelessness that you are moving toward, then, can be a sign of maturation, in spiritual terms. When you perceive that "Ultimately, *nothing really matters*", self concern falls away. When the (small) self is absent, what is present? When That is present, the light shines that has an effect on the selfishness that is all around it. That is *all* that one can *hope* to do.

Suchness

Duality, which has been referred to by many sages, basically defines a condition wherein exists "more than one"—generally, two (which, in Latin, is *duo*). In Buddhism it is usually synonymous with "manyness", multiplicity.

The two (or more) things which comprise duality can be any two (or more) things. The proposition that there is "good" at one extreme, and "bad" at another extreme, is an example of duality. If I say that there is "this" over here and "that" over there, two different or "separate" things, that would be a dualistic expression. If I say that "I" ("me") like spaghetti ("not-me"), this is dualism. To hold the view that there is something identifiable as "me" and something identifiable (or unidentifiable) as "god" is dualistic.

However, even if I say that "I" *am* "god", I haven't yet exceeded the boundaries of duality. In the same way, if I say, "*I* feel *fear*", that is duality; if I say, "I *am* the fear that I feel", that is still duality.

The nature of normal human thought is divisive. A mother opens the door and steps into the room: all of the stillness and all of the motion in the room are summarized into one immediate, pertinent sentence in Mom's mind; observing little Andy holding a ruler, and hearing wee Carol crying, Mother's initial thought is, "Andy hit Carol."

Typically, human thought finds its expression in sentences, and these sentences are composed of words. Each word "means" a "different" "thing": *Andy* is one thing, *Carol* is another thing, and *hit* is yet another thing.

Andy is the subject of the thought, Carol is the object, and hit is the action which connects the other two, subject-versus-object, things.

Even in the shortest sentence (in the Bible)—"Jesus wept."—Jesus is one thing, his weeping is another thing...although "related".

Primary to all relational, or relative, thought is the self-conclusive thought, the "I" thought, which predicates the existence of the subject of the thought. The formulation of the thought "I am angry" presumes not only that such a specific entity as anger exists, but that there is a particular entity—I—that recognizes anger and has cause to consciously note its presence.

The unquestioned (and in some minds unquestionable) assumption, or conclusion, that there is in reality a separate "self" which exists, is the very foundation of all of our common, relational thinking.

143

To whatever extent that one cannot (at least experimentally) suspend the "certainty" of the sense of self, one cannot appreciate the perspective which the sages have described as non-dual. This is referred to, in contemporary terms, as oneness or wholeness, and in Buddhism as suchness, in Taoism as *tao* (the way it is).

To minds limited to the mechanics of duality (self versus other, this as opposed to that), even to say that "all things are one" will not transcend the perspective of duality—because they envision that "one" (entity A) *containing* "all things" (entity B). *Not-two implies that there is not ever, under any circumstances, more than (if any) one thing or entity: "all things", and the "one" thing that they are, are the* same *thing.*

The yogi Patanjali is credited with saying, "It is the observer-observed phenomenon which is the cause of human suffering." Krishnamurti was known to have stated this more succinctly, in equation form: "The observer is the observed."

This statement sometimes engenders confusion in a mind which cannot (even temporarily) suspend its attachment to the dualistic propensity of thought. Its first reaction may be, "If I—the observer—look at a tree—the   observed—am I the *tree?*" To suggest, in response, the true implication is that there is, quintessentially, no I (other than as an isolated, thought-created entity) and no tree (ditto) will likely be resisted.

I cannot truly *be* the tree and have my I-ness remain. And if I, the observer, am the observed tree, the tree is likewise the very same thing that the observer is—which is to say that it no longer retains exclusive tree-ness. My separate identity has vanished into the tree (the observer is the observed), in this manner of speaking; and the separate identity of the tree—both of which identities were only the distinctive creation of thought—has vanished into me (the observed is likewise the observer). Two separate, dualistic identities have evaporated. If we now feel compelled (as thought will) to find a name for what is no longer the observer/observed contradistinction, we can call it suchness, oneness, "not-two, not-one", etc.

The mind which is enmeshed in duality is the psyche which is reluctant to surrender its sovereignty; that is, to re-examine the certainty that "I"—me, myself—exist as an entity which is independent and in a subject-object relationship to every other supposed entity.

To realize that the observer does not categorically exist (nor, by definition, that which he alleges to observe) is thoroughly to reorient one's entire mode of thinking. When the observer is actually the observed, there can be no "self" nor "other". Any such distinctions, however subtle, are the dualistic assertions of divisive thought.

"No self?! No *right* and *wrong*? No *past* and *future?!*", one exclaims. Is it any wonder that duality is a pattern of thought which man finds it exceedingly difficult to relinquish?

At death...or possibly *before*... that which *thinks* it is an independent, isolated entity (and that which it thinks it separately and "objectively" observes or identifies)—"self" and all "other"—will disappear: there is not any thing which stands apart from suchness, not one thing.

Meditative Mind

That sense of peace *can* be yours wherever you are.

And it will be, when the divisive perspective ends.

That the divisive perspective is present is evident when we find one setting more satisfying than another.

This does not mean that we have to *try* to be "peaceful" in a raucous setting. It means that *discrimination* is no longer the *stimulus* for our "unpeacefulness".

When the divisive perspective has dissolved, one circumstance is not viewed as more preferable than another.

This is not an abstract understanding, it is a practical understanding.

When we are desiring a particular condition, we are desiring a particular effect. True peacefulness means being okay with whatever condition or effect is *present*. To be in whatever the present condition is, and to be dissatisfied with that condition is not peaceful.

This may seem obvious, but people often don't follow this obvious pointer to its logical conclusion: when one circumstance is *not* viewed as more *preferable* than another, then we are *not* desiring a *particular* effect; therefore we are at peace with *whatever* condition or effect *is* present—even if the present condition is *not* one that would be *defined* as "peaceful".

A true example, from a recognized master (Ramana): He was sitting quietly, after dark, doing nothing—"meditating". He heard someone enter the enclosure where he was. The intruder began looking around, evidently intent on theft. Ramana approached, to tell the man that nothing of value would be found there. The man, seeing him, struck him on the leg with a club. This did not make Ramana "happy": he shouted, "Now hit me on the other leg, if you must!" Startled by the shout, the man fled.

The sage, in mediation, is neither at peace nor *not* at peace: he is *one* with whatever condition happens to be present. He is not desirous of one circumstance being present over another.

Thus, even if the mind is agitated—and seemingly not at peace—the awareness of the sage is even "at peace" with *that*.

Even when Ramana shouted out in anguish, his innate "peaceful state" was not disturbed.

Nor was it to be further *disturbed* by emotional or mental turmoil resulting from his awareness that he *had* shouted in outrage.

With whatever condition or circumstance that happens to be *present*—his *agitation*, or even *regret* for that agitation—he is uninterruptedly *undisturbed* in his all-inclusive awareness.

With nondiscriminatory serenity, it matters not *where* or in *what* condition one abides. All is the same. Peacefulness is *there*, not somewhere to be *sought* and subsequently "found".

The key is not in *cultivating* a meditative mind, but to recognize that a meditative mind (as Krishnamurti would say) is "*choiceless*".

Choiceless awareness is the basis of incorruptible meditation—freedom in meditation, meditation *without limitations*, such as "time" or "place".

This is yours, in relinquishing the dualistic (here/there; better/worse) perspective.

Sexuality

Very little is said, in spiritual literature, about sexuality. Psychologists have pointed out that mankind's activity is fired by two basic drives: the pursuit to preserve personal identity, and the expression of sexuality. Both could be said to be desire; the latter, an instinctual desire. Being so basic and integral, sexuality is at the core of physical existence—collectively and individually. Being so fundamental to our humanness, where does one begin in discussing it?

When one's life is whole and unfragmented, one's sexuality is not a separate and troublesome fragment. Put another way, when one's life is in order, one's sexual life is in order.

So what is implied, in terms of sexuality, for one who is attentive to the moment? In order to consider this, let us examine some of the elements which are involved in the traditional boy-meets-girl sexual encounter.

Typically, there is a subject/object relationship. One or both participants view the other as a means to an end. Even though the end result may be cooperative, mutual gratification, the partner is primarily viewed as a means to an end, in time, an object in the quest for gratification.

There normally is the element of expectation. There is an idea, in the mind of one or both, that a memorable sexual experience may unfold; a hope for fulfillment, an expectation of agreement and cooperation from the other party. As a result of an initial pleasurable experience, there may be the hope or expectation for a repeated experience.

There often follows attachment and dependence. This may be combined with conformity to tradition, which can translate into the obligations and responsibilities of marriage and child-rearing, accompanied by an idealistic projection of the couple's life together into the future.

Even short of this, basic to a sexual encounter is the pursuit of pleasure as the goal or "gaining idea", in itself, with the reaffirmation of one's ego as a side benefit in the experience of seduction.

None of these developments are "sinful" or "wrong"; they are certainly typical, as a result of our conditioning, in today's world. But like so many other reactive patterns in our culture today, their observation can be instructive in contemplation,

The sexual instinct is natural and not to be denied. Can we be open to our sexuality, in our relationship with other persons, without acculturated preconceptions? Can we view the other person as a sexual being, like ourself, without imposing upon them the objectification of a desire for sexual gratification? Can we explore the development of our relationship, from moment to moment, without expectation, without ideas, without longing?

Are we ever really dependent upon another person for sexual expression and satisfaction? Can we engage in sexual activity without the restrictive bonds of attachment? Can we end each encounter without fantasies which remand us into the future? Can our sexual expression be an extension of our capacity to live wholly in this moment, and not merely another disjointed activity of fragmented behavior? Can we be free of the pursuit of experience and achievement and reinforcement of our ego, which characterize the typical activity? Can our sexuality be the natural expression of an inalienable instinct, and not the compulsive culmination of inflamed desire?

Describing the Indescribable

There is a distinction that might seem trivial, but makes a difference semantically.

The literature often describes the Absolute as "all that is"— which is an appropriate description. It could be paraphrased, "everything is That".

An alternative way (that the Absolute is often described) is as "nothingness"; the Absolute is the "void" of Buddhism: it can be said that it is, by its nature, "nothing". The *nothing*, in this sense, is meant to be the literal meaning of the word; no *thing*; not an entity, or object.

As said above, however, the Absolute can also equally be said to be "everything that is"—because, by its appearance as *all* that is, it has no separable identification of its own: it cannot be pointed to, apart from something that it (already) exists as.

But if we preferentially stress its aspect of being *every thing*, we focus on "thingness"; our attention is drawn to the (myriad) *things* that it is. In other words, our consideration is on *multiplicity*.

From the standpoint of contemplating nonduality, it is more efficacious to preferentially regard the Absolute in the sense of its nothingness. This brings our attention to the condition of no "thing": the absence of separativeness among the apparent phenomena (all of which That essentially is). This holds our attention on its *non*-dual nature.

So, being all that is—every *thing*—it is nothing, in that it transcends identity apart from the phenomenon it appears as.

It's noteworthy that an enlightened person—whose sense of being is *all-inclusive*—does not exclaim, in conclusion, "I am something!", but typically, "I am nothing!"

Vedanta in a Nutshell

For those of us not raised in India, reading some of the Vedanta material *can* be confusing. What (in its truest sense) the Christians call God, or the Muslims call Allah, or the Buddhists call the Void, etc., is the same as what the Vedanta teachers call the Self. This is also the same as what is universally called the Absolute.

And all of this is only the *beginning* of many names for this same item. All such names are, basically, merely *different* names for the *same* one item.

In many cases, these names are meant to be somewhat *descriptive* of what they're naming. What they are naming is Existence, in its most universal form. What they are naming is Reality, in its most general form. What they are naming is the Sub-stratum, the essence of this universal or general Reality or Existence.

In many other cases, these names are *not* descriptive in the sense of being definitions: Ram, Allah, God, for example.

So, all such names that you read can be understood to *all* be simply different names for the One: Existence, Reality, Substratum, Void, God, Allah, Ram, Absolute, etc.

Vedanta texts commonly use—for this same One—the word Self. Obviously, when the word self is not capitalized, it is meant to represent the same as the word "ego": *ego* is Latin for "I"; *self* refers to what you identify as that I.

Self with a capital S, of course, is meant to represent the *Substratum* of the I: what we *are* that goes *beyond* the ego, beyond what we identify as I or "me".

So, in answer to your first question: this Self is considered, in Vedanta, to be the source (or, as Source—capitalized—another way of descriptively naming the One) of the entirety of Existence, the entirety of Reality.

If a ball of dough is the "source" of a loaf of bread, the ball of dough and the loaf of bread are the *same* (one) thing, though they each may *appear* to be *different* things.

So if the Self (One) is the *source* of the *entirety* of existence, it is the source of the small-s self, the source of this thing called "I", or "ego".

Ramana says imagine a movie projector. Like the Self, it is the *source* of the light (*Light*—capitalized—is sometimes another word for the One) that appears on the screen (the screen representing our world, or the universe in general). The *images* that appear on the screen *seem* to be figures of substance: but the cowboy who is shot and falls dead is not a "real person".

So, this example suggests, the *Self* (or One) is the source which *projects* what we identify as the "I", or *self*. The *basis* for self-reality must be traced back to the Self, the *source* of Reality for *all* Existence.

When the self traces back the *source* of its *reality*, it discovers the (One) source of *all* existence: the (Vedanta's word) *Self*. In short, the "I" is nothing other than a *projection* of (or "by") the Self. This is what Vedanta is saying will be discovered in getting to the *bottom* of the *question*, "who am 'I'?" (Really, *what* am I?)

When "categories" are spoken of, it means *differences*. Differences are obvious when considering "opposites": white is different than (and the opposite of) black; day versus night; good, as opposed to bad, etc. White is "in one category", black is "in another category".

Most categories, or differences, are more subtle. The unenlightened view the *self* as in a separate *category* from the *Self*. Vedanta is saying that such categorization is false; there is only One thing: Self/self is actually the same One thing.

When *sheaths* are spoken of, these are categories. Along with this word, a Sanskrit word is sometimes seen: *samskaras*—which stands for "tendencies", such as result from our conditioning. A tendency to be competitive, for example, is due to our conditioning that our ego ought to prevail over that of others. Resentment is a tendency, due to our conditioning, that our ego is fragile and can suffer. So samskaras are also categories: such as competition, resentment, etc. The "ego" is composed of layers of such sheaths—which are said to be "covering up" what is at the real core of the self (that being its source, or Self).

One can attempt to remove the "layers", by—for example— "practicing tolerance". Or one can "cut through" all the sheaths, all at once—by discovering that the self is actually a (false) image. If the item at the center of the sheaths ("me") is a false image, from the start, what need is there to worry about the so-called sheaths that are "hiding" it?

The key to everything said in Vedanta is found in just one sentence: The Self (the one Reality) is *all* that there *is*!

Being all that *is*, the Self is *you*. "You" actually being the Self, "you" *do not exist*—except *as* the Self. You. Are. *That*.

And not anything exists *except* That (Self).

Perceive *this*—and lay all books aside!

. . . .

Real Romance

Each monograph I have written has been intended to spark contemplation in the reader, as it has in the writer. Therefore, this purpose has been served whenever that has been the result: in other words, the reader need not necessarily agree with the observations of the writer in order for the effort to have justified itself.

In the monograph entitled "Sexuality", the point that is intended is this: the dynamics of the typical romantic relationship may at times be inconsistent with what is generally considered to be a spiritual outlook.

Specifically, in ten short paragraphs, the considerations that were suggested are these:

To one (or both) of the partners, is the other partner essentially a means to an end?; in terms of sexual gratification ; as provider of some form of security; as a comforter and help-mate, etc.?

Is the relationship based primarily on the pursuit of pleasure (in its myriad forms) and/or the aversion of discomfort (in its many guises)?

Are the partners (at least in their own mind) dependent upon each other, in any way? Does either partner (or both) find themselves with attachment to some worldly aspect of the consequences of their union?

Is expectation involved; such as in performance, by each other; or concerning the eventual nature of their relationship; or in regarding their future jointly, etc.?

In what degree does either of them operate on the basis of preconceived ideas and fixed beliefs and opinions?

Now, obviously, none of these items, to be considered, are inconsistent with the typical notion of romantic relationship that is prevalent in the world today. Indeed, such questions as these would not even normally be considered seriously. But all of these items, I submit, are inconsistent with a spiritual point of view in which any particular person (including oneself) is not persistently held in greater esteem than another.

This is not to say that two people may not be in a relationship which is beneficial to both. But why should either person limit that relationship to one other "special" person? Why would not both persons be equally in relationship with everyone they know, in the same mutually beneficial way? What obligations ought I to have, to someone whom I regard dearly, that I do not have to all my fellow beings?

You may comment that such considerations would wreak havoc with the conventional marital institution, as we know it. And I would agree. This is not a treatise on how to find oneself conventionally married, or in the role of a family founder. There are some to whom there are more urgent considerations than those of marital felicity or family fraternity. Yet even among these, I propose, felicitous and dear relationship is not disbarred. It is not, however, of primary importance, nor viewed without non-attachment.

Nor is this to say that an attitude of nonattachment to others is superior to an attitude of attachment. It is possible, in one's lifetime, to move between these positions. (I have been involved in two "normal" marriages; therefore it is not impossible that I could be involved in another.) But there is a factor, here, which makes that unlikely.

The essence of spirituality, in our lives, could be said to be the realization of the interconnectedness, or "unity", of all things. This realization is a fact in our lives only to the extent that it is reflected in our moment-by-moment behavior. And it will dictate our behavior only to the extent that this realization is the prime mover of our behavior. In other words, to a person who truly perceives the unity of all things, his behavior is affected by that perception.

To one who recognizes the inseparability of all things, no one person—including oneself—is more significant, or singular, than any other. In my own case, after an active romantic life of some 30 years, I have not been romantically involved with anyone, for more than 20 years. This has not been a matter of avoidance or abstinence, since—during these years—I have continued to respond to each moment just as it is, and have not held predetermined notions as to how I should or should not respond in any encounter. It is merely the consequence of the revelation, about twenty years ago, of the inseparability of all things—in which profound love is not confined to any particular individual or personality. In any generally accepted sense, I have been far more loving toward all whom I encounter, than I had ever been in the previous long years before this unifying revelation. I have not ever, in this later period, felt lonely, alone or isolated. And concern for security, the future, the past—and even the present—has not been at issue. Under such circumstances, what need has one to arrange romance? And yet, moment-to-moment, I am not closed to any of the possibilities which life could offer. This even includes marriage and family involvement, at this late stage in my life. I do not, however, expect that that will come to pass.

To quote: "They put their individual lives in order, and then perhaps they may or may not run across someone else who has done the same." To me, putting one's life in order suggests the realization of universal (spiritual) Truth, as the first order: and all else flows from that. Assuming that two people meet who have done this, it seems likely to me that they will not find themselves intentionally and permanently committed only to each other.

A. In spiritual writings—especially those of Krishnamurti—there is often a reference to "choiceless awareness". What is being suggested?

B. What does choice mean to you?

A. A preference between two—or more—things.

B. "Two, or more, things." What does *duality* mean to you?

A. The existence of, at least, two things.

B. And those two things can be two things that are alike, such as neutrons, or two things that are considered to be unalike, such as man and god. When we suppose the existence of any two—or more—"things", then there is always the possibility of preference for one as opposed to another. In other words, as soon as two "distinctions" are conceived (such as "me" and "you"), the dilemma of choice arises: shall I concern myself with *your* welfare, or with *my* welfare; with *our* security, or *their* security; et cetera. The proposition of "choiceless awareness" is a suggestion that there is a way *out* of that *dilemma*... a matter having to do with non-preference.

A. So, it's a matter of not "preferring" one thing, or event, over another.

B. But how could that condition of "not preferring" come about, without making a choice?

A. You mean, one would have to, at least initially, make a choice to "not prefer".

B. Then, the choicelessness itself wouldn't be "choicelessness", would it? If we say that "as long as duality is the primary condition, choice will persist", how is "choosing" to be ended —without making that a choice?

A. By putting an end to duality.

B. Could you "put an end to duality" without choosing, for yourself, to do so?

A. Perhaps a choice isn't necessary. Some say that the ultimate condition of actuality is non-dual—"not two, not one"—from the start.

B. If you were to actually realize the full truth of that—not as a handed-down supposition, but as a profound recognition— would that not put to rest the confusion of "dualism", for you?

A. Could that, itself, be done without making a choice?

B. If non-duality is the true nature of actuality, of absolute actuality, what choice can be made?

A. Perhaps that's one of the choices we make: to ignore the true nature of actuality.

B. Which is why Buddhists call it 'ignore-ance'. When one is aware that, ultimately, there are no choices—there can, from the absolute standpoint, *be* no choices—this is the "awareness of choicelessness". One is not choiceless by choice, but because it is recognized that choice, finally, is meaningless. As Suzuki Roshi put it, "ours is to see things as they are [non-dual]...and to let everything go as it goes [without preference]".

A. Ah, choice-less awareness.

Clagle. Clagle.

Water. Water.

The word *water*—even the sound, the vocalized pronunciation of the word *water*—means nothing, of itself. What caused you to think that you *understood* what was *meant* by the word *water*—but not the prior word, *clagle*? Hundreds of generations ago, we humans (that includes—included—you and I) arrived at a mutual agreement, regarding the sounded word *water*. We uttered the sound, ordained it as a 'word', and concurred on the substance (or substances) that it would include. We agreed that 'lake' and 'rain' were included, but that water was yet *apart from* mere 'lake' or 'rain'.

We arrived at no such agreement concerning *clagle*—which I, just a moment ago, contrived myself.

We, likewise, did arrive at an agreement that water is 'wet'; but that wetness is somehow *apart from* water, considering that we acknowledge that other liquids—such as syrup—are 'wet'. So *more* than mere water is included in *wet*—even though *wet* is a shorter word-sound than *water*—because of an agreement, or social contract, that you and I bought into as tots (before we were even cognizant that we had done so).

Water and wet are not abstract concepts; we have been physically immersed in a bathtub of water, and we know firsthand what it is —at least, what it *means*—to *be* wet.

Clagle. Clagle.

God. God.

We have also, collectively and generally, agreed that the latter word-sound is a representation of "an immortal being with special powers over the course of nature; typically worshipped as a male deity". For any of us who have not sat in a tubful of warm god, and splashed god onto the bath mat, this allegedly "hallowed" word-sound can be nothing more than an abstract representation, or symbol, for a speculative idea about something. Not anything about god—as far as the word or its meaning is concerned—is in the least concrete. Though this word-sound is even as short as *wet*, it connotes far vaster implications; anything that's wet is considered to be simply a ramification of nature—not wielding "special powers over the course of nature".

Perhaps, someone might reply, the meaning of *god* has been refined by recent well-educated generations: "Almighty Being, regarded as omnipresent, omniscient, and omnipotent." Would this ever-present, all-present being *not* be present in the phenomenon of sound itself; that is, would *it* not be the very utterance of the word *god*—and all additional words as well? Would this Being, having "all powers", not *be* the power—the *organism*—which expresses any, and every, sound?

If so, we could say that it is the (meaningless) *sound* which defines god—long before, even, any significance is *attached* to the sound. Or we could say that it is *you* who *utters* the sound who is the definition, or re-presentation, of god. In fact, under the circumstances, the only reasonable conclusion here is that it is *god* who is defining, or representing, god. For what reason do "we" need to agree on the meaning of such conceptual abstractions? Since the word-sound *god* is you—*and* me—why do we need it "between us"? This word won't even keep us from getting wet!

For two years, I lived in a Zen farming commune, in a monastic setting. We sat zazen (meditation) two 40-minute periods in the morning, and two more in the evening—a total of some two and a half hours a day. I also took long walks (a couple of hours) in the woods, on trails, in between.

In my opinion, the former "practice" was of no value. The latter (which I would call "contemplation", in contrast to meditation), I feel, was of *some* value perhaps.

To confine oneself to sit in one spot with some purpose in mind is generally counter-productive. Even at best, there will always be distractions from the "purpose"; and having a purpose for disciplined meditation is itself counterproductive for allowing a condition of non-attachment. To observe the workings of the mind—which is about all that meditation can provide—one need only attend to what appears on the screen of consciousness throughout the day (or, while lying in bed, at night). What appears are thoughts: thoughts are separative, divisive. There has to be something that takes place (for enlightenment to unfold) beyond the mere observation of thought.

One can engage in contemplation without a compulsive purpose or a rigid discipline. While involved in any "mindless" activity—such as taking a walk—one can observe the workings of the mind, even while "distracted" by "distractions". Without attachment to concerns for results, the mind is free to ponder (in an unrestrained way) the interconnection between the observer and all that is being observed: "I am actively experiencing life, right here, right now. Why is there this perception of 'separateness'?" Contemplating the source of awareness (whether it is awareness of 'separation' or of 'unification') can bear greater fruit than can simply observing one's thoughts for 40 minutes.

Briefly put, I do not recommend formal meditation of any sort. I do, if anything, support an introspective contemplation which can take place any time, and for any length of time, during the day. Introspection means that the subject is not contemplating an object; the subject is contemplating the subject itself: "Why is this activity being engaged in? What is the expectation involved in it? What is the supposed benefit, and for whom? Who or what is it that is *observing* 'the observing' that is going on?" Etc. Such contemplation needs to wander out of the range of the divisiveness of thought. It will be treading in an area of intuition (an area over which the calculating mind does not have control), from whence arises the "Aha!" recognition.

This kind of deep contemplation accompanies a deep, naturally-occurring questioning. "Who am I? Why am I here? What is this life about?" These kinds of questions lead some into structured meditation; but the structure itself restrains the psyche from allowing the intuition the freedom to resolve these questions. As Krishnamurti would say, for there to *be* freedom (enlightenment), you have to *start* with freedom (non attachment to conceptual structure).

Once the "unitive" Aha! awareness *is* present—indisputably—it does not *cease* to be present: the contemplation (spoken of here) is a fixture of *waking* awareness. With the (nagging) questions resolved in one stroke, contemplation *now* is a matter of conscious presence: attentively aware of the fluctuating "here and now". It is absorption in this continual awareness which presents as "placidity". Its real core is non-attachment; not a non-attachment which is willed or "enforced", but the non-attachment which is a consequence of the dissolution of the image of a separate self.

Even the persistent, aware realization, which is observed to be in place, is not "my" realization. That is why its "maintenance" is effortless.

Adyashanti had (for many years) practical experience with formal meditation. Like many others, he gave it up. Now, instead, he suggests that one "get comfortable and simply allow everything to be as it is": contemplate *whatever* arises in consciousness, and allow *everything* to be *as it is*. No agenda.

As Suzuki Roshi said, "The true purpose of Zen (enlightenment) …is to see things as they are…and to *let everything go as it goes*." This results in the serenity which practitioners *hope* to acquire from meditation. If they *were* letting everything go as it goes, what would be the need for continual meditation?

It's Vital

Astrophysicist Paul Davies has written about a "new universe" revealing itself through "changing ideas about space, time, and the nature of the cosmos…

"The revolution now in progress could alter, forever, not only mankind's perspective of the universe, but also (your) own place in that universe."

He comments: "Maybe our descendants…will arrange their lives very differently from our own.

"…without expectation, remorse, fear…their conception of the world might be incomprehensible to us. It is probable…we would be unable to communicate much of common understanding."

Throughout human history there have been those who have asserted that indeed there is truly a realm where fear has no relevance. And, furthermore, that it is possible for each of us to live the duration of our lives in that realm.

As Davies indicates, these persons attest that there is a fundamental connection between that realm and a change in "ideas about space, time and the nature of the cosmos".

This alteration *does* depend on, they say, a "revolution" in one's "perspective of the universe" *and* one's perceived "place in that universe". And what follows is that these "realized" persons arrange their lives, as Davies suggests, "very differently from our own". (One is reminded of a Krishnamurti book title: *A Wholly Different Way of Living*.)

Such a "conception of the world" is generally "incomprehensible to us". But those who have spoken of the existence of this realm claim that this need not be the case. However, there tends to be an inbuilt difficulty—relevant to "real world" perspectives—in communicating "much of common understanding" about a realm in which fear knows no place.

In summary, there may be more in human existence than seems immediately to be apparent to us. If that is so, what could that be? And more importantly: if so, what are the implications for the way in which we currently live our lives?

Let us speculate here about a few tangential possibilities.

In mathematics, by not skipping or ignoring any of the computations, we arrive at a conclusion (however unexpected that conclusion might be at which we arrive).

However, it is very difficult for something to compute which by its nature tends to escape, or supersede, the bounds of logic.

If we posit that "there is not anywhere where Q is not", then it is not entirely logical to speak of the existence of Q, from that start. For if Q is "everything", by definition, then it is not anything in particular: it is non-existent as an entity. So how could something which is extrinsically nonexistent be "everything"? And, so, there is a point at which we are required to accept tentative possibilities as probabilities—at least until we can explore where they might point.

For example, given what might be called the factor of Q, in a situation which is utterly devoid of any *separate* thing, there is no such "reality" as "movement". There would not be some "thing" which moves within (or about or around) some "other" thing. There is, in effect, only *one thing*. (And semantically, as we have described, there is not even that "one" thing.) Where there is only one thing, absolutely, there is not anything into (or out of) which it could move.

This propositional difficulty becomes even more profound, given one especially "impossible" aspect of Q. The more impossible it appears, the more likely we may be overlooking an astounding possibility.

Q, you surely appreciate by now, in its *manyness* is never for an instant apart from its *oneness*. Its manyness is in no way a contradiction, or contradistinction, to its oneness: they are both the same (to) Q. All things are inseparable, in Q context.

Please be attentive. *All* of It is wholly and entirely present, no matter where (or when) that happens (specifically, or particularly) to *be*.

It is because it is utterly space-less that It—all of it—is incapable of being designated in any distinguishable space. At any "point" that *any* of it is, *all* of it is. Wherever It is in its infinite diversity, it is indivisibly present in its cosmic wholeness.

Now, is that a "logical difficulty", or what?

If something could be said to be "miraculous", this surely is it.

There is no *point* or *instant* where the Immensity is not *wholly* and *indivisibly* Present. 100%: no matter how many "separate" points you choose to designate. It is there 100% at each and every point. Either that, or any attempt to describe the unknowable in terms of the knowable is, at the outset, doomed to insufficiency.

The thrust is that a) You are in no way *distant* or distinct from Q. b) You do not "share" in Eternity. c) You are not "part" of the Infinite. d) There is no way in which your "true identity" can be escaped.

In the profound sense, your identity is that, in actuality, you have no identity.

What would it be to abide—experientially—in this Present awareness?

The apparently extra-ordinary characteristic of the presence of "centerless" awareness would be (and has been) called "timelessness".

From the cosmic (or Q) standpoint, "past", "present" and "future" have no distinctive meaning. If there was any such suppositional framework, *all* of its components would be *simultaneously* present, or they would not be actual. If the past, present and future—in reality—"exist", they must (all together) exist *now*. Therefore, they would be (at best) one inseparable unit; which, of course, would completely void their meaning. The always-instantaneous presence of Q, in full, focuses all of possible duration into one point: and that one point has no more significance than any other point.

This confronts man with his most crucial dilemma. He has, consistently, acted—persistently—as if there was in reality some such proposition as a "past". And when not presently engaged in relationship to a past, he is acting as if there existed a "future".

The consequence of this misperception has been a concern for "his" security, for his "survival".

The consequence of *this* misunderstanding has been, and is, that man abides chronically in a general and collective condition of fear.

The consequence of *that* preoccupation has been that he—both individually and collectively—has not experienced the dimension of universal love.

Nor can he, or will he, experience universal love as an actuality while imprisoned, or limited, in the chilling bonds of fear.

To the extent of one's awareness of his *true*, primal and inescapable identity, fear cannot compute. One cannot comprehend the implied nature of the Immensity and continue to entertain the notion that there is actually anything to fear.

To choose to continue to live in fear is to choose to continue one's accustomed way of responding to the universe. It is to choose to "try to love" while contradicting what can be perceived as Truth. And trusting that Truth.

"Realization" is the resolution of fear. To remove the limitation of fear is to open the organism to the presence of limitless love.

The Infinite represents freedom from limitation. Wholly.

Now.

What Jesus *Knew*

You are beginning to look at things from the standpoint of how (we *might* say) they are seen by the Absolute; that is, beyond their relative appearance (or forms). And that is what "awakening" is all about. Also, the questions you are posing are much more to the (pertinent) point.

Regarding your comments on forgiveness, and being in the position of not being forgiven by others, it seems to me that the critical question is, "Have you forgiven yourself?"

Concerning your query, which I will summarize as "How do you know, when you're doing something, that it is what That opts to do?" This question is viewed from the standpoint of "me" in *relation* to It. But consider that there isn't a Robert, a "me", that is doing anything. Whatever is done is *That* doing what it does. Robert is the eyes through which That is experiencing ("conscious of") what is being done by its "Self". Therefore, Robert (aware of this as That) doesn't question what is being done. If a question *were* to arise (to Robert), it would be That which inquires.

This is why, for Ramana, self-inquiry is always *Self*-inquiry. When you perceive who is the source of the inquiry, the inquiry itself no longer has a meaning or purpose. The "who am I?" question is seen to resolve as "no who; no I".

You referred to the Book of John, Chap. 17, in which Jesus is reported to have said aloud what his disciple(s) heard: Jesus' description, as you say, "of the Absolute" (as "You", rather than That). "Everything you have *given* me comes from you." *Every* would include thoughts, motivations, behaviors. Why? Because even "*I* came from you." So much are the two one that "*all* I have is yours, and all *you* have is mine...we are one....you are *in* me and *I* am in you": there can be no separate distinction whatever.

Not just the two are one, but the "three" are one. "We are one: I in *them* ("others") and you in me....complete unity." Jesus' words.*

"Though the world does not *know* you, I know you...I have made you known to them, and will continue to make you known...that I myself may be in them."

Not only is Jesus and That emphatically the same, but it is That which is (also) "in" others. "I", as That, am in "them".

How did Jesus know, when he was doing something, that it was what That opts to do? Because he *is* That—and nothing beyond that.

Jesus was pointing out (again) how things are viewed when they are perceived from the standpoint of the Absolute: which he made *clear* was *his* standpoint. We could say, how the Absolute views its Self through this being's eyes: all forms recognized as the formless (*including* one's "own"). That is "illumination", en*light*enment: *Self*-awareness.

The Theory of Unity

B. In theory, I fully understand what is meant when we speak of "nonduality". But I am aware that if what I know to be theoretically accurate were to be translated into practice, I would likely be living my life in a radically different way. I am

---

* from the New International Version Bible

also conscious of what it is that is the barrier to translating theory into practice: it is fear. Even in theory, I cannot seem to uproot this fear.

A. And perhaps it will not be possible to uproot it until you come to the recognition that there could not possibly be anything to fear. How could there be—even in theory—anything to fear, where it is clearly understood that there are "not two things"? There can be fear only where there has been a "self" retained to be feared for. If there are not "two things", how does one live one's life?

B. Without a confirmed sense of separation from anything— such as a conscious sense of separate "self".

A. If you were to live your life—in practice, as you say—free of a sense of separation (as a separate self), do you suppose that your general behavior would be different than it is now?

B. I suspect that it would be radically different.

A. What are you separate from right now?

B. I perceive that my fears have separated me from the actuality in which no fear really exists.

A. Where there are no two things, what becomes of "you", "fear" and "actuality"?

B. This is something that I understand, on one level. But I continue to pursue a lifestyle which I perceive to be self-centered, to be principally concerned only with my own security and survival. That does not seem to me to basically be "conscious of nonduality".

A. Can one truly be conscious of nonduality without having fully faced one's fear of insecurity? Where there is only one thing, what has become of *you*? As long as there is supposedly a you, there must be a concern for outcome. Where there is only one thing, what possible outcome can be feared?

B. That's the point. When I acknowledge that there is only one thing, I acknowledge that I no longer have a "personal" life. And this recognition seems to dictate a change in current lifestyle. *And* the fears that consequently follow that recognition.

A. And therefore your life remains in *theory*.

Shall I Read Further?

Concerning your question, "Each day, there are new books, added to the list of the classics, which are meant to guide the seeker on the spiritual path. Where might one start, in reading this material, whether old or new?"

Consider that there is no need to read anything at all.

One could spend the balance of one's life reading about "the way" and how to "find" it. If it is the way that you want, the only way is to live it—and that means starting this instant. Insight is too quick for the literal mind.

When you have so fully perceived the truth that it affects your very movement, you will be acting out of an awareness that there is absolutely no division. When there is no division, you and the way are not, cannot be, parted. You were never apart from the truth, and you never will be. When will you *realize* that?

To real-ize means to make the thing real. If you realize that you and truth have never been separated (except by the veil of illusive thought, which is entirely the product of your "self"), what will you obviously do to make that truth a personal reality? You will *live* that truth, won't you?

If you were to start, this instant, living that truth, would you still ask that same question? An answer is implicit in a question: if there is a "seeker", then that seeker is viewing herself as separate from something—from that which is sought. There is *me*, the subject over here; and *awareness* (or enlightenment, if you prefer), the object, over there. The question becomes, "How can I manipulate (what is the technique), to make them one?"

A seeker has a desire. The surest way to bar yourself from living a life of awareness is to leave where you *are* and to set out in search of that which is *already* yours. And what will you do when you've found it? When you finally compare it with something else, and conclude that "Yep, this must be awareness", will you change the way you live your life—your actions, minute to minute? If so, ask yourself this: "If I were to begin this moment to *live* a life of awareness, would I be aware?"

One reads spiritual literature because one has a desire to attain. The spiritual literature *tells* you to give up *every hope*, including the hope of attaining. Give up the self that *would be* enlightened, the self which hopes.

The reason why there *are* spiritual classics is because, from the day they were written, readers have refused to acknowledge the message: stop reading, stop seeking, empty the mind of the self.

When the mind is empty of the self, who is there to read, and for what reason?

O. What is it that you're looking for?

X. I want to get to the bottom of this question, which I've been exploring for years now: what does it really mean, when all of the spiritual teachers speak of 'liberation'...'awakening'? What are they saying to *me*? It seems to be something that I'm not connecting with!

O. And what do you expect to do, when you find the answer to your question: when you've found what it is that you're looking for?

X. Ha! I don't know; I've never thought about what might come *after* that. I mean, in a general sense, I'd say that I'd hope to live in a life of peace—free of conflict, confusion. Is that idealistic?

O. It could be. What if what you discover results in unpredictable changes in your life? You might untie a ribbon and find that what's underneath is not what you expected: what you discover could totally change your life, in ways that you're not imagining.

X. Yeah, I suppose. You mean, letting go of control; not following the predictable agenda that I've set up for myself? I have thought about that. If I were to surrender *everything*, like they talk about, that *would* be unsettling. But that seems to come with the territory: I look at the lives of some of these people. They seem to be saying that you have to be willing to put everything on the line.

O. Well, that may be so; or may not be so. If it *were* so, how high is *your* risk quotient? What are you willing—or not willing—to let go of, in terms of what you now consider to be important aspects of your life?

X. You mean, what am I totally attached to—like, family? Well...I guess the one thing I wouldn't want to lose is my sanity!

O. What I'm getting at is, how high of a *priority*, in your life, is the discovery of what you say you're looking for? Is this interest somewhere down the line on the list of "Things I Hope to do before I Die", or is this the matter that needs to get resolved before any other, meaningful matter gets resolved?

X. Oh, no. I feel like what you *just* said. I'm sure that there's something that I'm not seeing—something that others have seen, or *are* seeing. I feel if I could see what's behind all this, as some say they have, I'd be making the right choices. It's the inner guide, the inner compass, that I want to be able to rely on. I don't want to waste any more time in my life, if that's what you're asking. I think of it as going back to Square One. And getting it right this time. *First* priority. Is that naïve?

O. Not at all. To me, it's realistic. But what you're talking about, I'm suggesting, is leaving the past behind *and* having no discernible future. See what I'm saying? Therefore, we're not talking about finding what you're seeking at some time in the *future*. We're talking about the "you", that you know, coming to an end. Not at some comfortable time in the future. Now. The question that needs to be asked is, "Am I prepared to die today?" That's how one needs to live one's life. Each day as the last. That's what your inner guide will tell you: your compass that points true north.

X. I understand what you're saying: a radical change in outlook, and experience.

O. Behavior, really. How do you live your life, when you no longer identify yourself as a "separate individual"?

X. Yes. I know there's something false about our egocentric point of view. But what am I, if *not* a separate individual? How do I make a connection with what I *really* am, underneath everything else?

O. You're saying there's something *real* beneath the *appearances*? Something that exists even when "you" no longer exist? How would you describe that "something"?

X. Well, a mystery!

O. How mysterious is it? What animates your body, your mind?

X. Life, I guess.

O. What activates other forms, in general?

X. Life, or energy.

O. What would you say is the source of activation of this entire cosmos?

X. That same energy, or spirit.

O. So, what is not clear about this mystery, to you?

X. My connection with it.

O. What is the source of your existence?

X. That energy.

O. So, how are you not "connected" to it?

X. But it's bigger than me: it's connected to all things.

O. Universally so.   That's the connection *you're* looking for.
    You're connected to—*in* and *with*—it. Your connection to it
    is established already, by the fact of your presence in this
    universe which it entirely activates.   You can't *escape* a
    connection with it.   And *because* of that connection, *you're*
    connected to all that is.   That source, of all that is, is the inner
    guide of all that is, the energizing or actualizing element
    common to everything, cosmically: "life", existence. When
    you die to who you *think* you are, what's left? Life?
    Existence? A "connection" that *always* existed, universally?
    Isn't *that* the "mystery"?: already being *inseparable* from the
    source, you "fail" to find a connection to that!   Can you see
    what's involved in the mystery?

X. The *appearance* is of a separate individual.   The *real* is a
    universal interconnectedness. The "me" is a coordinate of the
    two.

O. You could say "interdependent": there is no cosmic
    interconnectedness without all that is—including you—
    being an element of it.   Whether you view yourself as a
    product of the source or the source of the product, either
    view is appropriate in certain circumstances—and the choice
    is yours.   One of the choices, the choice we know best, is
    limiting your sense of yourself to a "separate individual".
    You've seen the perennial consequence of that, or we
    wouldn't be talking: divisiveness, and conflict.   The other
    possibility is to recognize the vital *reality* upon which all that
    appears, stands: the vital reality upon which the existence of
    "you" stands. In other words, you can identify yourself—in
    any moment—in a limited, limiting way; or you can

relinquish that identity, and not identify yourself in any *particular* way. (Long pause.)

X. The extent to which I focus on what appears to be my individuality is the extent to which I ignore my vital reality. The one is a separative view; the other is a unitive view. "Unit" means one, doesn't it. This is the recognition that they say brings peace?

O. Peace is not brought. Peace is here. Could the ultimate reality produce this universe, divided against itself? The key to your mystery is to remove the separative, divisive viewpoint.

Not to Worry

The Vedas, compiled as early as about 4,000 years ago, contain the Upanishads, those later (and once secret) portions that are collectively called Vedanta.   (Though Hindu, these were eventually to also influence Buddha.)

Guadapada (6th C. AD?) was said to be the predecessor of Shankara's teacher (Govindapada).   As the reputed author of Mandukya Karika, a commentary on the Mandukya Upanishad, he promulgated ajata-vada: *a-jata*, non-being or non-manifestation; *vada*, teaching. This can basically be summarized as "nothing ever existed (or happened)". As Ramana once put it: "no reality or absence of it".

Shankara (788-820 AD) propounded *advaita* (non-duality), and subscribed to the principle of maya-vada (also a Buddhist tenet) : the presence of the dualistic illusion, called maya—the phenomenon of the unreal appearing to be real.   This was a concession meant to serve as a bridge in teaching: from the original standpoint of ajata, there can be no such phenomenon as maya. The empty, ever-present "void" is formless; it cannot be the propagator of the changeable, temporal form called maya. Maya thus is *itself* unreal, and not a true principle; there being neither the "real" *nor* the "unreal" in ajata, maya is an unsustainable concept.

There is no justification therefore, from the standpoint of ajata, for an active relationship with a teacher. This is the viewpoint from which an enlightened teacher speaks: maya is a deluded creation, and there is no individual that can be "freed" from it.

Ultimately, it can be said, for this reason, that "nothing really matters". Not even ajata—"no existence or non-existence"—need be a principle of concern for us.

> *When Ramana gave out teachings that appeared to assume the existence of a world, and those in it who needed assistance and guidance, he was not speaking from the standpoint of the reality that was his own permanent experience (jnana).*
>
> – David Godman

A Self-Created Myth

There is an ultra-thin sheet of transparent paper that stretches throughout the infinite universe. Imprinted on its expanse are images of everything *in* the universe, both the tangible and the intangible. Therefore this sheet has been given the name Totality.

A monkey, for example, is one of these images superimposed in impermanent ink. A tree, for example, is a different image. But a monkey in a tree are, both, figures connected by their scroll. Beneath their colored ink, both are (in substance) the paper, Totality.

We could cut some of these images out, right now, and play with them. Ah, there's the character for "me". And look, there's *another* for "you". Hey, here's a name: "Adam"; I'll take this one. And, umm, "Eve": you take that one.

Wow, look : here's "concept". Yeah, clip that one out: "ego". What fun! "Mind"... "thought"... "choice", "doing", "awful", "bliss", "transcend", "Totality"—what a *wonderful* concept!

Oh, great, you've picked out "death", "dream", "sun", "Gestapo" (?), "Pope", "fear", "cancer", "Shiva"—gosh, you've latched onto some of the big ones—even "*million*". Oh, I thought *I* had *this* one (maybe there's more than mine), "self".

So, we end up with quite a collection of these scraps of Totality, *pieces* of the whole nine yards. Sorting through our accumulation, we study these pieces and we puzzle, "What is the relevance of this one to that one, what is their relative *relationship*? How do we assemble these into some kind of sensible *order*? What is most *significant* here? This is confusing! Help!" We try to sort these fragments out between us ("obviously, 'I' comes first before 'you'!"), but only disagreement results.

What if we just put all these flash cards back where we got them —*all* of them, starting with the very first?

Thingness is *man-made*: it's something we tend to do as a species. We are the ones who attempt to read all the isolated images—our "selves' being nothing more than one of the common symbols. None would even have a *basis*, were it not for their unifying underpinning, which has been called Totality.

Spiritual Joy

In the English language, the word *joy* is defined as "happiness; great pleasure".

The word *bliss* is defined as "spiritual joy". The qualification "spiritual" is *intended* to set the meaning apart from *mere* "joy".

Spiritual bliss is the *transcendence* of all opposites: such as, happiness/unhappiness; pleasure/pain, etc.

A jnani would not describe her condition as "happy" or "unhappy", "pleasurable" or "painful", "joyous" or "joyless". Bliss is the *absence* of such divisive perceptions, and limited conditions.

(Dis)Solving the Problem

In terms of societal behavior, it must be obvious to any student of world history that destructive means can never establish constructive ends. The failure to acknowledge that the means or methods utilized determine the ends or objectives realized, this is the staging area of intrahuman disturbances. Couple this with the fact that future objectives are typically envisioned in *idealistic* terms, and the formula for failure is certain.

But the compounding failure is that of focusing on "fixing" societal "problems". The drama that your mind participates in the devolvement of, this is no more of significance than a dream. Like a dream, the drama proceeds as long as a mind continues to reflect it. The only momentous change in a dream is when the mind disengages from its "reality", and it thus is rendered meaningless, ended.

The relater of the drama is "you". When "you" vanish, the dream ends.

How to respond to societal problems? End the dream: dissolve the dreamer.

Sometime, after writing a letter, read again all that was written. At every "I", pause: reflect; is *this* element perpetuating a dream? How could that entire letter be re-written without resorting to a single "I" subjectively?

The Energy of Intelligence

"Aren't you saying that there is a power which watches over and guides us...a power which heals the ills of those who are willing to await its help?"

Your question is an example of the care which needs to be taken in attempting to express the unknown in words. For instance, while we normally use the words *power* and *energy* interchangeably—because there is an obscure point where they overlap in meaning—they subtly tend toward different directions.

Power may be understood as a controlling force which overcomes opposition, in the same way that energy can be defined as contrary to inertia; we refer to hydroelectric "power" as dynamic "energy". But power can also refer to stable or nonaggressive strength, as the power of a sequoia tree to remain upright; and we may speak of *energy* as a potential in the expression of action: confronting a wind, the power of a sequoia tree *is* its energy.

And so, by way of illustration, what is in truth the energy of reality —such as the capability of the sequoia tree to stand—has traditionally been construed to be the "power of God".

Whenever we fail to clarify the difference between the implied meaning of such things as *power* and *energy*, we generally find ourselves far adrift at sea when using such words as "heals", "guides" or "helps".

For example, we may truly say that the universe is not without intelligence; but we may also truly say that the universe does not operate through an intellect. By *intellect*, we commonly understand that word to refer to the "part" of the (human) mind that devotes itself to pursuits of thought. In other words, *intelligence* can be defined as "an ability to retain experiential knowledge for use in solving problems or directing one's conduct"—something which the universe does *not* do; or as "the capability to respond effectively to new situations"—something which the universe *does* do.

As a noun, *intelligence* is "information" or "news" (as insight can be said to be informatively new). In one word, this nuance of intelligence is related to "discernment": to *discern* is to "clearly regard" or "perceive"—to attend with complete awareness.

Though humans may *express* this intelligence, it is not an intelligence that is possessed by *us*—it is not separate from an intelligence that "God" exhibits. What has been imputed, of course, is that man has an intellect because there is a God that possesses an intellect. (In actual practice, it is the other way around.)

The energy which pervades the universe can be described as "intelligent" energy (or even as the energy of intelligence); but it is an energy that is not saddled with an intellect: that is a peculiarity by which "man" may be said to be different from (while not *separated* from) "God". This unearthly intelligence can best be understood as a choice-less intelligence; it is not driven by such mundane considerations as, "How might this individual assist/resist my plans, and what shall I increase/decrease to make him more/less miserable?"

This energy has no center, and so it has no repository for the storing either of plans or memories: it recalls not who you last believed yourself to be, nor who or what you now define as your ally or enemy. It has no investment in the products of temporal assistance or guidance, having always been free of the need for control; it has—being all things—no fear of that which is uncontrolled.

Although the universe is not without awareness, when we suggest that it is "watching over us", we are ascribing paltry human characteristics to a limitless, transcendent energy. Were there anything "watching over", it would be watching over without purpose—impartially "looking on".

Does this show you, then, the direction that your question takes in regard to "healing" or "helping"?

Karma: In the Dream World

Karma is an idea that is rooted in dualism. Its relationship is entirely to the relative (dualistic) world of appearance.

In our (relative) dream world, we fail to see the connectedness of *all* things, in terms of *inseparability*. We, instead, isolate an "event": and give it a name; such as calling some particular movement an "act", or an "action". Think of an infinite ocean (not "different" at any point); think of a wave appearing (it is not different from the ocean, except in appearance); think of the occurrence of this wave as an "event" or an "act" or "action"; think of the wave subsiding back into the ocean: upon its disappearance, what remains of the "event", or "action"? Only so long as we think dualistically ("ocean", on the one hand; "wave", on the other hand) does there *seem* to be a significant "action".

For those who isolate some particular movement and think of it as a (separate) "event" or "act", there will also appear to be "consequence" to a particular action. A movement (in our dream world) following the initial movement (the "act") we— additionally—isolate, and call that the "consequence" of the act.

Since those who are mired in dualism think in terms of "good" and "bad", they will evaluate acts as "good" or "bad". They will likewise evaluate "consequences" in the same manner.

Therefore, the idea is that "good acts" are followed by "good consequences"; "bad acts" lead to "bad consequences".

This is the (dualistic) idea of (separate) "cause" and "effect": a "good act" (cause) leads to a "good consequence" (effect). Herein is the *idea* upon which "karma" rests.

What Ramana is saying is that *all* "events" or "acts" or "actions" are none other than the Absolute, or Self, in its endless appearances. "Good acts" are Self-expression. "Bad acts" are Self-expression. "Good consequences" are (more of the same) Self-expression. "Bad consequences" are (the same) Self-expression. "Karma" is just an idea, based on the dualistic ("ignorant") assumption that there is something (nameable) *other* than the Absolute, or Self.

An example (Christian): Believe that Jesus rose from the dead (your "action") and your person-ality will survive *your* dead body and be transported to a paradise ("consequence" of your action).

Another example (Hindu): Do puja every day, and your person-ality will survive your dead body and be successively born into a new body, as many times as necessary until every one of your worldly (dream) actions is perfect.

These ideas appeal to those who think in terms of (separate) actions: "birth" event; "death" event; for example.

What you've quoted (first) says that such dualistic thinking will only lead you further *astray* from the (nondual) truth of Self-realization: "Find the *root* of karma", *dualistic thinking*, "and cut it off"—relinquish the supposition that there is a "this", on the one hand, and a "that", on the other hand (such as "cause/effect", "birth/death", "good/bad", etc.).

The second quote: For some, Siva is another of the names for the "divine", representing the Absolute. Ramana was sometimes referred to in connection with Siva (sometimes given too as Sivan).

"Drink of the nectar of Siva-knowledge": Taste, or experience, the unifying wisdom of self-realization...and "you are the *same as* Siva"; the Absolute and the organism reading these words are no more different than the "wave" on the "ocean".

With nondual awakening, all separative ideas—such as karma, reincarnation, cause-and-effect, etc.—*disappear*: then you will "conduct yourself as you please", meaning without any concern for (isolated) "consequences" of (separate) "actions". Free-dom, in other words!

- -

Where Are You?

The distance from the sun to the earth is about 93 million miles. Pluto (the farthest of the nine orbiting bodies) is 40 times *that* distance.

Rule a line 13½ inches long. If this represents the distance from sun to Pluto, the *nearest* star (like our sun) would be about 1½ *miles* further. And the center of our (Milky way) galaxy would be 10,166 miles from your paper.

Light travels some 186,000 miles per second; or about 6 trillion miles per light-year. The *nearest* big *galaxy* to us is 2.4 *million* light-years away. This galaxy can be seen with the naked eye; the light which hits your retina set out 2.4 million years ago.

Some galaxies are 7 *billion* light-years away. The photographs that we take of them are showing them as they *were*, 7 billion years ago. Yet, what we see out there in the distant cosmos is not dissimilar from what we see right here, now, in our own galactic neighborhood.

Multiply 7 billion (light-years away) times 6 trillion (miles per light-year) and you'll have a sense of *your* place (relative to 1 mile) in this cosmos.

Present Right Now

What is meant by such sayings as "You are the World" is that if it were not for you, the world would not exist.

Consider: you fall down on the floor and die. You—as the body —no longer see anything, hear, smell, taste or feel anything. For you, every means of perceiving that there *is* a world has vanished. Therefore, for you the world is non-existent (and for all you care, under these circumstances, never *did* exist: you have no way of *knowing* if it did, or didn't).

Thus, you can understand that the world *depends* on you for its "existence" or *reality*. *You* **are** the world, in *any* sense that it is an "actuality".

If the world depends on you, and you die, and it thus ceases to exist, does it have any reality in any substantial sense? No.

One might say, "But if I die, it is still an actuality for others." No. It is still an unreality, in that it depends on the perceiver or sensor. If a plague killed every thing on earth, who or what would there be to say that there was a world in *any* respect? *

The point of this teaching is that one ought not to be "of this world"—concerned about worldly phenomena: one of which is your body.

When you *are* alive, that which is perceived (as the world) is perceived, as such, dependent upon the senses: it is seen, heard, smelled, tasted and felt. This *sensory* perception of what is "outside" of our skin, or body, is what we identify "inside" as the perceiver: "me". "I see the world", we say. But who am I? The sages answer, "The Self" (Absolute). So, "I" being ultimately the Self, "who" (or what) is "seeing through the eye, hearing through the ear", etc.? "The One", as you put it.

The body is as good as dead, in deep sleep. Awareness is void of seeing, hearing, smelling, tasting, feeling—nothing exists, as far as you know; not *even* your body, nor the world or the cosmos.

Yet, something about you is present, and has constantly been present throughout every instant of your life. Even when, in deep sleep, the body, world and cosmos cease to exist, this something remains constantly present.

If deep sleep is a death-like condition, yet something persists, is there any reason to suppose that this something will not persist despite physical death?

---

* "The world is there, because you are there"—Steven Harrison

It won't be "you" that persists: "you" were not even a reality (as far as you know) even in deep sleep. The "something" does not depend on "you"—neither in your waking hours, sleeping hours or absence of physical existence. This "something" the sages call your *true* nature, that which transcends "you" and is not dependent on you for its existence (unlike, for example, the world, as described above). You will not—and do not *now*—see it, hear it, smell it, taste it or feel it. But it is present, whether you are *able* to *know* that, or not. Present right now.

Upstaging the Actor

If one were to attempt to pinpoint the major difference between the dualistic and the nondual perspective, it could be said to be the subject/object bias. Where I, the *actor,* am viewed as one phenomenon and my *actions* are considered as another phenomenon there is a sense of separation: duality.

The realization which is said to embody the nondual perspective (so-called enlightenment) is that the subject is the universal Source (by whatever name one calls it: for example, Ramana uses the term Self) *and* the object is none other than, in actuality, that very *same* Self. The references to subject and object are not intended to *exclude* any 'two' (or more) 'things', whether material or immaterial: a prime example, "I" 'down here,' and "God" 'up there.' The so-called Father and the so-called I are one *inseparable* Reality. So, when clearly understood, there can no longer remain standing an entity or phenomenon, such as "I" *or* "God". Ramana would say, "There is *only* the Self." The essence of any nondual teaching is that "There is only_____" (whatever name the particular teaching is comfortable with). When Meister Eckhart says, "Who sees not God everywhere, sees God nowhere", he means to say: There is *only* (That). The "subject"—whether material or phenomenal—is That, manifest. The "object" is That, manifest. There are *not*—nondual teachers say—*two* actualities: despite appearances, all the named 'things' can be traced back to an illlimitable Source which encounters no opposition.

For those to whom the subject/object duality has not been discovered to be a false perception, the "me" (subject) still remains. The barrier to realization, for most people, is that they propose to *remain* as "me" (Ramana would say "pose as") while they seek unity with "the infinite".

The *realization* is, if "the observer *is* the observed", there no longer is an *observer*. Where there no longer is an observer, there is no longer an *observed*. Where "I" have 'disappeared' as a *subject*, everything 'about me' has disappeared: I no longer maintain the notion of "my body", "my mind", "my actions", "my karma", "my reincarnation", and so forth.

Where there is no independent subject, there is no independent object. "God" is not cloistered somewhere in the cosmos, studying daily briefings on your behavior, thoughts, actions, motivations, etc. The Essence of all that is, is not—in *any* way— apart from *all* that is. I am that, you are that, your brain is that, your thoughts are that, your actions are that, the consequences of your actions are that, ad infinitum. *This* is what nonduality *means*! "All that is, is That." No subject. No object. No dualistic propositions ("Well, you're That, except when…")

The *dualistic* proposal is, "I [not being That] want to unify with That [not already being That], so I will act in such and such a way [my actions not already being the actions of That]."

You *are* That. Therefore, your actions are the actions of That. Hence, no actions will being you nearer to, or send you father away from, That.

But this will not be realized as long as there is a "you" which remains as something *other* than That.

If you *are* a subject, you can be the "cause" of an "effect" on an object. Where the perspective of subject and object has *dissolved*, there is only That. If one were to propose a "cause", That was the cause. If the "cause" had an "effect", it is That which is affected. From the standpoint of *nonduality*, there is no meaningful proposition of "cause and effect". Cause and effect is a dualism based on subject and object. Where "I" am not a reality, I am not the cause of something; where there is no "you", you are not affected.

No "you", no actor. No actor, no actions. This is precisely what the Bhagavad Gita is all about.

This is what is meant when Ramana Maharshi says, when questioned about "the fruits of one's actions": "One should act without thinking that oneself is the actor....The question arises only if there is the *actor*. It is being all along said that you should not consider yourself the actor." And to another: "Let us not pose as the doers."

The Empty Page

Take a piece of paper and draw two horizontal lines on it from edge to edge, with a vertical gap between them. In our "mind's eye", this is typically our conception of time, a ribbon running continuously and evenly from one point to another.

Were I to say, make a mark where we are now—in the "present"—you would likely intersect the two lines somewhere toward the middle. Directed to add "past" and "future", you would probably write the first word about midway to the left of the "present" intersection, and the latter word toward the right-hand side.

This is our usual, linear image of time. Now, if we were to discuss the concepts of "past" and "future", and you were to agree with me that in reality only the present truly exists, we could erase those two words.

And, considering that the present is all that there is, we could even erase the intersection which represented the present.

What, now, if we were to come to the realization that time is really without limit, without borders? You are ahead of me: you have already erased the two lines.

The picture we have of time as a continuum is not unconnected to our image of the self as an entity which has continuity in "time", a self which operates within the limitations of "its past" and "its future".

When it is clear to you that the past and the future are a fiction of an ego which seeks endurance, it will be clear to you that the self can be nothing more than an aware presence in any given instant: and so it possesses no particular, fixed construct from moment to moment. You are, in reality, only what you are in any particular instant (and even that which we determined that you "are" is a definitional matter): that is all that you are, ever have been or will be. The moment is constantly changing, you are in the moment, and so there can be no fixed, static entity that you can lastingly identify with.

When your perception of self/time is such as this, your perception of the temporal world is different, effortlessly.

What Is Needed?

It has been said that generosity is not in giving someone something which you don't need, but in giving them something which you need.

The ownership or hoarding of property or possessions which you do not need is based on fear of the future.

A spider may locate itself next to an ant trail, yet the spider will not capture and kill more ants than it can eat at the present moment. Without concerning itself about the future, it exhibits no greed, it does not hoard.

Even though the Indians knew how to smoke fish and to make jerky, they knew that the longer each animal lived, the greater the chance for procreation by each animal. To hoard was to affect the food supply of oneself and others; greed is inimical to life.

"Give us this day our daily bread" means that we do not need what we need until we need it: "Take no thought for the morrow."

A few decades ago, a woman known as Peace Pilgrim walked the roads of this country, for many years, on foot. She owned only the clothing she wore, and the few items which she could carry in her pockets. She fasted until she was offered food; she slept along the roadside until she was given shelter. She would not accept anything which she did not need. If someone gave her money, she dropped it in the collection box of the next church she passed. She advised, "Consider not what you can get; consider what you can give".

Indeed, the question for those who lead a spiritual life is not "What did I acquire today?", but rather "What did I relinquish today?"

The idea that there is such a thing as "property"—either individual or collective—is the basis for personal security and its concomitant conflict and isolation.

Attachment to the idea of ownership—even ownership of a future for ourselves—is invidious to the harmony of the cosmos. This universe both gives and takes what is needed.

Homily for Sunday School

If God is all that is, the interactions of all that is have to be God's too.

The Good Samaritan rescues the man in the ditch: God's work.

The man had fallen into the ditch: God's work too.

Were the robbers caught, and the money returned?
God's work.

Did the robbers escape? God's work.

All things *being* God, God is the good Samaritan; the victim; the robbers; their captors too.

In all things, present everywhere, God animates all the players; winners and losers.

It is by *being* all that is, that God *knows* all.

It is by being all that is, that God is *all powerful.*

Was God *surprised* to see the Good Samaritan come upon a man in the ditch?

Was God *powerless* to prevent his being robbed?

Not a sparrow falls to the ground without God's involvement, Jesus says in the Gospel of Matthew.

Call the First Witness

Your descriptions were objectively clear and your points were well-considered. In short, your letters seem to be reflecting a change (less tension?) in your psyche. So I would just like to make a few comments on things that interested me.

Even if for nothing more than a short-lived experiment, it seems to me that it would be worthwhile for you to (as you say) limit your responses to Yes, No and Thank You.

You indicate that now, in *addition* to reacting, you are consciously witnessing "your" (or, the) reactions. *I* know this mode: it is my "waking" experience. There is this organism, which answers to the name of Robert. The organism's ongoing daily routine is to act and react (or, a more productive word, respond): this is what Robert "does". But there is that which is continually *aware* of what Robert does, as if it were abstractly witnessing a street scene outside the window; simply with disengaged interest.   This awareness is unconcerned with the development of what it monitors, and has no inclination to pass judgment on what is noted: "Hmm, look at what Robert is doing now.   That's interesting!" This, actually, is my "normal" awareness.

Not only is this witness aware of Robert's actions or inactions, but also consequently aware of the interaction of Robert's psyche in these developments and processes: the verbalized thoughts which appear on and pass across the screen of consciousness; the verbalized thoughts which *could* be expressed vocally (and awareness that some are, some aren't); the bodily sensations which Robert feels; etc.

By disengaging from "what the organism does", attention is (without effort) on what *is actually going on*—not what I *think* is going on. It's similar to *watching* a documentary, as opposed to arguing the position of one of its protagonists. One of the visible consequences of this is that I generally have very little to say. In fact, rarely do I express an "opinion"; rarely am I *reacting*. More often, I am responding; one of my most common expressions is, "Whatever you do is okay with me." *Without* making it a "practice", I'm often heard to say only Yes, No and Thank You.

I bring this up for a couple of reasons. By removing my attention from my so-called thinking mind (John Sherman says, "The *only thing* you *can* control is where attention is directed"), I am in a "neutral" condition where I am observing Robert and the person or persons in view with equal dispassion, and I am hearing what Robert and the other(s) says with equitable dis-interest. With no significant *self*-involvement, there is exceedingly little disharmony between the Robert organism and any non-Robert organisms. The Robert organism is so (un-self-consciously) passive that there is little which disturbs it.

But the point I want to make about this is that it's not a "program", it's not an "item on my agenda" ("I will do this; I won't do that."). If I set out to make this passive behavior a credo, I would be setting myself up for distress every time that self-promise was breached. By having no idea, or *ideal*, of what my behavior "should" be, there never are any violations of my personal canon. Awareness is on/of what Robert does; whatever Robert does (or is doing) is an actual fact. No attempt is made to *change* the fact of what this organism seems to think or feel that it needs to do: there are no prior, established rules as to what it "ought" to be doing, or "could" be doing, or "should" be doing; only awareness of what is being done by this organism which objective awareness is witnessing. No "plan" as to what will be done, merely spontaneity. Therefore, there is not a "personal" reaction to cause contrition and distress.

When you can be this unconcerned about your own behavior, you can (and likely will) be unconcerned about the behavior of others. Those who harshly judge others, harshly judge themselves as well. Double whammy.

It's interesting (as per another point of interest in your letter) that profound mystics (e.g., Teresa of Avila; St. John of the Cross; Ramana, and a host of Hindus) generally confined themselves to "cells", or caves. Your cell, unfortunately, is beset by noise and continual disruptions. But the cells of the mystics had their own, though varying, impairments and disadvantages. With food delivered to your door, if you prefer, what *do* you want outside of your cell? What was it these others found that made them happy to be confined in their holes? Quiet, yes. But there is a quiet, they would all say, that has nothing to do with anything external; that encompasses or envelops all. Krishnamurti often remarked on this, while in the madhouse that is India.

Also, consider Jesus' reputed "reward"; here's a guy—like Ramana or Buddha—who reportedly didn't do harm to anyone (quite the contrary). What was given to this young man for his last day on earth? In addition to all the other persecution, while immobilized he was jabbed with a spear. Ramana died with a painful cancer. Buddha died painfully, with food poisoning. This life is "unjust".

Unless you're under sedation, or in "denial", you're bound to feel the pain of your circumstances. There's no law, even cosmic, that says you have to like what you're experiencing. But you can note, in awareness, the dislike or the anger (expressed or unexpressed), moment to moment, realizing that—like an incurable, chronic illness—nothing can be done that is going to eliminate the pain or discomfort. We came into this world with no promises made that we would even wish to endure it. The sooner we face up to the fact that, whatever our condition, "It could be worse", the more stoic we become. (I find myself saying Thank You—vocally or silently—many more times during the day than I say either Yes or No.)

And, yes, to add to the frustration are these many insensitive (if not unkind or cruel) and self-centered (if not selfish and inconsiderate) persons we are obliged to interact with. How can we help them to comprehend that there is a more life-enhancing way to live? The obvious answer is to "start at home"; set an example. I liked your line from Dr. Hora: when it comes to the much-vaunted virtue of compassion, are we "speaking from our filing cabinet", or are we talking about "hands-on" application? Are we "visualizing" love of "fellow man", as you again evoked Hora; if so, any result will be a fantasy too.

When you can remark, "Maybe now the [personal] war can end", light is beginning to glimmer at the end of the tunnel; the *end* of battling is already underway when the internal desire for it is present. These lines are from *your* letter, not mine:

> *I will have no needs that require something to be done (now or later)....What I heard...was Do Nothing...stop everything [except] make the utmost intense effort...to discover the truth of one's identity....There is no other source of healing than absolute realization of the Self.*

To be "respon-sible" is to "respond". Your words above are *responsive* to your particular situation. (Perhaps this situation has been required, to bring you to this level of individual responsibility. How much have *each* of us contributed to the insanity around us: I know that I did *my* share of creating misery in the world.)

. . . .

Radical ("the root")

Your view of politics seems sound to *me*. How can we effect long-lasting change in the human condition? My view is: when each individual identifies the self with "all That is", and thus relinquishes selfish motivations. Therefore, I consider that transmitting the dharma is the most politically/socially radical activity one can be involved in.

"Principles" tend to be ideals—which are simply ideas about what *could* be, in the future. When one operates from Absolute awareness, inflexible principles are unnecessary. Right/wrong is replaced with "abiding as the Self".

Re: your essay, "Be Encouraged": I think it would be more practical to compose an equal number of words addressed to the issue of "non-interference". I once read that what allowed the native Indian populations to operate without police, courts, lawyers, jails, etc., was their individual commitment to—as a general policy—non-interference.

Let's take your questions in order.

1.

Yes; before awakening, one assumes that it is the individual entity —the "person"—which makes the choices.

Upon awakening, this person does not disappear. It is simply that the person no longer conceives of oneself as an individual entity. It would appear (to "others") that this person is still "making some choices". However, the *person* realizes that there is not, in actuality, an "individual" (anywhere) in existence: there only *appears* to be. Therefore, there is no (in awakened awareness) individualized, individuated or "person-al" decision-maker (or, choice-chooser).

This is what the sages mean by the phrase, "*you* are not the doer". Why? Because what appears to be "you" is, in actuality, That. So, it is That which is doing all that is being done. The sage takes no *credit* for what she does, nor does she accept any *blame*. The organism that you recognize as the sage is the very same organism *after* enlightenment as it was *before*. But the awareness of identity is no longer that of "me", but of the Absolute. Being now aware that the "me" and the Absolute are the same actuality, one is now cognizant that while it *appears* that it is "me" that is acting, *all* actions are universally those of the Absolute.

2.

Once this Absolute awareness is present (Nisargadatta: "I am That") it is clear that one's essence—*being* absolute—is not limited: absolute *means* infinite and eternal; that is, without beginning or ending anywhere in space or time. Everything that *is*, is *included* in the Absolute: not included as separate parts, but inclusive because all things are *permeated* by this infinite Presence.

Like the "me" that is, in its true nature, the Absolute, *all things* in their true nature are the *same* indivisible Presence.

So, if *all that is*, is merely different *forms* of the Absolute, then "you" are not apart from what you "see"; "you" are not apart from what you "hear". The hearer ("doer") is the Absolute; what is heard is the Absolute: no division, no separation: *all* that is, is That.

With this realization, one no longer views "reality" in terms of "this" as opposed to "that": such as, "me" (subject) as *apart* from what one "sees" (object). So-called subject and object are viewed as essentially the same one indivisible actuality: That (Absolute).

This is what sages mean by, "The observer [me] *is* the observed [seen]": no *real* distinction can be made, from the standpoint of Absolute awareness (enlightenment).

3.

The question of what is "alive", in all of this, now answers itself. *If all that is, is That,* then if we say that "I am alive" we are, in actuality, saying that the Absolute is alive—since I *am* That.

But, in terms of the Absolute, can we assign *any* qualities to it? No. Because, being *all that is*, there is nothing apart—separate—to *compare* it to. (Vedas: "It is One—without a 'second' [one]": incomparable!) Therefore, as the sages say, we cannot state that it "exists" or "does not exist". If we say that *it* exists, this implies that there is something (else) which does *not* exist. But there is no thing "else": all that is, is That. So, whatever "does not exist" is That; whatever "does exist" is That.

Whatever we say is "alive" is That. Whatever we say is "not alive" is That. Such either/or distinctions *evaporate* in Absolute awareness. Put another way, you are not "alive": you are *That*—

and That cannot be described as *either* being alive *or* not being alive.

Thus, "fear of death" ends for the sage.

4.

By now, you can answer similar questions for yourself, maintaining the inseparable awareness of the Absolute. What are the "images" which the "self" produces, you ask.

Who *is* the "self"? It is That (which Ramana calls Self, *capital* S). So, who is producing the images? "You"? Who are *you*, in actuality? The images—as are *all* things—are the product of the Absolute. *All* that is, is That: the producer ("me"), the producing (form in transition) *and* the produced ("images"). All being *That*, producer and produced (like observer and observed) are simply That, in its many forms.

5.

Once it is *clear* that "you" are That, it is clear that what is "seeing through your eyes" is That (*and* whatever it views is *also* That). So, with viewer and viewed disappearing into the Source (That), only the viewing is *present*; and this (that remains) is self-cognizant (or, Self-cognizant): That is *self*-aware. This is what we humans refer to as "awareness": Presence ever present for itself (its Self). To describe this to the seeker, the sage speaks of "witnessing". Like a spectator looking down impartially on the activity of an ant colony, the sage observes "the world" without the notion of "personal" involvement in what is viewed: his awareness—as a "witness"—is that "all that is, is That—doing what it does" (*including* the "witness"—so-called "me"—witnessing).

So, what the sage calls "pure awareness" and witnessing are the same. But bear in mind that there is *no separate individual* who maintains this awareness (or, who *is* the "witness"). *All* that is, is *That*—doing what it does; that is all that is happening, in truth.

Ramana:

> *The Self* [Absolute] *is the basis* [source] *of all experiences* [seeing, etc.] *It* [That] *remains as the "witness" and the support* [existence, or life] *of all.... the "witness" is to be experienced* [by the awakened] *as a form of Brahman* [Self, That, or Absolute]*; and Brahman* [Self, etc.] *is to be experienced* [viewed] *as the "witness"* [awareness].

Get Over Your "self"

As with most presentations on nonduality, Bernadette Roberts' *What is Self?* is attempting to persuade you to see that your *separative* bias, or mindset, is what is at the root of your confusion (or, "ignorance" in Buddhism).

She's pointing out that the mind, as subject, is aware of itself (its self), as object. (Why? Because this is the way that—what she calls—the divine [Self, God, Brahman, Absolute] "operates".)

So, it *seems* there is what the mind projects (self image) *and* the mind (as projectionist): the "object" in the mind *and* the "subjective" mind. (Object; subject: *separation!*)

But mind and self (an image) are not two different—separate—things.

When a mind *recognizes* that the self does not *exist*—as an entity *other* than a self-fabricated image—the "self" disappears (*dis*appears).

When it is *recognized* that there is no "individual self", "it" (a self) can have no (separate, distinct, individual) mind.

So, the idea "this is my mind" *also* dis-appears.

With no "mind", no God (a self-created image) can be "known" or *objectified* (by a *subjective* mind).

As she says, with this realization "there is no self, or 'self'-*experience*, remaining; and so, no *other* self." (As Ramana would say, no 'non-Self'.)

Because: "directly *underlying* our ego (mind/self) *is* the divine": you are *that* even *before* you realize that you are not a "self".

How can that be? Because, "the divine", she says, "is *everywhere*".

"The ego cannot hide the divine; the ego experiences (as Itself) the divine." If the divine is everywhere, then *all* experiences are the divine's.

When *you* say (experience) "I am *this* (self)", it is *God* (shorthand for "the divine") saying, "I *am that*" (an experience of my Self).

An analogy she uses: a circular piece of paper, with a dot (self) at the center—the paper representing consciousness (which includes mind; self-consciousness).

With the disappearance of the *idea* of the self (review the above), a hole appears where the dot had been. Now we have, she says, "the absence of the self *and* the presence of the divine"—the hole that was "behind" the dot all along.

So, if the divine was behind the dot, it's behind the rest of the paper (consciousness). When we "let" the rest of the paper disappear (through realization of truth), *only* the divine remains (exists). Meaning what? All consciousness is nothing other, in fact, than the divine. "The whole of consciousness has been affected", she says, not just the center (ego/self).

Thus, "there is no 'self' anymore to 'experience' the divine" (only the Divine is experiencing the divine)—"there's just a silent void in ourselves, our own *nothingness*" (which is what "you" have been, from the start).

Follow? The only experience there is, is God (Self, Absolute, etc.) experiencing whatever it is that appears to be experienced.

"My *being*" is *God's* being. "The divine is the *center*", she says, "of *all* that exists"—and you *are* the Divine.

The realization is that the self is *now* merely *being* the Self. All *one*. Now!

Once *realized*, if the form ("you") identifies its self as any *thing*, it identifies as That (formless Self, or God etc.).

Where the dot *was*, a permanent hole remains (rather, is "now present").

Therefore, there is no longer perceived an "individual" (self's) mind that focuses on the separation of "subject" and "object": there is *only* (always everywhere) *That* (which *includes* any supposed mind/self.)

....

Dying Daily

"Your original face before you born", the Buddhists poetically call it. Who—or what—are you, when nothing exists of who you *think* you are?

"Before you were born" suggests "before you were alive". Who are you when the "you" that you know is not alive? "Alive" means "alert; aware".

Is there a time when that presence which you know as "you" is *not* alert, aware? Is there a time which equates with your presence "before you were born"; *before* there was a you that was alert, aware, alive?

Synonyms for death include "inanimate, insensate, immobile, indifferent". When you were an embryo in the womb—before you were "alive, aware, alert"—something was developing which (your "original face") was not quite yet animate, sensate, mobile or interested.

After you are born, is there a time when you revert to—return to —this condition, this "death-like" or "unborn" condition?

Yes, on a cyclical basis: daily (or rather, nightly).

Yes, you die every night; and are re-born every day.

Much attention is given by us to our dreaming state, because it is seemingly a graphic extension of our waking, aware condition. But, for obvious reasons, little attention is consciously given to our condition when we are in such a deep state of sleep that even the animation of our imaginative dreams is suspended.

There is a time (or times) in our sleeping cycle when the presence of our life force is analogous to our condition as a gestating embryo. In the deepest of sleep, each night, bodily processes are proceeding as programmed by an organism in its particular phase. But the vitality that is essentially present is no more "alive" than it is "dead". It is nothing more than neutrally existent, suspended.

Think about it. In your deepest sleep, you are as oblivious ("unmindful") of everything as you were as an embryo. You are as death-like as any condition which you can imagine to resemble death. The only difference—which you are not in appreciation of at the time—is that you will arouse from deep sleep, in the morning. Until you *have* aroused, you would not consciously know (unmindful that you are) whether you were "alive" or "dead"—just as, when in embryo, you would be unable to make a conscious distinction between whether you were "alive" or "not alive". There is not even a "you" in consciousness to entertain such distinctions, in either situation.

When all else is stripped away (*or* added *on*), this is your *essence*. At your most fundamental condition of existence/nonexistence, there is nothing more that is present than a vitality—an energy ("potential force; inherent power")—that continues to move the organism through its biologically programmed cycles. In the deepest of sleep, bodily functions continue—respiration, heart beat, digestion—while the sense of personal presence is entirely un-conscious. In this condition, there is only "the void"; and even the void is not a presence, in the sense that there is not an awareness which is active to reify its presence.

There is, in this condition, nothing. No time, no space, no "movement", not even an awareness of the absence of these parameters. The only difference between this and what we associate with death is the (unacknowledged) functioning of the autonomic nervous system. Were this system to cease functioning, as when one dies in deep sleep, the fundamental "difference" between life and death would be nonexistent.

This most-essential level of vitality—awareness in suspension—is your condition before you are "alive", as an embryo; while you are "alive", in unconscious slumber; and after you are "alive", when no longer a momentarily-functioning organism. "You" come from nothing; you regularly return to nothing; and you go back to where you came from, in the figurative (or relative) sense.

Where did you come from? The void; a condition of vitality *en potentia* ("un-real-ized"), vitality in suspension ("undetermined"): inanimate, insensate, immobile, indifferent. It is a condition, a circumstance, you have "known"; "know" now; and will never not "know". It is your essence ("essential being"). It is "that without which there is not".

This condition which we all share in common is the same, singular condition. It has no (nor needs no) means or purpose of maintaining separation. Your presence as essence (in the embryo, in deep sleep, or after bodily consciousness has transpired) is indistinguishable from that of all other forms in this condition, just as it is indistinguishable between these "alternate" forms. It would not be proper to say that you are thus joined to all others in this condition; you, nor any others, have ever been disjoined, just as your presence as this essence has not been disjoined between the seeming phases of pre-life, life, and post-life.

Nor is this a condition from which any of us "come" or to which any of us "return". We have not at any time been apart from it.

Neither is it a condition which "comes" to us, at some point, and "leaves" us at another juncture. It is we—impermanent, transitional *materia*—who appear, express, and disappear *within* it.

You won't go anywhere "when you die" that you're not already. Nor will you know that you are where you are, any more than you do in deep sleep. You "are" where (what) "everyone" is, whether they are considered to be in pre-life, life, or post-life. There is but one, indivisible essence. Not anything escapes its inherent potential, which is ever present. Whether you call it pre-life, life, or post-life, it is present for or with—rather, *as*—you now. None are born, live, or die apart from this essence.

This essence that *has* been with you; *is* with you; and *will be* with you—*as* you—cares not who you are, what you've done, how you've lived, or died. It is you; it *is* these impermanent conditions which are expressions of the permanent, underlying condition, the *potentia infinitum*. Though we speak of this ubiquitous presence as a condition, it is without condition, unaffected by anything. You've been it *before* there was a "you"; you've been it *as* a "you"; and you will be it when there is no "you" to be aware of what you are—just as you are, nocturnally, in the deepest of sleep.

Whence God's Will?

We say that we are conscious, and we say that we have a mind. What is the relationship of this consciousness and this mind?

Consider it from the perspective of the presumption that there is a Supreme Being. "God" is said to be omniscient. This would indicate that God must be aware of what is occurring in every mind. Thus there are no barriers between one mind and the next, to God; all are equally accessible, hence all are connected indivisibly as one mind. And since God's awareness is not apart, or separate, from the minds of which God is aware, it can be understood that all minds are only one mind—whether called "God's" or not.

Put another way, what is going on in God's mind is what is going on in each individuated mind. Each mind that is conscious of existence is universally (indivisibly) conscious, because it is the omniscient God who is conscious of its inseparable existence. Since all minds are God's mind, it can be understood that *God's* mind is *all* minds. "Omniscient" means *all*-knowing; it does not necessitate that some *one* know all, any more than "consciousness" suggests that only "one" is conscious. Your "mind" and your "consciousness" are inseparably universal and *are that* of the omniscient and omnipresent "God". Thus your "will" is "God's will".

Through our "consciousness" and "mind", we (individually or collectively) can will things to happen; but only within the relative, and limited, domain of our existence. In the universal (unlimited or absolute) realm, our willfulness has no effect. What we refer to as "God's will" may have a *temporal* application—it is based on the limited notion of a God which has a discrete will—but that which is omnipotent, omnipresent and omniscient has no need for willfulness; God has no need for a will, since all that could be willed (including your individuated will) is already inseparably what it would have been willed. In other words, it makes no difference whether one distinguishes it as "God's" will or "your" will. Your consciousness is the consciousness of God, your mind is God's mind, and all will—every will—is God's will. Thus consciousness, mind and will have no real "relationship" at all; they are ultimately the same universal thing—as are *all* things.

Love or Fear?

Your question is: *"Does it not mean that, when one loves, one opposes war, oppression and bigotry?"*

It must be clear to you, surely, that there is no collective human reaction—such as war, oppression or bigotry—which will end completely, whether opposed or unopposed, until the individuals of the particular state, religion or race have abandoned the fears which motivate them.

If I am in opposition to your behavior, will that help you to overcome your fear? If my opposition is forceful enough, it might temporarily *restrain* you from acting out your fears. But opposition, of itself, will not effectively put your fears to rest.

Is there any way in which an individual's fears can be ended, except for personally facing the reality of fear, as it exists in one's consciousness, and perceiving its source in the concept of identity?

Strip away all that we identify our self with, and where is the ideological core of that collective which goes to (or goes against) war? If I do not know if I am an Iraqi or an Israeli, how am I to know which side I am to fight on? Or which ideals I am to die/kill for?

When we come to the end of the idea that there is a separate "self", we come to the end of the idea that there are separate nations, religions, races and ideologies. We come to the end of the idea that there are "others" who need to be manipulated by "us" to achieve some commendable "end"—such as an end to war. We abandon the idea that there are some things external to us which we need to fear.

Those who wage war are in fear. Those who oppose war are in fear. It is not war, or opposition to war, which we must address: it is fear. An end to war will be an end to fear, simultaneously.

The first fear we must address is our own, personal fear, our fear for the security of the self (and other selves).

There is a difference between negation and opposition. While we cannot "oppose" our self, we can negate our self. When we have negated the assumption of the self, and ended our fear for its "safety", we are then free to act from a place of selfless, non-ideational love. This love knows no opposition—it is not in favor of or opposed to any particular thing. It harbors no ideals or idols which are to be defended.

When we free our self of fear, we are, at the same time, dispelling the fear of "others". One need not oppose war, to negate war.

One need not oppose others, to affect others. And one need not oppose the self, to see the self change.

....

At Oneness

a) Let us start with what you know to be true:

aa) You are alive, at this moment.

ab) You are alive in this universe, the only universe of which we are presently aware.

ac) Anything which exists, so far as we know, exists within this universe.

b) This universe—where you and I exist—contains everything that there "is". There is not anything in actual existence which cannot be considered "in" this universe.

ba) Therefore, we could say this universe is a container for everything that actually exists—there is not anything that we can suppose that is actual that is *outside* of this universe.

bb) The true actuality of this universe is that it encompasses everything which either exists or does not exist. If this is not so, then there is something that may be beyond or outside of the universe of which we are speaking—which would not be a concurrence of ba).

c) By our definition here, the universe is *composed* of all that actually exists and does not actually exist: whatever there "is", we are saying, *is* the Universal. There is not anything which exists apart from the "is/is not", there is not anything that is not the Universal.

d) Since all "things"—whether actually in existence or in actual nonexistence—are in the universe, everything (or anything) shares in *common* its universality. There is not anything which can be named, or thought of, which is apart from universality —in any way. There cannot, under the circumstances, be *any thing* which does *not* represent—or is not represented in (or by)—universality. The fact that anything which we can describe is represented within the whole of the universe (which, by definition, is "all-inclusive") means that anything which we can name has, by its very actuality, at least one commonality: that it is *among* the all-inclusive.

e) That which is all-inclusive does not exclude the "container"— the universe—itself. Universality is not something, not a characteristic, which is in any way apart from any particular thing which we can say "*has* universality", nor from any number or collection of things which "share universality in common". This *universality* does not exist as something *outside of* the universe, which is brought in and added to things in the universe. The common universality of all of the things in this universe means that the "package"—the universe as an entity, of itself—is not somehow removed or distant or apart from the things which it contains. Both container and contained have the same, and equal, actuality, or commonality.

f) All things (the universe and any of its supposed contents or lack of contents) share something—"one thing" in common. And that commonality, or "oneness" of actuality (or "existence") is *not apart in any way from any of these things. "Oneness" and actuality are the same thing.* Anything of which we can speak "shares" its Universality, or commonality, with any and all other things; there is not anything—including "oneness" *itself*—which is outside of or apart from this "unity".

212

g) The one thing that universally exists is that anything which conceivably "is/is not" partakes of this condition of actuality, with any and every thing else which conceivably is/is not. In this commonality, there is *indivisible* unity or "oneness". And the existence (or nonexistence) of oneness itself is in no way apart or separate from this actuality, this condition of unity or oneness. The point is that *not anything can be apart* from this oneness, *under any condition.*

> ga) The sense of this is that there is not anything which "you" do not have *something* in common with, or a *connection with.* Likewise there is *not anything* in the universe which is not commonly connected to you.

> gb) In the sense of this commonality of connectedness, *you* and anything *other* ("not-you") are the *same* thing: universal.

> gc) In a likewise manner, *you* and *commonality* itself—being inseparable in this way—can *also* be said to be the same thing.

> gd) In fact, *you* and *commonality* (or universality or "oneness") and any *other* thing, or things, are all complementarily the *same* thing: all *actuality.* And in an actuality that encompasses all that is/is not, even "actuality" itself does not stand distantly apart from this universality or "wholeness".

> ge) Therefore, it can be proposed that all things which share actuality are a "unit"; each and everything—of *whatever* possible sort or kind—is a component of the same oneness. This being the *primary,* unifying *identity* of all "things" in the universe, each and every thing basically represents (and is represented by) *one* thing: oneness, or "nonduality". Thus we can

comprehend that *all* things are *one* thing. *The one thing which you and I share in common is that neither of us are in the least way apart from this* one thing. Nor can *one thing* be disconnected from us: unity.

h) The term "oneness" now can be refined. Any reference to "one" automatically seems to suggest or imply that there could be something "*other* than one". In our "universal" context, if there was actually a "not one" (or "other than one") that was in opposition to our "one", it would still fall within our unity of commonality—being that "all things that are" (or "are not") wholly exist commonly within the very same actuality. In other words, we can say that "oneness", or nonexclusivity, encompasses and incorporates not only itself, but any possible "opposition" or counterpart which could be supposed for it.

Put another way, we said in ge) that all things really are one thing. Said conversely, the "one thing" *is composed of all things*. You and I are among all of the "things" which share a common actuality, or unity (or wholeness, or "oneness"). Likewise, "one" and "not one" (or "two", etc.) are among all of the things which share a common reality. In this sense, both "one" and "not one" are encompassed by (or share) the same "oneness"—because it is the reality of their *existence* which all things have in common. There is not anything that is/is not which stands outside of this oneness of universal existence: it defines all things, including its own existence.

Though some of the other terms can be no less confusing, oneness is ofttimes referred to by other names: for example, nonduality, indivisibility, suchness, nothingness, presence, essence, etc.

But all names are the names of *Oneness*.

If, like a mantra, you have taken as a reference point, "There is no self"—no "me" or "you" as a separate entity—that can serve your purpose. Why is there no me? Because, from the standpoint of nondual realization, all that is, is That, the eternal, infinite actuality which is formless.

When the nondual realization is fully present, one begins to re-examine the separative, divisive views or ideas, concepts or beliefs that one had previously held. This is an automatic, effortless development, a consequence of a change in perspective. (Hence, the arising of the expression, in Buddhism, "This *too* is it!")

Before long, we may conclude that we need not re-examine every possible situational construct on a case-by-case basis. Wherever a proposition of dualistic "separation" (separateness) arises, we can recognize that this is merely a false *appearance* that disguises the actuality that transcends all forms. Thus, to the awakened, all references to "self"—"mine" or "yours"—are recognized as ultimately meaningless or contrary to realized truth. (As Krishnamurti said simply, when you see the false as the false, you are seeing truth.)

To use your example: the idea that there is a pre-arranged "destiny", and/or "control" by a "God". Such propositions are immediately recognized as false, from the standpoint of the formless nonduality. The perceived truth being that "there is no self"—no finite entity (beyond appearance)—for *whom* would there be a personal destiny? There being no separate reality, no isolated entity, there is no "thing" in control. Where, from the standpoint of formlessness, would there be a "center" from which control would be directed? No control is even necessary: what is *actual* must be perfect as it is, *however* it is. However "it is", it's the Absolute doing all that is done: It represents both all causes and all effects. "Control" is a separative idea of there being a controll*er* and a controll*ed*. Even if there were such things, both must be That, which is the *essence* of all being, to begin with.

So, the importance of your query is to recognize that it is not necessary to *examine* every proposition in which "two" or more elements are present (as was done in the paragraph above). All such questions which come to mind concerning a "this" and a "that" are instantly resolved in the awareness that "this" *and* "that" are both merely names, or aspects, of the fundamental indivisible actuality. "All is *One*; One is *all*."

Then obviously, it will be clear to you that this applies to shaktipat (saktipata). Who is the One that could give it?; who is the One that would receive it? How could the indivisible One give its "self" some thing? To the one which is all that is, there can be no part-icular things to be given: It *already* is all that could be given *or* gotten. Shaktipat is an *idea* about truth; it is not *truth*. Truth cannot be given or received, being *already* ever-present. If there is a "you" and its "experience", this is not a *nondual* perception. For those who seek phenomenon—shaktipat in particular—Ramana said, "Abiding peace will not result. This is gotten only by the removal of ignorance." The removal of ignorance, he goes on to point out, is the removal of the supposition that there has ever been a "self" to "get" any "thing".

So consider all questions from the standpoint of nonduality: all questions are dualistic in *content*. Where is there a "self", or some "thing", supposedly in relation to some "other" thing, in the question? "There is no self—*or other*." Bathe awareness in that truth and all questions will answer themselves. And conflict will effortlessly be resolved.

Don, it appears to me from your letters that you are permitting the past (at least pre-prison) to, slowly, begin to fade into obscurity.

What is past, is past! I sometimes look at someone who has lost a limb and I try to envision the kind of psychic adjustment that must be required: you look in the mirror and you see, undeniably, that the limb is absent. And you know that the fact is that this is never going to be any other way. What, really, are your choices under the circumstance? To spend the rest of your life agonizing over this development? Or to accept the hard fact for being as it is, and to decline to indulge in *pointless* agony?

You are in prison; not an enviable place to be, but you are there— like it or not—and no amount of agonizing is going to change that fact. Every event which has occurred—right up until the moment you read these words—is a fact, and an *unchangeable* fact.

Every wisdom teacher has said at least these two things: Let go of thoughts about the past. Let go of thoughts about the future. Why do they say this? Because it is imperative if one is to ever have peace of mind.

Among these things of the past which you relate to are what you consider to have been Divine interdiction; in particular, what you believe to have been inspired "direction", instruction or guidance. If there were such guidance and the guidance resulted in a lost arm, then both the lost arm and the guidance are facts. What can be done about something which is a fact? Will any amount of agonizing have any positive effect?

If there is a Director who gives you directions, do you have any choice in whether you follow the directions? If not, why concern yourself about the outcome? Or if so, is the director *responsible*?

If there is a Director giving directions, this supposes that there is a "purpose" for it. How are you to know what the purpose is, or whether it has been, is being, or will be effected? If you can't know, then why concern yourself about it?

It is given to some to have two arms. It is given to some to have one—or no—arm. There is no Entity which consults us about how we would like things to be. Things will be as they will be—whether we like it, or adjust to it, or not.

If there were a Voice, and we stopped complaining and listened to it, perhaps we'd hear: "Get used to it!"

Guilt, shame, forgiveness, repentance are surely on the minds (consciously or not) of many—or most—of your neighbors. How simply and easily these matters (and all others) are resolved when one awakens to the truth, the actuality, of their nondual nature!

Supreme Be-ing

There are no suitable "brief" ways to answer wide-ranging spiritual questions. However, I'll keep this as short as possible.

"I am" is your "spiritual" state: pure *be*-ing. That is why "I am" and "God" are said to be the same. It is what you *really* are, when you take away what you *think* you are ("I am *this*, I am *that*").

This "I am" condition, pure be-ing, does not change or fluctuate: the ever-present Reality ("God") is always the ever-present *Reality*. The "you" that you suppose exists *does* change and fluctuate ("I am *this* today, *that* tomorrow").

Different books (different teachers) may have different premises when they say "you": one book may be speaking of you in your true condition ("I am", or as *God itself*); another book may mean you as you think yourself to be (a falsely-identified form): the "*I am separate*" idea—separate from God, or "I am".

If you stick with one teacher, this confusion in *terms* is less likely to occur.

On First Base

Ask and it shall be given; seek and ye shall find; knock and it shall be opened unto you.

Your intense interest in this subject will carry you through.

However, some questions will occur to you meanwhile which you will not be able to resolve until you have a solid basis for their revelation: one must have a basis in math before exploring algebra.

The enclosed material will be of assistance in orienting your attention in the most productive direction. Questions which proceed from this material then can be equivalent to exploring algebra.

At this point, I can merely provide the following quotations from the fountainhead of nonduality in our era, Ramana Maharshi. These will simply suggest the direction in which your query about karma can most assuredly bear fruit:

> "Let us first understand what karma is—whose karma it is; and who is the 'do-er' (of actions).... There is no karma without a doer (actor). But on seeking the doer (self), it disappears: where is karma then?.... Discover the 'who' in karma. You will find that you are not the doer. Then you will be free.... There will be karma until

there is Self-realization. After realization, there will be
no karma.... The (enlightened) mind...cannot contain
the seeds of karma.... He will not be bound by karma
either now or ever."

Someone suggested to Nisargadatta that "karma prods us toward
perfection".

Nisargadatta replied, "You are already perfect—here, and now....
But you imagine yourself to be what you are not: stop that....It is
your refusal to examine (Self-realization) that creates karma!"

That which is said here can become crystal clear to you—and
much more yet.

But there is a truth (an eternal truth)—right before your eyes—
which will need to be apprehended *first*.

Buddha's Advice

Of Buddha's Four Noble Truths, the first truth is that "Life is
suffering." Buddha didn't say that "life is suffering sometimes"; or
"life is suffering until we do this or that". Even for one who
becomes enlightened, suffering is not something left behind, like a
bag of old rags in the dumpster. Buddha, in fact, died a painful
death (food poisoning); as did Jesus; and Ramana (cancer).

What changes for the enlightened is not the presence of suffering
itself, but how one responds to it. Notice that I said responds: not
"reacts".

The first noble (Latin: "well known") truth is that life *is* suffering.
Not "life is what we want it to be", or "what we hope it will be", or
"what it *could* be". So, Buddha's advice is: Number one; recognize
that as long as you are alive, some form or degree of suffering will

be a co-existent fact. The second noble truth: determine what your response will be, in the face of this fact.

What Buddha suggests is forsaking preference. Considering that suffering is a fact of life, he suggests that we do not wish, hope or prefer that life be anything other than it is.

He proceeds to point out that this matter-of-fact disposition saws both ways: when one is completely dispassionate, one has no preference at all, one way or the other. In other words, one is not elated at good tidings (yours or others'); one is not dejected at bad tidings.

When one accepts everything just as it is (positive *or* negative), hope withers away like a dry leaf. One no longer hopes or wishes for any particular thing (or event): being satisfied—content (from Latin: "contained")—with things just as they are.

This response—as opposed to a (negative) reaction—doesn't make suffering disappear; it makes it less disturbing. No law says that you have to like 'what is'; even mice squeal, cats squall, and dogs whine. But that which is the witness to the suffering body, does not itself suffer. One can observe both one's liking and disliking without doing anything more about it than that. In a sense, this is the end of suffering, because what is viewed with *equanimity* is no longer seen as "suffering". It is this counsel of dispassionate nonattachment which has made Buddha's teaching practical, over 2,500 years.

One form of suffering is to expect to find "meaning" in life, or to suppose that life should "make sense". The words *should, could* and *would* all point to something other than what presently and actually *is*. If there *is* meaning in life, it must be present *now* and need not be longed for. If life doesn't "make sense" *as it is*, what alternative can one hope to discover?

Buddha's emotional suffering—while a do-or-die seeker for an end to suffering—led to physical pain. It was in response to this pragmatic reality that he concluded that, no matter what one attempts for an escape, life is bracketed by suffering—from the moment we are torn from the sea in the womb. What he showed others is that we must begin from this stark assessment, in calibrating our psyche to the reality we expect.

Forgive? Or "Forget"?

How does one go about not identifying with his or her suffering?

The obvious answer, of course, is by not identifying: period. There is only one thing that is ever going on: "That", doing what it does. One of the things that it does is to re-present itself as a "person" who "thinks". One of these thoughts, among the infinite variety, is "I am (or, they are) suffering." Another such thought is "I am (or, they are) not suffering."

"Suffering" and "not suffering" are both That doing what it does. *Thinking* there is suffering/not suffering is *also* both That doing what it does. In fact, the very "thinker" itself re-presents That doing what it does: it "persons" (among other things).

Why "identify" anything: That which does the identifying is the very same as That which is being identified. "You" can't even actually "identify" with *That*: you *are* That. All identification, as Ramana might say, is Self identification. Realize the truth of this, and separative distinctions evaporate.

What all this is pointing to is that you (as a "separate entity") are not the doer—or sufferer/not sufferer: all that is, is *That*. Since all is That, even if "you" *do* identify with suffering, that *too* is That doing what it does.

(So, whether or *not* you realize the truth of this, and whether or *not* separative distinctions end, That is still always continuing to do what it does.)

This is not to say that, in terms of *physical* suffering, the body will not register pain. But who/what is it that is identifying (with) the body and/or pain? In other words, as long as there is a retained "you" (or "other"), there will be "someone" to whom pain/suffering applies. (Or *doesn't* apply, as the case may be.) This is the *only* way that identification with suffering can possibly end.

Find out if this is true!

As per the words of your song: *Peace is there waiting, Surely to be found. It's there in every moment, Especially for you. When you really want it, It gives itself to you.*

In this context, while we're looking at it, it seems to me that it is time to re-consider your emphasis on forgiveness. The endeavor to "forgive" is embedded in a "me"/ "other than me" mindset. Even in terms of "self forgiveness", there is a *me*, on the one hand, who presumably forgives *my self*, on the other hand. All of these "individual" entities are illusions: all there is, is That.

"Forgiving/not forgiving" are merely ideas about what That is doing (*by* That, doing it): just like "suffering/not suffering".

"Forgiving" is a prime example of the machinations of separative conceptualizing: "to give up resentment against; to stop being angry with; to pardon or not exact penalty for an offense". Only where the me/other construct persists can there be resentment for; anger toward; the desire to penalize; and personalizing an offense. Who/what is the doer that represents "me"? Who/what is the doer that represents "the offender"?

"Who" is doing the forgiving? "Who" is being forgiven?

Is forgiveness really an act of Love? Or is the dissolution of the me/other conflict the presence of Love?

Lastly (if you're still with me), I hope you will come to recognize the difficulty that occurs when one objectifies what you have referred to (though by many other names as well) as the Entity. This conception, in particular, *means* "a thing that has definite, individual existence outside *or* within the mind". I just want to emphasize that (this which I call) That cannot be considered as *apart* from *anything* ("individual"); nor appearing *partially* anywhere (outside, as opposed to inside); nor, in actuality, can it be *confined* to a concept in the mind (it *being* the mind, in addition to all else).

Only where there is a "me"/ "other" (Entity) can there be a communiqué, one way or the other. Seen another way; *being* That, we cannot *experience* That. The experiencer *is* the experience.

"You" are not, in any way, *apart* from that. Who or what would "communicate" what to whom or what? And what would be the point? This, that *is* all that is, need not rely on communication.

I can acknowledge that you attest that you have had such communication. When you come to recognize that you *are* this Entity, and there is *only* one such actuality, consider: *from* whom and *to* whom could the experience of communicating occur or pertain? Who, actually, are "you"? You signed your letter, "Not at war." How about "Not at"?

....

How They Died

The lives, as well as the teachings, of four sages in particular have been instructive by comparison of both the similarities and the differences: namely Buddha, Jesus, Ramana Maharshi, and Krishnamurti.

Among the informative comparisons of their similarities is that of their manner of dying: specifically, the message which is inherent in their non-resistance to physical death.

The cause of death, in Krishnamurti's case, was a cancerous internal organ (pancreas). He was restricted to his bed after he had become too weak to function otherwise. By this time, his condition was untreatable. He had not sought treatment, nor notified associates of his condition, although he himself could not likely have been unaware of the development of significant internal symptoms.

After he was confined to bed, he consented to analgesic life-sustaining medication; but when he had completed the business which he needed to attend to from his sick bed, he halted the medication and succumbed.

Ramana Maharshi's death resulted from a cancerous limb (arm). He permitted doctors to treat—but not amputate—his arm. Otherwise, he did not concern himself with treatment nor with the predicable outcome of such a condition.

When he became so weakened that impending death was apparent, he was held in the arms of disciples and comforted. Aside from a smile, it is said that the only sign of his death was the cessation of breathing.

While the details of the death of Krishnamurti and Ramana Maharshi have been documented, having occurred in the Twentieth Century, the details—indeed the history—of Jesus and Buddha are subject to less reliable reports.

However, tradition tells us that Jesus was not unaware of his fatal trajectory, but made no effort to resist it (not even so much as to encourage acquaintances to defend him). As with the aforementioned, he willingly acquiesced to the unfolding denouement of death.

The detail of Buddha's death is (having occurred approximately five hundred years earlier) at least as obscure. There is an implicit instruction, though, in this common account.

Buddha and his attendants were invited to a meal, prepared by a goldsmith. When the main dish was served, Buddha silently observed that it contained wild mushrooms, of a poisonous variety. He insisted that he alone partake of this dish, that the remainder be buried.

After the meal, Buddha and his retinue traveled on, but was forced to stop increasingly as he became weaker. After giving some last words of teaching, while being comforted by his most faithful attendant, he lapsed into a final meditation.

In all four instances, the lives—as well as the deaths—of these prominent sages pointed in one direction: non-attachment to all concerns of life…including life itself.

Expose Shadows to the Light

Evidently, your recent impulse to look within has served as a laxative for the psyche. What we have been calling That has been engaging in witnessing the *images* of what *appears* to have been experiences in the life of one of its manifestations, Don; and that imagined person is being purged in awareness. This visualized drama is revealing the pain and suffering which self-centered behavior visits on "self/others".

The consequence of this retching introspection is that you are beginning to see the fruits of desires in an objective light—rather than as they *could* have been, or *could* be.

This might develop into the seeing of things *as they are*, instead of "how they *ought* to be".

There are a couple of areas in which this honest apprising of 'what is' can be instructive.

One: you do not know that you will ever leave the place where you are now.

Two: conditions there are inhumane.

If these are *facts*—'what is'—then how practical is it to focus concern on how "things should not be this way"?

If tomorrow you fell into a coma, were taken to an internist, were tested and found to have a malignant brain tumor that was untreatable, to focus attention on "this should not be" would obviously be pointless.

To dwell on what "has happened" or what "I hope will happen" is pointless. Attention to what *is* the fact functions to keep our awareness in the realm of survival.

We are animals. Non-human animals don't torture themselves about what they have previously done, or agonize over how situations might develop in the future. They survive because they are attuned to 'what is.'

Stripping away past and future projection is the only way you will wholly survive.

The shadows of the past are being exposed to cold light, and are disappearing. Expose the fantasies as to how the future (tomorrow, through the end of your life) ought to unfold.

Out of Busi-ness

Thanks for the worthwhile excerpts you sent, particularly "The Ultimate Nature of Mind."

Ontology is not a word that I use. The dictionary speaks of it as "an argument for the existence of God, asserting that the conception of a perfect being implies that being's existence outside the human mind". And *God* is defined as "eternal, infinite, all-powerful and all-knowing; supernatural, having powers over the course of nature" (and, implicitly, human nature).

Could that which is infinite ("without limits, bounds, beginning or end") exist "outside the human mind"—"outside" *anything*, for that matter?

And if That existed inside *and* outside the human mind, what would be left that was not It?

In other words, what could be making arguments for the existence of God, and asserting conceptions of a perfect being, but that which is in no way apart from God?

What is described as God is the equivalent of Khenpo's "just one great sovereign, the master of all activities" (even those of arguing and asserting); "the ultimate nature of reality within" and "not something you need to find outside" (the body, mind or presence).

By whatever name—and he cites ground, essence, emptiness, nondual presence, clear light, rigpa, Buddha-mind or -nature, etc.

—"there is nothing superior to this". It "pervades all", is "the absolute...beyond the relative mind", immanent everywhere in time while transcendent of time: "something that has been with me forever...unborn, undying, beginningless; not something to be sought, the heart of our being".

Not something to be sought and attained, he says, it is inseparable from our uncontrived every day awareness, beyond willful alteration, free from conceptuality, unadulterated by effort and modification: "What could be simpler than this"?

"In that light, how far is that fabled 'other shore,' nirvana? So, get out of the construction business!" Relax, "just go with the primordial flow, *however* it occurs and happens"—even if you *don't* go with the flow!

So, it always puzzles me how a person could "realize" that rigpa (or whatever name) is the fundamental essence of everything that is—already—and yet concern themselves about the workings of the (supposedly) individual mind: theirs, or others'.

It's God's mind. Let God worry about its conceived "short-comings".

> "Everything is pure and perfect from the outset. This is the absolute truth....there is nothing that need be done or accomplished."– Khenpo

Anything the perfect God could worry about perfecting would already be its perfect Self.

Your Choice of Words

The word *metaphysics* is a vague term. *Meta* means "beyond", similar to the prefix *trans*. *Physics*, of course, is the study of the nature of matter and energy and their interrelation.

So, metaphysics, then, essentially means to look beyond physics: what is "behind" matter and energy, and what is the nature of *its* presence?

Some physicists today feel that you can't really understand physics without an appreciation of metaphysics—the reality of the universe in which matter and energy are merely manifest elements.

Since physical postulates can be "proven" in the laboratory and metaphysical ones can't, the latter is often described as "mystical".

The dictionary says that metaphysics, as a general term, suggests a discipline involving "subtle or difficult reasoning". (The more modern term is ontology—*ont*, Greek for "to be" or "is"—the study of ultimate being or reality.)

For thousands of years before these descriptive titles came along, sages (often called mystics) have investigated what "be" or "is" means, implies or suggests: what *is "real"*?

Based on their discoveries, the word *subtle* ("not on the surface") definitely applies; but *reasoning*—in terms of linear constructs $(1+1 = 2)$—can only be of use to a limited extent; especially "difficult" reasoning, if that suggests a proliferation of concepts.

Basically, what physicists are revealing today merely reinforces what sages have maintained since before scientific proof was available. Physics is a narrow window into an infinite presence.

Those who see the connections, beyond the glass, are metaphysicians; when they describe what they see in limited terms, they're ontologists. When they have disappeared into what they see and describe, they are sages.

Un-Conditional Awareness

Your last few letters have been both shorter and more objective (less woe-is-me subjectivity). It seems to me that you are viewing circumstances with a more open mind. Thus, I want to comment on some of your considerations, from the perspective here.

You ponder, "Is the belief system of my friends anymore absurd than my own? And just what is my belief system, and where did it come from?"

In regard to the last phrase, it likely resulted from your conditioning—which is what "guides" most everyone (at least until they question it).

Why cling to even a particle of a belief? Belief is defined as "faith in something that has no solid basis in fact". What is—that which is observably present in each immediate moment—is a *fact*. Remove what "has been" or "will be" and any belief dies on its feet! A fact, in present actuality, requires no belief. When we no longer think in terms of things being any *other* way than they *are*, beliefs have no relevance! As you state, "Obviously, I have expectations of *something else*, or am waiting for some change to take place". Change is constantly taking place: it is the substance of the *fact* in, or of, each moment. But when you are expecting (or waiting for) some *other* fact, disappointment is inevitable!

You comment, on your quandary, "I begin to feel as if I am quite a hypocrite." A hypocrite is a person who doesn't live up to their professed ideals. Hypocrisy is unavoidable as long as we cling to ideals. *Ideals* are "ideas" about how things should be, could be or would be, if..! That which unfolds moment by moment has no interest in how we think it could be or should be. 'What is' is not an idea, it's a fact. An ideal is, by definition, never a fact. As long as one's focus is on that which is presently *not true*, there will be dissatisfaction!

Do Unto Others

For most of my life, I was conscious that I was not relating to other people in what I would have defined as a loving way. I could find justification for this ("I'm too busy", etc.) but basically I yearned for that situation to be different, and I sometimes made a conscious effort "to be a loving person".

The turnabout came (without effort) when I no longer concentrated my attention on becoming something that I wasn't, and when I ceased to analyze and compare and judge my behavior as being either correct or incorrect. It was not until I could accept (or love) myself, for what I was, that I could accept (or love) others for what they were. With the barrier of discrimination erased between myself and others, relating to others, with the same concern as for myself, became automatic.

To "be loving", when you are not loving within your being, is a dichotomy; it is fragmentation, it is hypocrisy.

The highest value which you give to anything is that which you give to your self. There is nothing higher which you can be than a seer—one who sees truth so clearly that he acts truthfully on what he sees. When you are not living what you are seeing, you are not truly seeing it. Once you have perceived that which cannot be diminished, you will want to share it—by your example—and that is love.

I continue to see changes in your letters that (for lack of a better term) I would call "more grounded".

The only condition I can imagine that would appear to be analogous to your circumstance, in physical terms, is terminal illness. The situation is not likely to get better—and could get worse.

It would seem that the only sensible course of action is to "accept" what you cannot change.

The problem with this point of view is that "acceptance" is automatically on one end of a (value) scale, on which "rejection" is at the other end.

As Krishnamurti would say, is it possible for us to go beyond—to transcend—the pull toward the polarities of "accepting" or "rejecting"? As long as one category is present in the mind, the other category will be indubitably present.

Can you reasonably "reject" some situation that you cannot change (the loss of a limb, for example)? If the option of rejection is not a possibility, of what meaning is it to "accept"? These are two words—concepts, actually—that can best be dropped from the mental vocabulary (along with good/bad, right/wrong, just/unjust, and so on).

To say that "I should, or I need to, accept" something is to set yourself up for conflict. To eliminate the adversarial categories of accept/reject is to remove one more source of inner contention.

Similarly, why think in terms of "being still 24/7"? There will come a time when you will achieve that (idealistic) goal, without even your heart beating. Meanwhile, is stillness (psychologically) going to be present while you are fretting over whether it is present without relief? If there comes a time when (inner) stillness *is* present, it will be when the mind is "dead" to all such strivings and yearnings ("desires", Buddha called them). Stillness and goals are not compatible. A "goal" of "stillness" can only result in conflict.

"Who" Understands it *All*?

> "What I find really strange is that early yesterday I went to the shower, and for a brief few minutes, I seemed to understand it all. That it was exactly as it needed to be, each piece of every aspect. The place was quiet, and I was still. You would think I would have more of that here, now. Not less".

I suspect, from some of the perceptive changes you have been describing lately, that you will find that this moment of clarity will not be a one-time experience. And that it will be noticed when you least expect it.

It can't be produced, so don't *look* for this occurrence. It is an "experience", in that it comes and goes. What you are looking for is *not* an "experience": it is permanent (without beginning or end); it cannot come from anywhere or go anywhere, because it is infinite, eternal, timeless, without condition. It is All That Is.

The value of such a moment of clarity is that it demonstrates that such omniscient clarity is possible. If seeing through the eyes of the infinite is possible for "a brief few minutes", it is possible for a lifetime. The momentary recognition that "all is as it needs to be" is a "clue" that this Truth is the actuality *in which* we exist. *And* that *it* exists *in* us . The awareness of this Truth is evidently operative in your psyche, even though you may not consciously be cognizant of it.

The essence of the "experience" can be said to be Truth recognizing Itself. Not *you* recognizing Truth, or Truth communicating to "you". There is no you, in this equation. It is a reminder that there is an *awareness which has nothing to do with "you"*. You, in actuality, are not an element in noumenal awareness, or "pure consciousness". In deepest sleep, you do not even ask, or concern your "self", about whether everything "is exactly as it needs to be" or *not*. This absence of "you" is the space in which Truth presents, unobscured.

Focus your attention on the actuality that your *true—deepest—* identity is this Truth which is self-aware that all is Perfect as it is. And that Perfection persists even in the absence of "you".

The Crossing Over

Yes, love is the issue... the only real issue.

To love more than your life is the crux of spirituality, if crux implies crossing place. This suggests a love which goes beyond life, as we know it. It is, therefore, a love which does not manifest with "you" as its center.

When "you" love, there is invariably an object to that love: a what or a whom. You may love "mankind", or "god", but it is a limited love, which owes its virtue to you as lover.

With whom is the lilac in love when it scents the air; the pear tree when it produces abundance; the lark when it whistles curiously its song?

Can love, as essence, be withheld from anything or anyone?

When your love is not withheld, it knows no division, it is boundless.

If such love is boundless, can its origination be in the bound?

If the bounded is who you are not, who then are you... when you and love are without identification? Love is expression of who you truly are—not of who you are as a *result* of love.

Love, in that case, is without intention... without intender or intendee. To *be* love is to be without objective.

In being love, there is no receiver of love who is outside of yourself, and no giver of love who is outside of yourself.

There is no "you" where this love originates. That which presumes to be you cannot be the source of love.

- -

Be As You *Are*

Your insistence upon "looking deeply within" is motivated by your presumption, your expectation, that you will find something that will *change*—the hope is, *improve*—your life.

This is the motivation of the ego. You want to do that which you think is necessary, in order to become a better—"more whole", "less confused"—person.

When the ego looks within, it will see what it *needs* to see in order to perpetuate its position. It will see all that is "good" and "remarkable" about you. It will see all that is "bad" and "despicable" about you. It will rest satisfactorily upon the former, while busying itself about "working on" the latter.

What is *behind* the ego—*aware* of the ego that is rummaging around within—is the "you" that was aware even before your ego (your idea of who you are) was constructed. This you—this *awareness*—is *unaffected* by what it sees. Were *it* to look within, it would observe neither "good" nor "bad", because it is free of judgment.

This you—this *observer* that is aware of the antics of the ego and its "looking within"—is unblemished. It *cannot* be blemished, because it is neutral to all that it observes. If *it* were to look within, there would be nothing special that it would see to report on.

Recognize that the ego is an *idea* of who/what you think you are. Awareness has always been there, *before* any of your ideas ever arose.

This *core* of your being cannot be "improved" upon, therefore no amount of looking within will affect it.

What is looking within hopes to find trouble. So doing, it can ignore the disturbing information that you are perfectly okay as you are (whatever the balance of good or bad).

In *touch* with who you are, you won't be *looking* for who you are. But then you will have nothing to improve, and the ego will suffer.

When you look within and you see good and bad, that's who *you are*—but you/ego are dissatisfied with what is present; you don't want to be who you are, you want to be something *else*. Through this desire, you will suffer.

You do not need to get rid of the ego. You do not need to get rid of your desires. Just discover what it is that is *aware* of ego and desire. *That* is unchanging—always aware of *all* of your activities;

yet it is not *affected* by any of them. Give your attention to *that*, and stay there.

You will not have difficulty discovering this ordinary, non-reactive, ever-present awareness. In fact, you can't escape it, because it is the core of who you are. Notice it everywhere. It is your self. Look for what is aware of being aware. You will be looking into a mirror that reflects all of your attributes with calm unconcern. Isn't that the change you really want?

Who's Responsible?

To view our existence from the perspective of the Self-realized nondual sages, one's own Self-realization is imperative. To attempt to perceive the nondual teachings from the standpoint of duality can lead only to confusion.

These teachings submit, in a nutshell, that "all that is, is That". All; everything; no exceptions: absolute. There is but one permanent reality, and it encompasses or over-arches all that is impermanent or conditional. Being itself (the only actuality that is) infinite and eternal, boundless spatially or temporally, there is not anything which exists outside of its presence. As a consequence, all that we cognitively consider to be *not* It, is a *subset* of it. *It*, being itself *formless*, is not a thing, an entity which is limited in time or space. All *forms*, whether material or immaterial, are *limited* things, or entities. *These* all have their meaningful identity, as varied things, in relation to all other things: therefore, we say that they are "relative". All relative things exist and/or cease to exist within the all-inclusive, absolute presence.

As such, while we cognitively consider each relative thing to be separate (or separable) from each other relative thing, not any singe thing is "separate" from the all-embracing Absolute. In fact, from the standpoint of the Absolute being entirely unrestrained in space or time, the Absolute not only encompasses every single thing but *permeates* all that is; as the Vedas declare, speaking of this *saturation*, "There is no where It is not."

Therefore, we do not have the relative on the one hand (or in one place) and the Absolute on the other hand (in another place). The Absolute and its "by-product", the relative, exist indivisibly and simultaneously. The limited forms, as we suppose them to be, exist "within" the Absolute; while the unlimited (and "itself" formless) Absolute exists "within" (and "without") every relative item.   Since each relative thing appears within the timeless presence and disappears within the timeless presence, these relative appearances are impermanent (in a supporting condition which is permanent).

With the arising and subsiding of the seemingly separate things within the expanse of the all-pervading, no thing is *ever* separate (*throughout* its existence) from the Absolute condition. Nor is the Absolute ever separate in any way whatsoever from any and all, each and every, existent thing.   This is why the sages say that ultimately the only reality, or truth, is: "All that is, is That."

This is what *non*duality means: there are no two (or more) things, from the nondual perspective. There is nothing *other than* That.

Those whose perspective is dualistic perceive our existence in terms of "this" thing (*whatever* it is) as compared to—or relative to—"that" thing (whatever *it* is).   Limited to their dualistic mindset, they conceive of the Absolute as "one" thing, and the relative entity or form as some "other" thing.

Thus, they presume that there is an "I" which is separate from "you"; and that "I" and "you" are somehow apart from "That" (by whatever name). The sage maintains that these supposed separate entities are a misleading appearance, a mistaken "identity". "You" are *That*, they assert; and all that "you" do (or suppose that "you" do) is That, doing what is done. By obvious extension, all living beings are That, doing whatever it is that is being done.

So, from the nondual perspective, if I hand you an apple, the ultimate reality is: That is handing That to That; "I", "handing", "apple", "you"—*all* That, doing what it does. From the most basic standpoint, not anything is even "happening"!

There being, in truth, no "I", there are no "others": this is the nondual perspective. Only where there is a dualistic ("two or more things") conception can there be an "individual", in actuality; or a "relationship" (of *any* kind) "between" one or more "other" individuals.

If one can feel good about the relationship of "responsibility" between individuals, one can feel bad about the *lack* of responsibility between individuals. This is why sages point out that separative *ideas* lead to conflict, "suffering"; and why sages point out that suffering will *only* cease to the extent that separative ideas are abandoned.

But—to penetrate more deeply into this matter—from the standpoint of the nondual sage, "all that is, is That...doing what it does". Therefore, to be concise, if one acts in a so-called (interpreted or defined as) "responsible" manner or form—or one *doesn't* act in a responsible manner or form—it is "not different". There are no "moral imperatives" from the perspective of nondual Self-realization.

There is an interesting consequence to this realization. If it makes no difference *what* one does, from the ultimate perspective, what traditionally have the enlightened sages found themselves doing? Exploiting "others" (in *whatever* way) for one's "own" gain? Acting *self*-ishly or self-*lessly*?

If this particular organism, (authoring this monograph) acts "responsibly", *whose* action is it? "Mine"? And *who* is it that is being acted responsibly (or "irresponsibly") toward? Something or someone "apart" from the actor? Is anything at all, ever, really "happening"?

Obviously, this perspective is not the perspective of the dualistically conditioned "individual" who concludes that it is "important" how "I" act toward "you". From their *relative* perspective (only), this may be a considerable issue. But that very fact points to the incapacity to embody the spiritual truth advocated by the enlightenment teachers, who say that dualistic polarities—such as "responsible/irresponsible"—are delusive ideas, "self" centered concepts.

· ·

"Nothing to stand on" (Buddhist pointer)

The pointer "The observer is the observed" suggests that we *are*, mysteriously, what we *see*. According to one's inclination, this can be considered in more than one way.

From the most elementary standpoint, all that we see (and even what we don't see) is composed—according to our best investigation—of subatomic particles. While these elements are termed "particles" because there are many forms, all have the same *non*-particulate character: they are not concrete, but are roughly described as patterns of energy, or vibrations or pulsations. Further, each pattern is not independent, but is dependent for its form on co-existing patterns. The infinitely interconnectedness of the overall pattern, or field or ground, is the matrix of the "orderliness" of the universe. That each element acts in a universal harmony with the whole can be regarded as intelligence in form.

As with all that you see, your own body is a galaxy of these subatomic particles. In fact, a particular particle from a star could be substituted for a particle in your body, with no modification. Therefore, in this sense, you and what you see are fundamentally nothing more than the same intelligent energy or omnipotent, omniscient presence.

Many Questions, One Answer

What is said by *all* teachers will *seem* contradictory. They are speaking with those who understand, and those who don't. For the latter, they must speak from the point of view of the *relative*. For the former, they are speaking from the standpoint of the Absolute. The answers to the kinds of questions you are asking will be obvious to you when you are viewing clearly from the non-relative. So, consider your questions before you ask: "Where there are *no two things*—which is said to be the Truth of (our) actuality—what is the 'answer' to *this question*?" All 'answers' are *self*-evident; questions are inherently dualistic. Until the Truth of non-duality is *recognized* and *acknowledged*, questions are endless.

Adyashanti speaks of ego to those who still suppose that ego "exists". If there is presumed to be "me" and (my) "ego", can you see that people are thinking in terms of "two things"? Therefore, Adya responds on the *relative* level. *You* are right: since "there is, in truth, no ego", there is no ego that makes "choices".

Since there is, Ramesh Balsekar says, nothing real except the One, are not the "do-er" and "what is done" merely "different" ways of describing that One?

242

I don't recall having *ever* said that I initiate anyone. In mystical religions, "initiation" is a secret ceremony by which one enters the "inner circle". There is no inner circle in regard to Oneness. We are *all already* One, if we but recognize that fact. And there are no "secrets" in regard to recognizing that fact. You are *already* what you seek: how could there be anything secret about that? "Initiation" has no relationship to recognizing your true nature.

I do *discuss* nondual awakening with people "on a one-to-one" basis, so I suppose *that's* what you heard—not that I "initiate" people.

As to "fact", "reality" and "actuality", some people use these terms interchangeably. I use them with a slight distinction, along the lines you've noted. A fact is "what is"; because it is something that *is*, it is not subject to alteration (if it changes, it is now a *different* fact, a different "what is"). If you have, for example, lost an arm, no amount of wishing it were otherwise will change that fact.

Since most people would say that this world and their "independent" existence in it are real, when I use the word "reality" it is usually meant in the sense of the appearances which we *suppose* unarguably "exist".

To distinguish that which exists whether or not there is a world, a person, or any manner of thought concerning it, I typically use the word "actuality". What is referred to as the Absolute, then, is to me an actuality. The person who supposes that they are somehow apart from the Absolute is bound by, in my view, limited "reality". And, to me, the one "fact" behind all facts is that unchangeable actuality which is generally called the Absolute.

True Self

Put this piece of paper aside, and look out the window: we could say that what you see or perceive is what you are aware of. If you focus your attention on any particular item in your view, you will still be aware of what is seen in the periphery…the movement of a lizard to one side of the rock, which you are studying. You will also be aware of the music emanating from the stereo, even though you may not intentionally be giving it your direct attention.

You can, in shifting the focus of your attention, be aware of your "self": your body; a mannerism or habit; a memory or thought or opinion, etc. But even when it is not the direct subject of your attention, an awareness of the self—the "attendee"—is persistent.

But what is it which is aware of the attendee, aware of the self? Clearly, there is an awareness which is "behind" self awareness. Consider anything which you define as your "self"; what is *aware* of this self?

If you are aware that there is an awareness which "stands behind" the self, what is it that is aware of this awareness?

If you say that "*I* am aware of this awareness", what is it which is aware of the I which is aware?

If there is something which is *aware* of the self that is aware, that "something" must be your *true* self.

To be aware is to be conscious of other than one's self—in addition to being conscious of one's self: one is persistently aware of the foreground, simultaneously with the background; one is aware of that upon which one's attention is focused, while also being aware of the "attendee" which is focusing the attention.

Are the background and the foreground actually separate? Is that, of which you are aware, and your awareness of it, in any way separate? If there is an observer of your self, is this self a separate identity; is the identity of the self not *dependent* upon that which observes it? If the self is dependent upon something beside itself for existence, is the self an actual, isolated entity? Is there an awareness that is apart from a self, or a self that is apart from awareness?

How is your self apart from *anything* of which you are aware? If the self is *not* apart from the not-self of which you are aware, what is the true nature of the self?

Idolatry

Krishnamurti is saying that an image is a representation—not a *presentation*, but a *re*-presentation—of reality. We have, for example, our actions, our behavior—reality, factual; then we have our subjective view, our opinionated critique of our behavior (couched in the past tense : e.g., "I shouldn't have said what I said; it made me look stupid"). In other words, there is our self as we *are*; and then there is our self as we imagine that we ought to be. It is this self-*image* which separates us from reality, and creates conflict.

The most ideal of all images is that of "God". The reality around us is not "perfect"; yet, the reality around us is the omnipotent in its visible form. Forsaking reality, we created the God of our image-ination: perfect, loving, creative—positive adjective, after positive adjective.

Having this established image of God (perfect) and our self (imperfect), we want to be "more like God": "in his image".

God (the Absolute) is not an idea: it is reality. But it is this "positive" idea of what God is *like* that is worshipped—not the reality which is manifest all around (and in) us: though I am as much that manifestation as are the heavens, I don't want to be as I *am*, I want to be the idol that I conceive in my imagination.

So, we have such things as consciousness (which we experience) and "super consciousness" (which we desire to experience); one is reality, the other is an idea of what reality could be like. Only one is—and will be—real. So K says, "There is only the self". Ramana, too, says the same thing: there is only one actuality, one thing which we experience to be existent; I *am*.

Buddha-mind is the recognition that "I am" is the only ascertainable truth, and the "I" is without a center—no locus for an image of what I *am*.

Or *can* be. Or *will be*.

See the World?

Awakening from a dream, thinking about it: a friend, who I was expecting, entered the room and approached the table near where I stood. I poured a glass of wine for each of us, and we tasted it and commented on its bubbliness and pastel color. Had the dream continued, perhaps we would have stepped out onto the patio and looked at the night sky, remarking on the moon, stars and heavens.

People suppose that dreams are contained in the mind; that the mind is contained in the body; and that the body is contained in the cosmos.

Dreams, like thoughts, are fleeting and unsubstantial. The body and brain or mind, of course, are impermanent; born to die.

Though the cosmos seems permanent by comparison, we acknowledge that it too was born (or created), at some point; and, by definition, anything which *comes into* existence will, sooner or later, *go out* of existence.

We presume that the cosmos is contained within something which is not subject to birth and death, coming and going. Indeed, the fact is—according to our best science—that all that we can detect, of the universe, is inhabiting an infinite realm. We deduce that within this infinity, the universe has arisen; and, consequently, could at some time subside. If and when all else were to cease to exist, that matrix (which we conclude must be beginningless and endless) would be the presence *into* which all existence would disappear.

This infinite and eternal condition, being the original essence, the only absolute permanence, the unchanging within which change takes place, has historically been considered the Creator or the Supreme Being.

Nevertheless, we consider that the Absolute exists within the cosmos; whereas evidently it is the cosmos which exists within the Absolute. If there were any such thing as a progenitor of the universe and everything manifest within it, the Absolute would appear to be its foundation, or so-called First Principle.

So, existence resides in the Absolute. But to that which is infinite and eternal, there is no such ascribable condition as *non-existence*. The possibility of non-existence being ruled out, the possible alternative condition of 'existence' has no meaning. The Absolute, in other words, cannot be supposed to be either existent or non-existent. Such *variable* states do not apply to it.

In fact, the only thing which gives anything existence is the discriminating mind, which presumes to segregate the Absolute universe into existent and nonexistent portions.

When asleep, the activities perceived within my dream are unquestioningly existent. My friend, standing across from me, is no less real in my mind, or consciousness, than I myself. The wine is poured, the glasses raised, the contents consumed and appreciated—the experience as real as any other seeming experience.

Later, when *awake*, the activities perceived are also unquestioningly existent. The mind registers a real body, in a real cosmos. If anything occurs to it to be *un*real, it is the insensible, the imperceptible, the non-existent.

Yet, what grants existence or non-existence to anything, but the mind? The mind determines that my dreaming state is unreal, but my waking state is real; the wine I drink in the former is nonexistent, the wine I drink in the latter is existent. Were it not for the viewer, is the "cosmos" existent? Is the "Absolute" nonexistent? Apart from the viewer, does anything *have* determinable existence?

Who's Answering Your Questions?

It is evident that you are apprehending the message of the advaita teachers.

To use your terminology, what is observing God's creation is God itself.* All enlightened teachers stress that the Absolute is omnipresent: ever always here (*wherever* here is) now (*whenever* now is). Therefore, all that arises (or is "created") springs from this ground of being—*into* this ground of being. In other words, *all that is* is inseparable from the Absolute (because it exists only

---

* Generally, I tend to avoid the word "God"; it carries too much dualistic freight: note how, in Michelangelo's ceiling, God is apart from man (kind).

within the Absolute). Therefore, you are as much the Absolute as the Absolute is the Absolute.

So, "God's creation"—you *as* the Absolute—looks out on a universe of "God's creation", of equally-Absolute manifestations. This is precisely why Meister Eckhart said, "The eye with which I see God is the same with which God sees me." Thus, whatever the organism observes is an aspect of the Absolute—with "another" aspect of the Absolute (you) observing it.

Likewise, what is *thinking* about God (as you put it) is God thinking about itself. Actually, no matter *what* you think about— since all things *are* the Absolute—it is merely the Absolute thinking about itself. Of course, since even the phenomenon of "thinking" is simply an (other) aspect of the Absolute, not anything—ultimately—is "happening". This is what Nisargadatta means when he says, "Nothing ever happens."

As you've indicated, if all "thinking" is God's, then all "will" must also be the same. Therefore, if a so-called individual wills to do "good" or "evil", that too is God's doing. And, as you say, the feelings or emotions that the acts of good or evil elicit in "other" individuals, it is—as you put it—"God who is feeling that." Why else would St. Paul say, "outside of God, there is nothing"?

References to "pure awareness" are merely pointers: from the standpoint of the awakened, there is no such thing as *im*pure awareness; all awareness is perfect (neither impure nor pure) as it is. The root of the word *pure* means "clean" or clear. In your deepest sleep, awareness is devoid of divisiveness. That fundamental awareness does not disappear when one wakes to the day. But it is a non-functional awareness when we set about to perform our "separate", relative tasks throughout the day: during that time, our awareness is focused on the organism and (acquiring) its needs. The "pure" awareness of deep sleep is not "superior" to the awareness of our waking (or dreaming) state; the *cognitive* awareness has its function to serve. But since most people are only appreciative of their waking awareness, the sages emphasize the condition of "pure awareness" because that is the basic condition to which our presence returns when all else has subsided as temporary (temporal).

All states or conditions of awareness are "That doing what it does", as (and when) it does it. In deep sleep (an experience of "pure awareness"), your sense of personal identity, "self", is absent. So, the sages are making the point that "pure awareness" is your most elementary condition: no I-thought as one's central reference point. They would say that when you have put the I-thought to rest in your normal waking condition, pure awareness is your operational awareness. Therefore, in answer to your question, when "observing" from the perspective that is consciously free of subject vs. object, the observing is in pure awareness: clean, clear.

Finally. Looking at matters from the standpoint of nonduality, you have seen through the statement, "For self-realization, there must be self-control". As you said, "Where there is no self, of what value is 'self-control'?" Realization is really a matter of recognizing that there is no separate "self". As Tony Parsons has put it, "There is no 'person' that becomes enlightened…. Awakening is the absence of the illusion of individuality." Where all is That, who could possibly be in control of what?: That being all that is, there is no *need* for extraneous "control".

The Devil *Claims* Responsibility

Someone once accused Krishnamurti of being responsible for (something on the order of) "leading people astray". K's reply: "I'm not responsible for *anything*." Why would he say that?

What does responsibility *mean*?: "answerable as being the cause or source of something; to account for behavior in terms of right and wrong; duty-bound or liable to an authority that sits in judgment". Underlying the presumption of responsibility is one of *control*: "the power to cause or prevent".

Isn't there a power that surpasses *your* power to cause and/or prevent? When you cease to exist, will *this* power be diminished? And what of the domains that you were responsible for? Does someone then take on a responsibility that is equal to what was your own? So how critical or enduring is your responsibility, when it can be absent and not even be missed?

It is arrogance to assume that we are the cause or source of anything which has meaning beyond our own thoughts or definitions. What are you responsible for in your true nature, when "you" as an entity are absent in deepest, dreamless sleep? Such a concept does not even *occur* in the psyche.

If you assume that "you" are responsible, who *are* you? You are That. So "you" are not even responsible for "your own" actions. And any *thing*, for which you *could* be responsible, is That. So, if That is acting as; causing; or preventing That, where does judgment of *responsibility* arise? If "you" are holding yourself or others liable for behavior that is beyond your ultimate control, this is merely another example of *That* doing what it does— *appearing* to be other than It is.

You're not even in control of your own destiny. If you were, you could will to avoid death. But there's a power that you must admit is beyond your control: to it, belongs credit or blame for what is caused or prevented—including the presence or absence of those who presume to "take responsibility".

You can't even "give up" control of your actions, because you've never been responsible for actions from the beginning. Are you to be "held responsible" for your actions in the womb? Are you to be held responsible because you died and left the world in the condition it's in? *That's* supposed to be the responsibility of the Devil!

Embraceable You

I wish I had a copy of one of your earliest letters to send you: your letters get "saner" all the time. You may not be aware of the change over the past couple of years, but I am. Even your handwriting is much clearer!

It's always darkest before dawn, it's said. You appear to be getting closer to *letting go* of *even* the anger. Don't worry about it: you are what you are, and that is exactly as it should be. "Let's see...call this one John. Fill him with, umm, nine parts anger, breathe life into him and let him play out his life as a catalyst in an institution in, uhh, Michigan." You and your anger are one, aren't they? Can you "accept" John without accepting all that *constitutes* John? Only anguish will result if you try to do otherwise.

Lozoff wants people to work on, and perfect, themselves—as if God made imperfect beings. *Is* there a "self" apart, to "work on itself"? Silliness. Wapnick says "embrace *all* people without *exception*". That would mean embrace the embracer as well, wouldn't it?

Who's Hurting?

Teachers of nonduality sometimes are asked this, in its variations: "If there's no me, whose pain is this?" The response to such a question can *only* be appreciated within the context of the nondual perspective.

252

Physical pain is basically the transmission of a signal of bodily damage or decay, communicated to consciousness through the nervous system. At least in death, even spiritual teachers are subject to pain: Jesus, Krishnamurti, Ramana, Nisargadatta, Suzuki Roshi, to name a few. That they were subject to pain did not affect the fact that they were enlightened teachers.

Pain, clearly, is conditional: it can be excised with analgesics (Krishnamurti was given morphine); nerve intervention (Suzuki utilized acupuncture); or dispelled in coma. In the coma-like state of our birth, pain is also generally dispersed.

Our conception of pain figures largely in our fear of death. The same dualistic perspective is common to both concerns: pain and the "victim" of pain; death and the victim of death. Pain, like death, is viewed in a different context by one to whom such oppositional propositions holds no significance.

A questioner asked Ramana, "Is there no 'I am the body' idea for the realized person? If, for instance you were bitten by an insect [such as a scorpion], is there no sensation?"

"There is a sensation [pain]", Ramana replied, "and there is also the 'I am the body' idea. The latter is common to both the realized and the unrealized—with this difference.

"The unrealized thinks 'I am the body only.' The realized person knows that *all* is the Self [Absolute]: 'all this is Brahman' [the questioner's surrogate for the Absolute].

"If there be pain", Ramana explained, "let it be. *It* is also the Self.

"The Self is perfect," he added.

In other words, the "body" that the realized sees himself as, is the Absolute. The body that the unrealized sees himself as, is this finite, ephemeral organism.

From the standpoint of Absolute realization, there is no separate phenomena such as "pain" and "me": both merely come and go *within* the inseparable completeness of the (perfect) Absolute.

For an analogy: physicists have discovered that there is energy in a vacuum. Why? Because subatomic particles spontaneously arise from the void, exist momentarily, and subside again into the vacuum—endlessly, and without dependence on any casual relationship.

The realized person considers that both the arising of his impermanent body and its transitory pain are like bubbles in the effervescent Absolute. Ramana says, Yes, I feel pain. But who am I? I am "embodied" in the Absolute.

So whose pain is it?, he would say: not mine. There is no me.

This is not to deny that there is a conscious experience of pain, or to suggest that the sage isn't aware of the physical body. It is to indicate that—unlike the unrealized—he doesn't *identify* with the pain as something in relationship to "himself" which he then supposes he can conclusively affect. His summary: "Let it be." It is pointless to raise the question, whose pain is it?; or to propose that "I" can do something about "it". There being no "you", whatever is done about it, Ramana would remind, is That doing what it does.

You've got it down to one question. One question can be the thread that unravels the ball of mystery, if the question is in the proper context.

The context is commitment—which is necessary.

Nine times out of ten, the questions themselves are based on a misunderstanding of what one perceives the "spiritual" proposition to entail.

The "shattering of the image of the self" is not urged so that one may then experience a "more rewarding" life. The world we live in does not become more benign for the awakened. It is merely that this world is seen in a different way, by the enlightened. If there *were* a "reward" for the shattering of self image, that would be all that it is.

So, when one asks, "How does one get rid of the 'me'?", there are several threads to look at in this question. Is there an assumption that, in "getting rid of the me" the world will appear to be a better place? If so, don't waste your time. Is there an assumption that, in "getting rid of the me", I will have become a better person? If so, ditto.

The interpretation of "shattering the image of the self" as "getting rid of the me" is one of these misunderstandings that I referred to. To shatter the image of the self is the complete end of self-objectivity. There is no me *left* to now be "better". There is no me left to view the world in the way it has heretofore *been* viewed: *thus* it now is seen "in a different way".

So, when I say that unraveling the ball is possible only through commitment, I'm talking about putting what you conceive of as the me "on the line": at risk of destruction. If you're not willing to risk all, all that you hold to be of value, in coming to the conclusion of your question, this lack of commitment will not carry you through.

Another element to untangle in the question is the "how". This suggests that there is process in time: "Here's how we'll do this; first…" How long does it take you to blink your eyes open in the morning light, and recognize "I'm awake"? This is a realization, simply, that "I am no longer asleep." How long does it take you, once your eyes are open, to be aware of who it is that is now awake? If I were to pose the question, "How does one get to know who it is that says 'I'm awake'?", the "how" would represent an instant, wouldn't it? So, the idea that there is a "how" that represents a discernible process in time is another misunderstanding, in regard to this awakening.

But all of the above are rather minor misunderstandings: let's look at the *fundamental* misunderstanding.

The answer to your question is: There *is* no me!

You can discern this from your own experience. Tonight, you'll lie down in bed and the awareness will go from waking to dreaming to deep, dreamless sleep (and then reverse by morning). In the dreaming portion, there will continue to be thoughts about the sleeper and the world he daily inhabits. In deep sleep, this me and his world will entirely disappear. Clearly, then, this me is the subject of the retentive mind. It is not a permanent reality, because it disappears at times. *This* me is already "gotten rid of" for at least a portion of every day. This impermanent me is not something concrete or substantial that *can* be gotten rid of, actually.

So, what is "gotten rid of" is the *idea* that this phantasmic image (as in "imagination") is a reality of which one can be "in riddance".

There is no me of which one *can* be rid.

If one *were* able to be rid of the me, what would be *left* to acknowledge its riddance? In other words, if you *could* get rid of the me, "you" wouldn't know of it!

Set up a mirror. Place a candle in front of it. The candle in the mirror appears to be as authentic as the placed candle. But if the mirror is moved away, the *image* candle disappears. Likewise, if you shatter the mirror, the instant it falls away, the image candle ceases to *exist*. It was *never* a real candle, from the start.

The *real* "me" is the presence which persists even when all images (as in "imagination") have ceased in awareness—as is the case in deep sleep. There is no mentation there that asks, "How does one get rid of the me?"; there is no me *there* to be rid of. It is from *this* "one" that the me image arises: in dreams, and in waking. There is no "world" in this fundamental awareness: it is *from* this awareness that your world is "created".

This means that the me, that is *not* this one, can be dismissed as the inauthentic *image* that it is: one need not "get rid" of it; it was never real, from the *start*.

But this image is who you *think* you are. With its disappearance, "you"—as an image of your self—evaporate.

This is where the commitment comes in. There will be no you who will be rewarded by the evaporation. There will *be* no "world", as you know it now, that will then appear to "you" to be "better".

There will, instead, be a different view of what is present: the standing candle alone will be perceived, no false images; no "me's" to be rid of.

The Message from the Universe

According to cosmologists today, the most distant man-made object in the universe is the probe Voyager 1, now about nine billion miles past the sun (or twice as far from the sun as Pluto, its most distant "planet"). By 2020, it will have sailed completely beyond our solar system.

The distance from Earth to the center of our Milky Way galaxy is 26,000 light years. One light year is 5,880,000,000,000 miles. Our galaxy may be 200,000 light years across.

Our sun is a star. There may be as many as 400 billion stars in our galaxy alone (nearly the age of the universe, which is 13.7 billion years).

Since the universe is a living organism, new stars are being formed as close as one million light years from Earth (at a rate of about 1–3 per year) from cocoons of gas which collapse into stars like our sun.

And the death of aging stars, in this vibrant cosmos, is recorded daily on average, with gamma ray bursts detected as far as 12.8 billion light years away, emitting a million times more energy than light.

In our galaxy alone, there may be 10 billion massive planets near sunlike stars (169 such planets have been identified so far). As many as half of these may meet the basic requirements for life as we comprehend it.

The width of the *visible* universe is 156,000,000,000 light years, and contains at least 80 billion bright *galaxies*. Ten million of these galaxies have been identified so far, but little more than location and distance is known about them.

There could be 100 times as many *unseeable* galaxies, composed of dark matter; so there might be as many as a trillion *galaxies* altogether.

The universe contains 21% dark matter; and 75% dark energy—a ubiquitous but real, unseen energy threaded throughout all of space (and which appears to remain steady over time).

Ordinary matter makes up 4% of the universe, and just 1/10th of that accounts for all of the mass visible in the night sky.

You say your daughter stayed out past midnight, last night? Consider your (and her) place in the universe before you get too wrung out of shape about it!

A Major Shift

> "There's a major shift taking place in here with me. I would describe it as the merging of the darkness and the light into one. I no longer resist the streams of consciousness that *seemed* to be outrageous. There is a lot more to it than that, but I will go into it later with a couple of things in your most recent letter."

I consider this to be good news! Particularly your awareness of the darkness ("this") and the light ("that") as one (It). And "no longer resisting" are words that portend an ego (self-fascination) "no longer existing". And, lo, I'm sure "there's a lot more to it than that"!

> "I've been busy. Things are changing here. The chaplain and I have had several talks. He does want to turn his program around. And he is trying. I've really started to get involved".

And I consider this to be good news. *Things* may be changing, but that is only significant to the extent that *you* are changing. It doesn't matter to me *what* you're getting involved with, but one cannot remain self-centered and get involved with "other" selves, particularly where some cooperation is required.

Regarding the monograph "Mind", a series of questions meant to be provocative, "where can the mind be located" really means to say, "*can* the mind be located" (anywhere)? Can it logically—being considered to be immaterial—be a product of the brain, which is considered to be material? We have been taught to presume that the mind is an artifact of the brain; and the brain, of course, is in the body. But *is* (what we call) the mind something that is located within a body? If we suppose that "the mind" gives us our sense of being present, where could that mind be located? If it was located where the sense of presence is, how could it see that location ("presence") as "central" to anything: "presence" is not confined to a body.

The Need for Affirmation

In answer to your question, "Are *you* aware?"

If we were to say that a particular person has awareness, then the possibility would exist that the person might *not* have awareness, wouldn't it? Put another way, if I were to say, "I have awareness now", the implication would be that there is a time when I might not possess awareness.

If one could either "have" or "not have" awareness, then awareness would be a state or condition which is apart or separate from the person, correct? If it were something which was apart from the person, at any time, then presumably it could (at some point) be gotten, or gained or attained. If it could be gained or gotten, it could also be lost, could it not?

So, if you were to say to a person, "Are you aware?", and he replied, "Yes, I am," you could be certain that the answer to your question at some other time might be, "I was, but I am not presently."

What could awareness be, aside from the consciousness of the reality of 'what is'? When one is conscious that one is aware (or not aware), who or what is it which is experiencing this consciousness? Is it not the "self"; and is the self not a construction of thought? In other words, isn't the proposition, "I am aware (or unaware)"—or "He is aware"—merely a thought? Is thought, awareness; or does awareness encompass (or, as some would say, go beyond) thought?

While your question is proper in its context, as with any question, it is a delusive question. Is there a self—any self—that is to be aware? If there were awareness and there were the self, wouldn't they be, as we say, "one and the same thing"? If I were "aware" of reality, and reality is constantly changing, what could my awareness be but something which is constantly changing; what could I hold onto, or "have"? If I have awareness, and awareness is constantly changing, might I not have awareness in one particular instant and nonawareness—or unawareness—in another?

The question is not so much whether there is such a thing as the "self", or "awareness"—and whether they are separate now and can ever become inseparable—but whether we can be so attentive to the moment that questions of this nature do not even occur to us.

And the answer to that question is that you will not know personally unless you have found out.

The real question is, "Who is it that wants to know—and why?"

Who's Stressed?

You mentioned that someone had commented, "If I am God, why am I so stressed?"

Have there ever been times when you *weren't* stressed? Did you contemplate *then* that you were God?

We want to suppose that when we are aware that we are, in truth, none other than Oneness, that the only thing which we will experience will be *positive*.

As long as experiences of *any* kind are noted, they will be *relative* experiences; therefore, they will inadvertently be in the (dualistic) realm of "positive" as opposed to "negative".

Does God (or Oneness) not operate in *both* the realms of positive and negative; is there not (on the relative level) birth *and* death, pleasure *and* pain, joy *and* sorrow, etc.? Is the *Omnipresent* not somehow involved in *all* of these phenomena?

Do you ever ask, "If I am God, why am I so peaceful right now?"

God, or Oneness, *transcends* all opposites—is not confined, or limited, to *any form*: thus the synonym, The Formless.

Ramana knew that he was That. Nisargadatta knew so too. And Krishnamurti (in a poem, he even said, "I am God"!). Do you suppose that each, as they died of cancer, did not experience any stress?

Despite the relative, stressful pain, Ramana put their condition this way: "There is pain; but there is not suffering."

Why? Because the body (a relative form) experiences pain. But it is the "person" who experiences suffering. ("Why *me*?!")

For the jnani, the person—all "personhood"—has died. *Only* the omnipresent, formless Oneness (God) remains. Would we ever say (in Self-realized terms) that That is "stressed"? No.

Nor would we say that That is "happy", or some other (relative) positive term.

It should be obvious that in knowing that you are God, you know that all limiting descriptions are necessarily transcended.

But if one so chooses to make reference to limiting descriptions ("names and forms"), knowing that God "is all that is" (One-ness) one knows, as well, that the Omnipresent is present in the negative *as well as* the positive, in the drought *and* in the thundershower.

Fire Consumes Forms

I would not have guessed, prior to a nondual realization, what a change in life it would represent.

I have conversed with many seekers, in the twenty years since. If I were to surmise the most common barrier to their own realization, it would be typical unwillingness to allow their life to unfold in a radically unpredictable way.

In order for the unknown agenda to unfold, the known construct must come to an end. The crux of the known construct is our sense of being an individual, personal self.

The most misunderstood aspect of the unfolding of unitive awareness is that somehow it results in self improvement. To the contrary, the entire thrust of spiritual awakening is toward self erasure.

This is commonly referred to in spiritual teachings as "dying while one is alive." The death referred to, of course, is the demise of the "person" that supposes it inhabits a single, particular body or organism.

I made a point of this (central core of the nondual teachings) to a correspondent. His reply: "Oh yes, I'm familiar with these references to symbolic death."

It is not a *symbolic* death which is being referred to. When your car battery dies, there is nothing symbolic about it: "dead" means "no longer functioning". When you fall into a deep sleep each night, the "you" (that you think you are) no longer operates. It is that absence of the centrifugal you *while awake* that is spoken of as death of the ego or self.

The gravest error to be made by the seeker of freedom from limitation is to assume that this ending of self image is a poetic metaphor or a theory which bespeaks ideal terms but is not actual in practice.

Were you to die physically, there would be a radical change in the course of your history. To die to the image of the self while alive —the "me" that flourishes as this particular "person"—is to unbind this personage for a liberating change in the course of its life.

Striking iron against flint stone does not produce a theory or symbol. The flame that results can both warm and burn.

Ad Infinitum

A number of lines in your letter were noteworthy, so I'll just comment ad lib.

Yes, writing about the maelstroms of our life can be an effective way to purge their repressed energies. But this is to dwell on the past; which is devoid of reality. Better to spend the time considering whether that fictional character of the past is not an extension of the fictional character of the present. To whom did these things happen, and by whom were they precipitated? What is the source of all activity, including self/Self examination? You made the appropriate surmise, in my opinion: "They need to be let go of." And *even* the self (subject) that would be parted from them (object). As you said, "Those things are not *me.*" No "thing" is. Neti, neti. "Not this, nor this."

Again, in "feeling for" the guard, what is this guard's true essence (whether he knows it or not)? What is your true essence? Where do you find a difference, except in the mind? Where does he find a difference, except in the mind? Notice the *separative* nature of the mindset where individuality is considered before essence. Which is real, the transient forms or the unmoving ground from which they emanate? In essence, who is feeling for (or *not* feeling for) what?

Yes, to forgive is to "not take offense" (a dictionary synonym is "overlook"). Just yesterday, a neighbor insulted me: there was no need to forgive him, because there was no self-image he could offend. He was forgiven before he spoke.

"Nothing has changed", you remark, "but everything is different". Ah, yes! This is often exclaimed by those experiencing the Truth!

You are noticing the "pointlessness" of reaction. When you know who the actor *is*, *action* will supersede *r*eaction (even where "action" is to take *no* action). Even action is ultimately pointless; when ultimate Truth is realized, it is clear that "only your mind moves", as a Zen parable has it: action/reaction/inaction all depend on a doer.

"A permanent attitude of 'This too shall pass'"? In the sentence before, you spoke of "some ideal". Is any attitude permanent (or anything else, for that matter)? Why have an attitude ("opinion, mental set") about anything: isn't an attitude just another *idea*? And what if "this too" *fails* to pass? I often remark to myself, "This too is it! (or It)." But as the "this too" changes (or doesn't change), it is still it. How about an attitude that no attitude is necessary, to the nothingness that is uncritically observing each moment: The "witness" observes your every act and thought without discrimination; the individuated mind expresses an opinion (pro or con) about all of them.

Yes, "Why am I doing what I'm doing?" is a reflection which will often occur (perhaps followed by, *"who* is doing *what?"*). As one relinquishes the idea of being a doer, the "I" at the center of all doing (or even not doing) appears less frequently in the (fundamentally subject/object) thought processes. As a consequence, the "questioner" recedes and speculative questions diminish.

Thanks for that Wei Wu Wei quote. As you remarked, "If you have no experience of it, it (the paradox of being/not-being in simultaneity) makes no sense."

Ah, yes, you are in a place where the fruits of self-centeredness will never be lost from your sight: a *constant* "reminder".

As you mentioned, meaningful communication is about all you have left. But even the possibility for this too can be taken away. There is only one unassailable refuge, and the wisest unfailingly abide in That.

A major pitfall will be to continue to think in terms of someone (subject) experiencing something (object)—*whether* positive *or* negative. There is no I, other than That.

What motivates one? The genuine desire to end one's "suffering", confusion, conflict.

Have you ended confusion for yourself? Nonduality, to be "taught"—transmitted—must be lived. Ramana was *teaching* nonduality *secondly*; he was *living* it (in the way that his realization shaped every movement in his life) *firstly*.

There are those who are sincerely open to what such teachers propose—the death of the "self"—and they are few. Ramana's words *alone* did not affect them; his presence as a living example of realization was *at least* as vital a force. Consider that much of the time he did not speak at all. In fact, he had not said a word for years, when seekers first began to come to him.

Even among those few who comprehend that the end of conflict means the end of the individual "I", all that can be done sometimes is to plant the seed of truth (*you* are *That*) which may sprout at some eventual time. Ramana is more appreciated (more than half a century) after he spoke, than he was during his lifetime.

The No-Thought Experience

In terms of your query, I think we could say that there is a) unrecognized duality; b) recognized duality; and c) nonduality.

We could say that a) is the condition of the ignore-ant person: her perception is mired in a dualistic perspective; and she is not even aware that this is the case, because she has no inkling that any other perception is possible.

Let's say that, at some point, she becomes aware of her dualistic perception, and supposes that another perspective on the actuality of our existence is possible. She conceives of this as "oneness", which she *equates* with non-duality. *But* her comprehension of this is that "I am united with everything." Her conception is (despite her *assumption*) dualistic. There is an "I", on the one hand, and "everything" else, on the other. Item 1 and item 2 are "united". She is still impaled by her subject/object mindset.

Perhaps at some point—c)—the perception dawns that "non-dual" literally posits "not two;" no two "things". She has realized that the (conditioned) conception of "I" and (as opposed to) "other" is false. There being, in absolute actuality, no "this" and no "that", there is no reality that can be described as "uniting".

She has transmuted from not recognizing her dualistic mindset; to recognizing her dualistic mindset; to relinquishing her dualistic mindset (*and* the "I" who supposed that any of this pertained to her "self".) Her awareness is presently nondual.

In general, Dzochen characterizes the a) condition as "ordinary" mind; the b) condition as "alaya" (oneness as an "experience"); and c) "rigpa" (nondual awareness which is beyond "experiencing").

In comparable terms, the Hindu savikalpa samdhi is analogous to b); and sahaja samadhi to c). In b), through disciplined concentration or fixation (meditation) on "not-self", she can nullify "self" so as to *experience* its "non-existence". *But* there is an experiencer. When the phenomenal experience ebbs (as all do), the "not-self" is no longer a present actuality *and* the "self" is again a conscious entity.

Attendant to b) is the notion that (first) she is apart from something (desirable); and (second) is driven, by ego motivation, to "attain" or "achieve" it. Subject proposes to "merge" with object. But subject does not comprehend that in a non-dual "merging" both *subject* and *object* dissolve. The subject, here, expects to remain an entity to which an (unusual) experience is to be *added*. It is a stultifying, frustrating pursuit, a deadening cycle of "arriving" and inevitably "departing". But because of the (temporary) suspension of "conceptual", egoic thought, it is sometimes presumed to be the "liberation" which is spoken about.

The *true* liberation is in that nondual awareness of c). Where the inspiration is that "there are not two things", there no longer is a "self" which is apart from the "One"! Thus, no condition such as b); or a). In point of fact, even c)—when conceived as an *entity* (such as Self, Buddha-nature, etc.)—no longer has any relevance. There is no subject self *or* desirable experience (such as "no thought") in rigpa or sahaja samadhi.

"Jesus said..."?

All four of the New Testament gospels quote Jesus verbatim, as if a stenographer had been present recoding every word.

What most people aren't aware of is that the earliest of these tracts was written about 35 years after the death of Jesus, and the later one was written 60-65 years after Jesus died.

This later one has traditionally been ascribed, by the Church, to the disciple John. Another of the gospels has been attributed to a second disciple, Matthew. The gospel of Mark (the earliest) was supposedly written by someone who did *not* himself *know* Jesus, as was the other gospel, Luke.

Were the gospels of John and Matthew *also* written by someone who did not even *know* Jesus? Evidently.

A leading New Testament scholar and professor of religious studies, Bart Ehrman, says[*]:

> "Even though the gospels go under the names of Matthew, Mark, Luke and John, they are, in fact, written anonymously.

> "The titles of the gospels were not put there by their authors...we know that the original manuscripts of the gospels did not have their authors' names attached to them.

> "The titles...are *later additions*; they are not original to the gospels themselves.

> "It seems probable, then, that *none* of the gospels was actually written by one of Jesus' closest followers."

The writing attributed to John, in particular, quotes Jesus at great length—especially on the issues which have historically been the most controversial. (To apprise this, thumb through any red-letter edition of the Bible—where Jesus' reputed words are printed in red; for example, chapters 15 and 16 are *entirely* red.)

Another New Testament authority, a Princeton professor of religion, Elaine Pagels, addresses the gospel of John in particular[†]:

> "We do not know who actually wrote the gospels.... [thus] no one knows who actually wrote [the gospel of John].

---

[*] Bart Ehrman, *Misquoting Jesus.* Emphases mine.

[†] Elaine Pagels, *Beyond Belief.*

"Toward the end of the 2nd century, the Church leader Irenaeus...declared that it bore the 'authority' of John the apostle..."

Ehrman points out that Acts 4:13 notes that the John who was a follower of Jesus was "unschooled"; the Greek word this was translated into English from means, specifically, "illiterate".

Furthermore, even some of the writings attributed to Paul are known not to be of his authorship. (He, however, was not claimed to have known Jesus.)

It's no longer a question of whether the New Testament can be taken literally. Can it even be considered factual?

....

The Undoing of the Doer

Your letters are seeming more reflective/introspective, this last in particular.

Let's regard a few of your key observations (in their order).

"What happens when one...is powerless to effect the shift or change to a truer perception?"

"It seems that when the suffering is great enough (ego), self-loathing, self- hatred is the result."

"What is really being recognized at these times is ego (even though it is not understood as to what it is and what it does)."

"It is the suffering that causes the desire or willingness to surrender something *to* something greater."

"It does seem to me that Adyashanti and Bernadette Roberts posited that one does not make the decision to awaken (or, rather, when or how this is going to take place)."

The fundamental element in all these observations is *pointing* to the *core* of what you're looking for. And because it sounds so ridiculously *simple,* it has to be *repeated* over and over again:

What becomes of all these propositions when the idea of a *separate self* disappears?!

When one does not hold onto the conception of being a separate entity:

What could remain to shift from one (subjective) perception to another? What could remain to be either powerful or powerless?

What remains to *have* an *ego*? And where there is no separate self, what becomes of self-loathing or self-hatred?   (*Or* their opposites?)

What becomes of the idea of a personal ego when the idea of being a person has itself vanished? Why be concerned then with what it "is" or "does"—considering that it *isn't* ?

When the surrender*er* itself has disappeared, where can the question of surrender further appear?

There being no separate entity, no such self, what is there to awaken—whether "how" or "when"? *Could it be* that to *drop* the idea of being a separate self *is* the *totality* of awakening?

In your (recent) contemplation, you are focusing more clearly on the fundamentals. *The* fundamental is that there is no "person" *beyond* your *ideas* of such. Ideas are mutable. That is why the sages say that it is *possible* to "awaken". The "awakening" is that there *is* no *individual* to awaken! (There being *no* individual, there is no *need* to awaken; thus, there is "nothing to do" where there is no *doer*. Awakening is always only a "possibility" to the imagined "doer".)

. . . .

The Shadow World

In the context of the cosmic space in which the Earth exists, there is only sun light. If you were in a room with stained-glass windows, this pure and clear sunlight would appear to enter the room as light of many different colors.

Such is the appearance of reality of the relative world within the context of the Absolute all-encompassing actuality.

It is not that there are two separate conditions. It is that there is one fundamental condition which gives an appearance of having more than one aspect. The sun reflected in a tub of water gives only a limited view of the expansive presence of the sun. And it tells you little of the life-giving effect that the sun initiates across the earth.

Similarly, *within* the one actuality, there are what *appear* to be separate realties: "me", my "mind", "thoughts", the "world", "others", etc. These seemingly separate colorations—all expressions of the singular radiance of total presence—are what we perceive as the relative forms in our waking state. That which is *aware* of these varied colorations, or forms, is the formless presence that we have likened here to the invisible energy of the sun. That self-aware energy is present in you in the individuated manner in which sunlight is dispersed in tubs of water (by way of analogy).

The relative forms are merely appearances of the formless Absolute. The appearance of the forms owe their generation to the formless, like shadows owe their existence to sunlight. The "me" has no more independent reality than has a shadow. Everything that the light of awareness is aware *of* is dependent upon it for reality. The "me" that appears in awareness is nothing more than a seemingly individuated expression of the Absolute, and has no more significance than the shadow of one form has in comparison with any other.

Busted

Personally, I consider what you've been going through, recently, a good sign. I've begun to notice some change in your letters. John Sherman (after 18 ½ years in prison) speaks of "breaking open". Some people slide open, others have to break open. The tension builds before the breaking. You speak of yourself as broken; I'm speaking of broken open. The "open" indicates "nothing left inside", and nothing any longer able to be retained inside. The darkness has no place to hide.

The Eternal Freedom

A life free of conflict, strife, and confusion can be yours—*now* and always. The simple cause to the problems, which we humans experience, has a simple solution. Because it *is* so simple, most of us overlook it entirely.

An energy exists, in the universe, which is undivided. *Because* it is whole and undivided, it is manifested in everything. It is essential to all the myriad, endlessly-changing forms. It is, at the same time, *in* everything and *around* everything. Thus, in its effect, it *is* everything. It is not apart from you, and you are not apart from it. This energy is infinite; it is ageless. It is everywhere always, and so there is not anything which can be severed from it.

We view the different forms (the manifestations) of this energy. We see one form there (say, the mountain), another form here (such as the river). And we observe that physically they are distant from each other. However distant and however different though they may be, we recognize that they are not unconnected or uninvolved with each other. But through custom and habit, soon we begin to *overlook* the fact that there is not anything, in reality, which is truly divided from all else. Consequently, we come to view *our self* as isolated from every other thing around us. The "I" becomes an island; every interaction is with some thing "out there". Instantly, we have divided the universe—in our mind —into "self" and all "other". This tendency can be observed, for example, in categorizing "humans" and "nature" as conflicting phenomenon. We find ourselves considering each as divorced and alien from the other.

Another notable example, of our definitional divisiveness, is to be seen in the unwitting separation which we make between *ourself* and that universal energy which we actually *are*—and which we cannot, in any way, ever be apart from. The attitude we take is that "we" are here, and "God" is "out there"—somewhere. But instinctively, we surmise inwardly that we cannot in Truth be separate from this primal energy, and so we long to be "reunited with God". You cannot ever be "reunited" with something which you have never been apart from; and so we find ourselves in confusion and anxiety.

This habit of assuming that *different* forms are thereby *divided* forms, is also visible in our attitude toward "subject" and "object". I, as subject, desire what you have: you, then, become an object to me, in the pursuit of my desires. I, for example, want you to love me; you become the object for the fulfillment of my desires. Or: I want to "know God"; God becomes an object, to be known. You can view things as objects—apart—only when you view yourself as isolated—divided—from everything else that is.

The divisiveness of the human mind can be seen also in our concept of time. We have (for "convenience") arbitrarily segmented time into three different compartments: the "past"; the "future"; and—sandwiched between them—the "present" instant. In the universe, there is but *one* time: this very moment is, has been, and will be, an endless continuum. No point can be located at which the present began (except as an artificial designation in the human mind), nor can any point be located at which the present ends. No activity ever existed which did not exist in the present. There is only an eternal, unbroken moment—and there is the endless change of forms of the universal energy within it.

A treacherous consequence, of this tendency to divide things, is that inevitably we begin to *compare* one "separate" thing with another. One of the creations of our divisiveness, then, appears to us to be "better" (as an object to fulfill our subject desires) than another. All things are thus weighed, in each individual's judgment, and awarded a relative value on a scale of "better" or "worse". For example, having divided our conception of time into categories, we now find ourselves continually comparing the "past" and "future" to the present. The result is that we are completely *dissatisfied* with the present—and constantly attempting to change or "improve" it. We spend half of our time remembering the way things were, and the other half of our time imagining how things could be—which takes our attention away entirely from the the unfolding of the only moment in which we truly live.

We also create anguish and tension for ourselves by making comparisons between ourself and other persons: this is certain to lead quickly to a conclusion of insufficiency: "I'm too short"; "I didn't graduate from college"; "I'm too forgiving"; etc. When we are chronically dissatisfied with who or where we are, or what we have, life becomes a frantic scramble for achievement, an endless hoping and scheming to become happier, holier, healthier or richer than we consider that we are. Blithely, we exchange *the gift* of "being" for *the promise* of "of becoming". The means to the end, of our becoming, is "control", and invariably we attempt to manipulate circumstances for our "self" advantage. We strive to control and "improve" ourselves inwardly by employing disciplines and mental effort. We aspire to control circumstances outwardly, through the perpetuation of self-serving beliefs and social institutions.

We suppose that the illusive object that we define as security can be achieved, and presume that it can be found somewhere outside of us. Any security which is apart from us can at any time be taken from us. There is only one true security, and that is the lasting security which is yours when you recognize your indivisibility with the timeless energy of the universe.

When you end division in your perception, you will effortlessly end strife, confusion and conflict in your life. The reality of the universe is unity. The reality of the restricted, fettered human mind—which struggles to "create unity"—is divisiveness. Life is not a collection of broken shards. "Life" and "death", for instance, are not opposing chess pieces. Death must be an integrated element in our life, if we are to live completely. This means that we must die with each day, as it dies. We must die to expectations, so that we live with an open, unfragmented mind. The mind which is whole, is the mind of the whole universe.

There is freedom in this moment—or there is no freedom at all— and this moment is eternal. A life free of divisiveness is yours, *this instant*, when you perceive it. This freedom is an active freedom. Once activated, a life of wholeness, clarity and serenity is as effortless as is breathing.

"Self Generating"

"The difference between creation and manifestation?" What is generally meant by manifestation is "what is apparent to the senses" or "what appears to the senses" (including to the mind). So, all of the "named things", material or immaterial, are manifestations.

Made apparent *as* or *by* what? Not made apparent *by* the *senses*; the sense are merely the medium of apprehending (and are themselves among the named things, the manifestations). Everything is a re-presentation, an appearance in form *of* a formless, omnipresent actuality; the ground of being, as it's called.

Some would say that all of these manifestations are created *by* this omnipotent actuality, but this statement leads to at least a couple of false concepts.

The foremost among these is the idea that there is a Creator, apart from the created. The "creator" (the formless) and "created" (the forms)—as well as the "creating"—are the same thing, an indivisible (no "parts") whole.

Secondly, because the created and the creator and creating are all one immediate actuality, there is no "creation" in the sense that a plan or design has been culminated. There is no "intelligence" *apart* from all these manifestations that has (prior to manifesting) *desired* or *decided* that what is "will be as it is". All of the "creating" is going on at this very moment, moment by moment, without having to be accounted for (as a "purpose") to anyone or anything. The formless, being *without* a separate "self", need not even justify what is unfolding to its own "self". No matter *what* happens—without an "intent"—nothing can go wrong, as far as the formless actuality could be concerned. If there were any "going wrong", that too would be a manifestation of the formless.

So, we need not think of some engineer somewhere who is amusedly watching some inflexible, dead plan that has been set in motion. The formless is no more static (or remote) than the forms in which it manifests itself. What is there to restrain the *spontaneous* freedom of the formless? To whom do these manifestations need to answer to, for what unfolds? The formless *is* the unfolding, in these forms.

The above can apply to your question concerning Jesus' crucifixion. "The Father (Absolute) and I are one." The relative forms (bodies) are not a possibility, in the absence of the Absolute. "Son" and "Father", to Jesus, were one—*same*—thing (as he stated). You don't find the formless ("come to the Father") apart from the form ("except through me"). The body, the cross, the death: all manifestations of the omnipresent Being. Evidently, none of the disciples completely comprehended Jesus' message. Forms don't "go" anywhere; they merely change forms as manifestations of the undying ground of Being. If forms *were* to go anywhere, they could only "return" to their "source": but where could they "return to" when there is *nowhere* that this ground of Being *is not*? Would we say that Jesus "returned" to that which he was never apart from? His disciples never freed themselves from their Hebraic conditioning concerning a king-like Creator, despite hearing "The kingdom of heaven is *within* you."

The real message is that there is no "you" (named thing), to start with—*except* as an expression, or manifestation, of the Absolute. Nor *anything else* that is "other" than this. "I am (all) that I am": Being, alone. The Absolute is *in* its expression, not somewhere else.

"You": Not Actor or Acted Upon

The reason it is said "You are not the doer," is because it is also said "There is no you."

It is not that "you are not the doer" because some other doer is acting on (or through) you. It is that "there is but one thing"; the apparent entity that is acted upon, *and* the apparent force (causation) that is "behind" (or "doing") the thrust of the acting, are one and the *same* actuality: *neither* a "you", *nor* an "other" which is the instigating doer.

Under *these* circumstances, the idea of cause-and-effect disappears. What the organism (presumably) does is not "caused" by something (prior). Nor can the organism itself be viewed as "causing" some (resultant) effect.

Therefore, a question such as "Am I the doer?" or "I am not the doer, so how do I help myself?" does not arise. There is no "I"; there is no "myself". That which we refer to as "I", "self", "doer" or "not doer" is That which is doing what is done. And "That" is not an entity that is separate, or *apart*, from what is being done by the organism.

The "see" in Consciousness

Lie down on the bed. Close your eyes. Envision any thing you can think of, tangible or intangible. Discover for yourself whether there is anything that exists for you that does not exist within your consciousness. Is it not true that everything which you can say that exists can be discovered within your consciousness? In fact, *you* are among the things that exist in your consciousness, not so?

Consider this also. If your consciousness were to be removed, you would cease to exist, so far as you could verify, correct? In fact, *everything* would cease to exist: the entire universe would vanish, would it not?

"Oh, no, it would only vanish for *me*," someone might say. "But not for all the others." Yet, every "other" that you suppose exists, exists within your consciousness. Were your consciousness to be removed, every "other"—the entire cosmos—would disappear. Not even consciousness itself would be present, so far as you could determine, correct?

Then, wouldn't it be fair to say that not any thing exists outside of your consciousness?

Place your hand on your leg. Are not both your hand and your leg "known to exist" within your consciousness? Feel the weight of your hand on your leg. Is not that feeling a "reality" within your consciousness?

The experience is of seeing things "through" your (opaque) eyes: are these images not registered in consciousness? You can, in fact, *close* your eyes and still "see" them, in consciousness. Not even any concrete objects "discovered" by the eyes exist outside of consciousness, correct?

Has it occurred to you that the common denominator of everything that you can maintain as existent *or* nonexistent is (this presence of) consciousness? Why have the mystics claimed, "Consciousness is all there is"?

Is it possible that "you" exist only in consciousness? Is it possible that you exist, actually, *as* consciousness? Is it not clear that you have no existence *apart* from consciousness? Have you considered that consciousness is not "in you", but that "you" are in consciousness? Therefore, this consciousness is not "yours". You (and all else) can disappear, while consciousness persists: this is the experience of those who have delved into deep meditation.

So, if consciousness remains when you (and all else) are absent, consciousness is "real" and you are not.

In answer to the question about siddhis, all phenomena appear in consciousness. Only consciousness is real; *phenomenon* are dependent on consciousness, therefore they are not real on their own. As Ramana points out, your siddhis (supernatural powers) can be no more real than *you* are—merely appearances dependent upon consciousness. And when it is recognized that "others" are as unreal as "you" are, what would siddhis appear to have an effect on?

Are supernatural powers attendant on enlightenment? First, find yourself in the condition of enlightenment and then determine for yourself what powers, special or unspecial, present themselves. If you do not even "own" your consciousness, what powers will be "yours"?

Changes of Life

I understand what you are asking: "I considered sending the pamphlet 'Open Here' to my son. If he were to take seriously what you are suggesting in it, he might be prompted to leave his wife and child. Doesn't that seem to be a possibility?"

You have told me that your son "has the itch to find out the truth about life—above all else". Will he not find that truth, as reality, changes one…because it *is* change? Were he to perceive this truth in a manner which affected his every waking action, what truth would there be for his wife—or any other person—to discover? The perception of truth embraces risk, as do all eventualities in life—including *absence* of the perception of truth.

An element of this truth is that all bodies die, and all selves die: we typically expect them to die "together". But life does not accommodate itself to human expectations; the death of the self or the body (if we are to view them apart) could instead be consecutive. There is the possibility that any form of mortality (mortal: "person") may happen to anyone, at any time—and one of them is certain. There is also the possibility for one's self-image to "die" though the body is yet to meet it inevitable demise.

As far back as twenty-five centuries ago, it's been commonly known that an instinct for awareness may direct even a prince to forsake his wife and child.

Look Within

Your last couple of letters have seemed much more focused on present consciousness, and you are also indicating that some particular changes are occurring. You appear to be relying more on your own experiencing of immediate awareness (as opposed to habitual thought patterns) and less on quoting various scriptures. I am sensing some opening (as, for example, less defensiveness).

So, I wanted to make a few comments, especially concerning some of the things that are still "troubling" you (and would *likely* be troubling *me*).

Allow all the negative feelings, reactions, to arise full blown. Witness, on the screen of consciousness, *whatever* is present, whatever occurs. As you *attend* to what arises ("good" or "bad") without attachment, you will also witness its "playing out" *and* its disappearance. What is not held (resisted), will come and go. It may be that one episode (of psychic drama) will be followed quickly by another (particularly, if you are not resisting); or that the very same charged emotional tumult will recur, or replay, several times throughout the day. Let it roam completely free in your psyche, and observe, with the attention you would watch a bronco at a rodeo. Do not attempt to "intervene" by re-acting to what is occurring. Just ride each wave, like a surfer.

Bear in mind, there is no universal law which dictates that you must *like* whatever it is that is going on. But there is no universal law that requires that we maintain an emotional attachment to our *dislikes / likes*. We can safely assume that Jesus did not "like" being crucified. But he "didn't take it personally". Ramana probably didn't "like" dying with a painful cancer. But he didn't go around crying, "Why me, why me?!" You are in a hell hole, with no means of physical escape. Who, in their right mind, would like to be in that situation? But Jesus, Ramana and others have attempted to demonstrate by example that it is possible to comprehend that even what we don't like, "that *too*" is a manifestation of infinite Being that rains on the just and the unjust.

Cease viewing "your" ego as an object. Recognize that all "things"—without exception—are merely myriad *appearances* of the same infinite Being. "Ego" is that; "you" are that. You and "your" ego are essentially the very same be-ing. Forget "the ego", forget the "you": focus consciousness on its source—which *is* the source of all things.

Likewise, attend to this "self" which has its source in infinite Being, instead of *externalizing*. The power of the energy that you are focusing on "others" is immense. Like sun focused on a magnifying glass, you could burn away your perceived "bondage" (apart from the physical one, of course) if you didn't dissipate that intensity on critiquing what's going on "around you", as opposed to what you are overlooking "within you". (*Your* kingdom?)

The *phenomena* that you reported ("being that") has *gone*: what can "come", can "go". It may recur, but it will not remain. What you are intent on finding is *permanent*, eternal. However, that experience is not uncommon among those who are "dissolving" prior to disappearance as a "me". When glimpses of that "magnitude" are present, Wynn is present *as* magnitude. When Wynn is present as "Wynn", unlimited boundaries are not available for That to display its illumination. However, do not try to recreate any such experience, do not "hang back" in the *past*. The "sign" has to do with the development of dissolution of "personal" boundaries, with beginning to "forget" who you think you "have been". Continue to question who or what this Wynn caricature really is: what if all that you "knew" of him (*past* tense) disappeared? What might be discovered in the "vacuum"? *No* "self"?!

It's good that you've re-read Roberts; but you've read enough of that. What you're looking for is inside your door, dispassionately witnessing Its activities.

Self-Emptying Awareness

Persistently throughout recorded history, adepts have reported an ultimate meditative state. In Dzochen, it is characterized as "empty awareness", the "natural state". The meditator has evaporated; consequently, "meditation" is not what is occurring. There is "attending" *to* presence, *as* presence, but without the involvement or engagement of an entity as either observer or observed. *Be-ing*, without "being", is perhaps all that can be said of it. Any description of it comes afterward, like trying to recall the memory of a dream. The thinker not being involved, thought is not involved: non-awareness of any *thing*, including discursive, linear thought; or awareness without a center of awareness. Yet the bodily processes continue to function non-consciously. And awareness returns eventually, of its own accord, to the organism that is in attendance of, or present for, it.

This empty awareness is, some say, our natural state in our deepest, comatose cycle of sleep. The meditative state described above is the bringing of this natural state into the waking experience.

It is also suggested that this is our condition of awareness in the womb, and for an indefinite period after emergence from the womb, before the development of verbal constructs (that we know as thought) and self identification.

Though it may be a natural condition, prior to being conditioned, it is not a functional condition, in the sense of providing for the activities of bodily development. For this purpose, linear, discursive thought is a super-imposition which serves to provide the vehicle for the *maintenance* of the fundamental, natural state.

The basic condition (of empty awareness) is non-linear, non-conceptual, unparticularized. The ancillary or auxiliary condition is limited, separative and discriminatory; what we call the cognitive faculty.

Experiencing the ultimate meditative state, *empty* awareness, serves to make unmistakably clear how every single thought or conception is an intrusion on a trouble-free, ever-present, uncomplicated awareness.

Yet, from the standpoint of continual physical survival, the machinations of the human mind are a requisite. Consider the role that the mind plays in the propagation of the species.

The mind and its thoughts are not in opposition to the natural state. Unconditional awareness is complemented by conditional awareness. Were it not for the latter, we could not know what we know of the former.

But the natural state is our pre-existing state. It is also a reasonable conjecture that this will pertain as our ultimate state, the condition we "return" to when the organism is no longer engaged in the activities of physical survival.

Whether or not we, as conscious beings, emerge out of—and exit into—the boundless presence of the empty, natural state, the significance of the ultimate meditative state is that it tells us something crucial about our self.

The "you" is revealed to be a conceived, selective thought, an artifice of the mind configured to the concerns of physical survival. However, it is not merely a fleeting thought among countless musings. It is a pivotal, critically-central thought, the thought to which every other of our thought/actions pay homage. It is, furthermore, the exclusive distinction which transposes our untroubled awareness of awareness to an awareness of disparate, conflicting "things", that we counterpose as "me" and "not-me". The I-dominated thought process is, though not inimical, the antithesis of empty awareness.

Fortunately, we have the capacity to realize the utterly superficial nature of our self conception. We each know, if only from our experience in deep sleep, that our most fundamental state of presence is one of empty, untroubled awareness. It is evident that it is upon this indiscriminate consciousness that each of our waking thoughts disport, to dissolve again in that night's mindless slumber.

Knowing that the ego-I is an insubstantial thought, no less spectral than any other thought, we can be conscious *of* the ego-I, rather than being conscious *as* the ego-I.

Knowing what our basic, natural, prevailing nature is, we can reorient our attention away from the importance of the ephemeral I-thought and its attendant self-promoting constructs.

This is what meditation concerns itself with, in any case, whether or not one pursues it to its ultimate end—awareness which empties itself of itself.

The Final Question

I *generally* avoid the word *God*. It (even unconsciously) evokes Michelangelo's image from the Catholic Church's Sistine Chapel: God on one side, man on the other; the (talkative) Jewish Jehovah of the Bible, a "lord", not even *connected* to man.

I prefer the word *Absolute*, which a) removes all traces of human-like characteristics, and b) connotes that which is *defined* as "without limitation"—omnipresent: everywhere at all times, indivisibly.

The key to understanding the difference between the Absolute and the God of *history* is that the Absolute, by implication, cannot possibly ever be separate from anything.

Not being separate from anything, it a) *is all things*, and b) cannot be located in any central place, as a consequence.

Contrast that with "God" *who* (the Absolute is not a "who") is "in Heaven"; and by the implication of this removal, is *not* all things.

This traditional conception of a God permits a conception of its counter-*part*, Satan who is "apart from" God. This permits ideas of "good" and "evil" (and priests to protect you from the latter by serving as a solicitor of the former).

Contrast this with that which, by its nature, is *all that is*: good, bad and in between; no arbitrary distinctions possible.

So, to rephrase your first question: The Absolute is not only the inside and outside of everything, it *is* every thing in its entirety. This is what the sagacious *teachings* mean when they use the term Absolute (rather than God).

Being all things, no descriptive word or words *selectively* define it. It is not even—given *this* understanding—"good", "bad" or "indifferent": it is *just what it is*, without qualification.

Next. The notion of predestination is false, when we consider the Absolute. First, It (for shorthand) has no relationship to time: being limitless (by definition), it is absent of beginning or ending; time is a measurement, the Absolute is thoroughly immeasurable. So no "pre" or "fore" or "aft" can be spoken of in this regard.

Second, there is no *center* from which destiny could be planned and executed. *This* is what the (false) God does. The Absolute is not a "mind" some*where*, plotting your destiny.

What is meant when the slokas say "you are not the doer" is important to understand. They mean: the Absolute is all that is; *you* are not excluded; you *are* That (or It). Therefore, anything that the supposed-you does, is—by extension—That doing what It does. *Being* all things, it *does* all things.

Ramana would say, "*I* am not the doer." You might say, "I *am* the doer." Ramana *is* the Absolute; the Absolute is saying what he says. *You* are the Absolute: the Absolute is saying what you say.

As to karma, that is a (dualistic) "God" idea. The Absolute is not a tracking satellite somewhere in the heavens taking notes on your every move, and at some *time* in the *future* tallying the score. Karma has nothing to do with nonduality.

Ditto "rebirth". You are *in essence* That; and That is without beginning and end. It has experienced no birth, and suffers no death. Nor is there any *thing* apart from it which *comes* and *goes*. No birth of That, and no re-birth of That; it does not come *from* some place, and go *to* someplace—being omnipresent.

Also. Just as *you* are It, all "others" are It. Saints and sinners are absolutely alike in their essence.

It is *crucial* to bear in mind that all that is, is That. Therefore, to speak of an "individual person" is to speak from the standpoint of duality. In the condition of *non duality*, there are *no two things*; neither "men" nor "women", nor "evil men" or "good men".

A sage does not view him/herself as an individual or a "person", so could care less whether considered to be a "good" or "evil" person. Those are dualistic ideas, in their most obvious form.

Lastly. Equanimity is a word to describe the life of a "sage". What else, to whom there are no "ups" or "downs", no "pleasure" or "pain"—dualistic distinctions. To someone to whom pleasure is important, yes, equanimity would be boring. The sage refers to his condition as "bliss". Take your pick in descriptions.

Bear this in mind. Your questions will be endless, as long as you continue to pose them from a *dualistic* framework. Ponder one thing *instead*. If there is only that which is *all* that is, as the sages aver, *who is this* questioner?

There is no question that you cannot answer for yourself, once *that* question is resolved! By *not* dealing with that question *first*, your time will be wasted in pursuit of other questions, which—from the standpoint of Realization—have no value, in *any* case.

Were there existent any such thing as time, it would have to be present in its entirety *now*. Thus it can be said, "Any time that there is, is fully present this moment": however, this will not be accurately perceived by one who does not understand that this does not propose that there *is* time. One might tend to conclude that the past, present and future coexist simultaneously—which could only pertain if there were any such thing as "past", "present" or "future".

There being no time, therefore no future, there is not "predestination" (or any other destination). Where there are no possible distinctions such as "now" or "future"—where there is no time—there are no activities now which can determine one's future. Where there is no time, there is no cause and effect.

There is not anything which is *to* be. If the tide rises tomorrow, it rises: it does not rise because it is *to* rise.

Anything which is "destined" (Latin: "to be fastened in place") can be resisted. Where there is no time, there can be no resistance. One can resist only that which is separately identifiable; it is when "death" is identified, as the opposite of life, that we resist it. There can be no separation between life and death where there is no conception of time. Were one "destined" to die, one could be "destined" not to die.

There being no past, there is no place of departure; there being no future, there is no place of arrival. Because you have not (past tense) lived, you will not (future tense) die. In this world of reality, you are—without distinction—whatever it is that might be "living" and whatever it is that could be "dying". There can be no separation where there is no time for it.

Mind is in the I-Thought

To awaken to the truth of nonduality as the actual condition of our—rather, all—existence has always been the substance of enlightenment. In actuality (the nondual proposition states), *all* that *is* is That—the Essence which is the underlying foundation without which not anything has form or identity. Ramana sometimes used the word God, or Brahman, for this; but, more frequently, the word Self.

Ramana's means of pointing to the essential truth was to reiterate that, in actuality, not anything is permanently or finally existent *but* the Self. All things come and go *in* the Self; therefore all *but* the Self is not genuine or truly existent. When this truth is clearly perceived, the "I-thought" (the idea of self existence—for anything other than the Essence) falls away: no longer a "personal" psyche identifying with a particular organism.

Where there is no longer an 'individual' self in awareness, there is no longer the idea or concept of a *self's* 'body,' 'mind' or 'thoughts'. Anything which can be *named* is merely an alias for one thing: that Essence.

That is why, when a visitor complained that his "mind wandered", Ramana's reply was: "Is there a mind?"

"If the enquiry is made whether mind exists", said Ramana, "it will be found that mind does not exist. That is [how to effect] 'control of the mind.'"

To another questioner, he said: "You can never find the mind through mind. Pass *beyond* it, in order to find it non-existent."

Someone suggested, "The mind must kill the mind."

Ramana: "Yes, if there *be* the mind. A search for it discloses its non-existence. How can anything that does not exist be killed?"

If there is no existent mind, then there are no thoughts, either, existent in *actuality*.

Q. "Then thoughts are not real?"

R. "They are not: the only reality is the Self."

Only Essence exists. Ramana liked to point out that it is as Essence that we exist when the body is un-conscious. "What is your experience in deep sleep? There were no thoughts, no mind; and yet you remained then."

Ramana would proceed to point out that all that we conceive—all the named things and phenomena—are merely manifestations of Essence, or Self.

> "Mind is one form of manifestation of life.... The vital force manifests as life-activity and also as the conscious phenomena known as the mind....If the inquiry into the ultimate cause of manifestation of mind itself is pushed, mind will be found to be only the manifestation of the Real, which is otherwise called Atman or Brahman."

At another time: "Mind is only the dynamic power of the Self." [In Buddhism, what Ramana refers to as Self, with a capital S, is referred to as Mind, with a capital M.]

> "If one realizes that thoughts arise from the Self, and abides in their *source*, the mind will disappear....In their absence, there is neither the world nor God the Creator [as conceived]."

Thoughts are a manifestation of that Essence which cannot be conceived:

> "Now, what about thoughts?...Where from do they arise? Their source, ever-present and not subject to variations, must be admitted to be. It must be the Eternal state, as said..."

Clarifying further:

> "There is no entity by name of 'mind.' Because of the emergence of thoughts, we surmise some thing from which they start: *that* we term mind. When we probe to see what it is, there is nothing like it. After it has 'vanished,' Peace will be found to remain eternal."

The idea that there is such an isolated entity as mind, or thought, is a *self*-generated idea, an idea that follows on the heels of the "I-thought"—independent existence. "Thoughts cannot exist but for the ego."

> Q. "How may one destroy the mind?"

> R. "Is there a mind, in the first place? What you call mind is an illusion. It starts from the I-thought."

Further:

> "After the emergence of the mind, the universe appears and the body is seen to be contained in it. Whereas, all these are contained in the Self, and they cannot exist apart from the Self....

> "Its [mind] destruction is the non-recognition of it as being apart from the Self. Even now the mind *is not*. Recognize it!....It is not real, but a phantom proceeding

from the Self. That [recognition] is how the mind is destroyed!" Ramana's summation: "The individual confines himself to the limits of the changeful body or of the mind—which derives its existence from the unchanging Self. All that is necessary is to give up this mistaken identity; and, that done, the ever-shining Self will be seen to be the single non-dual Reality."

Dying is Collapse

This last letter is not from the Don that I originally began corresponding with. This is coming from a deeper well. It sounds to me as if things are beginning to fall into place. Your dream that "my house was being torn apart and destroyed by storms, even though no one (upstairs or down) was being injured" recalls a verse in the Gospel of Thomas: "Jesus said: I will destroy this house, and no one will be able to rebuild it."

As you say, "There seems to be a 'dying' fear associated with it." That is a good sign. *This* dying comes from within (self-activated), an implosion; the housing of ego collapses entire with its foundation—and none are able then to rebuild it.

When you are able to recognize, from your own personal conviction, "previous lives, and any anticipated future ones, have nothing to do with the Truth which can only be found in the now….Surrender needs to be understood as not only giving up of one's desires, but also the renunciation of every aspect of material (relative) reality….*all* things are equal, because all things are equally unreal"—when you are able to say such things from your own perception, a shift in perspective is obviously underway. When you can say, objectively, "Who or what *is* there to 'heal'?", you are speaking the dialect of the "dead".

It is such a one (like Papaji, Maharshi, Nisargadatta and others), as you observed, "Who has awakened and sits still for those who would seek him out to do likewise."

Advice from the Holy Spirit

I sympathize with the hardships that you have to endure. I speculate that if I were in your place, I would hope to expend as little energy as possible on things that are evidently beyond my control. (Under such circumstances, I usually cuss—to vent my feelings—then let the matter dissolve as "past".) I would probably also remind myself—*not blame* myself, but remind myself—that I put myself in the position to be without control of my circumstances; those in control are in control *because* of my own activities. Even so, yes, they ought to treat me humanely; no, they don't because of their own ignorance—which, again is out of my control.

But this is merely relating to the relative situation (of me vs. them), and not of the most help overall. There are some who say they're happier in prison than they were when outside—because, while in prison, they underwent a profound ("spiritual") change in perspective. So, I think I would focus as much of my energy as possible on discovering the liberating freedom that some attest is possible.

One of the ways that the nondual perspective is liberating, I have found, is that one no longer attempts to "make sense of life", to think in terms of cause and effect ("Why is this being done to me?") or positive and negative ("The world should be a better, kinder place."). But in order to gain that freedom, there is a seeming price to pay. As I repeated, the idea of being an entity has to dissolve entirely into the nondual Absolute. So my advice to any person in your situation would be to focus assiduously on that prospect: to disappear, as a person, into that which is without distinction.

My reservation about your enthrallment with the Course is that it's a false lead. Buddha, Jesus, Ramana knew not one word of what is written there; in fact, the advice of all sages is to throw away the Bible (no matter *which* one) that you're leaning on. What it is that you must know, cannot come from a second-hand source. If it is not first-hand truth, you will not have the *power* of conviction.

For reasons of your own, you are ignoring that what you seek is to be found contained in #300378. It will not *arrive* there in the next post. It is there as you read this.

Being without individuated form, it permeates all that is—and, as such, *is* all that is. It is not waiting until you read further in the Course: it is as it is this instant. You can close the book, use it as a coaster, and surrender the dream figure that once thought of itself as Wyatt.

Or, you can continue the dream, with Wyatt imagined as one entity and the Holy Spirit (or a guard) perceived as another entity.

When your suffering finally forces you to abandon the dream, you will find that nothing in the material, *relative* world has changed. The cell is *still* cold, the guards are *still* there, and they're still counting your stay by the calendar.

But if *conflict* (of any kind) is ever to end, I attest that *division* must end. Separation as an "individual" entity must end: yours, the Holy Spirit's, the guard's—all of it. Wyatt, and "Wyatt's life" (the good and the bad), must disappear just like Mariah Carey disappears when you wake up from slumber. The anonymous Wyatt, the Wyatt who never really existed as an individual. (Telling that to the judge won't do you any good now!)

What is one's perspective when he realizes that he no longer actually exists? If I were in prison, I think I would sincerely want to find out. I would be focusing my attention on, "What does it mean when all these sources maintain that there are *not* 'two things'?" If the author of the Course found out, good for her or him. But I would want to find out what they keep insisting *can* be *discovered*. I would waste as little time as possible (*especially* if I have lots ahead of me) to prove them either "liars" or "saviors".

But, then again, maybe I wouldn't, if I got juice from the *dream*. After all, I *have* had an *interesting* life. Who wants to have "no life?" Being at one with everything doesn't allow for much personal pride!

So, the Course is not going to wake you up from your dream. It's being *read* (and recited) *in* your dream. The Course and the dream are appearing *in* what it is that you are looking for, the infinite. I would recommend going *directly* to the infinite, which no written word will manifest for you.

And, hey, the best part is that you don't have to stir from your bunk to find the infinite: Buddha sat down under a tree, Jesus sat in the shade of a rock in the desert, and Ramana laid down on the floor. They all discovered that what they were looking for can't be escaped. "Not two things." Find *that* phrase in the Course, close the book and contemplate the significance of it until you don't depend upon any outward authority any longer. *All* the "sacred" sources would urge that.

Fear as Feeling

You ask: "You have talked about ending fear. Does this mean that you personally never feel fear?"

Fear is a complex element. Let's look at it closely.

The fear of which I have spoken is that which is the reaction of the self in its relationship to what it views as security. The self is a product of thought, an idea; and security—with a capital S—is a concept, an ideal, and so also is a product of thought; through the myopic lens of thought, we see security as something apart from our sense of self. Anything which threatens the self—such as a supposed "loss" of security (which is ephemeral from the start)— threatens thought, as our "mind"...since self and thought are interdependent.

The variety of thinking which has created the notion, or concept, of the self (one's "image" of one self) is what we've referred to as "speculative", or subjective, thinking. There is, precedent to this, what we might call technical or "mechanical" thinking, an activity of the brain which one does not necessarily think consciously about (or "register" as memory or imagination): you lock the door, and later can't recall whether you locked it or not.

As there is mechanical thinking, there is what we might call "mechanical" or instinctual fear: you are driving at fifty miles per hour, hear the sound of a blowout and your car swerves toward a tree. In this instant, there is complete attentiveness in which analytic or speculative thought is absent: action is direct, without analysis or internal debate—you do not *consider* turning the steering wheel, you *turn* it.

Speculative thought—which depends on the linear time involved in language, on the orderly chaining of appropriate words— catches up, in a fraction of a second, later. With the conscious cognition of your "close call", there is a flush of adrenalin, hammering heartbeat and self-congratulation for your "presence of mind".

Fear which relates to the physical safety of the body is instinctual; and probably no human being is—or, nature implies, ought to be —without it.

When we act through instinct, we are acting without "self-control"—we can't choose to act in a way other than the way we act. We are not *re*acting to the "prospect" of death, we are acting from a part of the brain which functioned even before we consciously "understood" the significance of "death".

Fear which involves the self—the "person" who believes he "inhabits" this body—is present when and where reactive thought is present. Thought (or "knowledge") has told us—and we have stored that "information" in our memory—that death is the end of the self: "It will permanently divide you from me, and thus from your consciousness that you *are*."

Where *this* thought is not, fear for the preservation of the self—as an ego that occupies time and place—is not.

In other words, as humans we commonly experience instinctual fear, and it is antecedent to our conscious thought. And, as humans, we may—or, however uncommonly, may not—experience subjective fear: it *is* conscious thought (even when it is repressed).

Can one ever be entirely free—permanently—of subjective fear…fear not specifically for the body, but specifically for the self (and its "fate")?

Can one ever be entirely free—permanently—of subjective thought? What can be permanent in a physical world in which all things change? If one were permanently "good", would one be "perfectly" good? Put another way, is any awareness a fixed state, a "perfect state"; or does awareness change, as that of which one is aware changes?

What we are searching for, is it not, is a panacea? It isn't happiness that we want, it is *unending* happiness that we want; it is not freedom in this eternal moment, it is freedom in the *future* moment. We are not willing to find out what it is to be without fear, until we are first assured that the result of our effort will be to forever be without fear in the future.

Have you observed your fears? Have you noticed that you are not separate from fear? Have you observed that where the *self* is not, this *fear* is not? Have you discovered that you can—or cannot— be free of fear....*regardless* of whether anyone *else*, has ever been or not?

Our first fear arises when we *confront* the thought that our sense of self is indispensable. Can we let go of the fear of the loss of the self of thought? Can we let go of the fear that the self may never be free of fear? Can we let go of the fear that even an absence of fear may be impermanent? When we can let go of fear and neither cling to nor resist it, we will not make conscious note of whether we feel fear or not.

Ac-tor: role-player

You say,

> "It would make no sense to me to claim that I was the source of this (action).... If I was not the source, then what is the source?...

> "Something happens, and you know that you're not doing it...and you know that you can't claim credit for it....

> "I feel that all of us are connected with this source, even though all of us may not be conscious of it."

So, what *can* you claim credit for? What have *you* ever been the source of?

This dilemma arises (as do all others) because of dualistic thinking: there is an "I" and there is "the source", and they are two separate things.

You are not "connected with" the source: you and the source are the same thing. *That* is your "true nature".

Even the word *source* suggests duality. (I generally try to avoid it.) "L.: that from which something comes into existence; the starting point for an emanation." We say that a spring is the source of a creek. But are the "spring" and "creek" apart from each other?

The fundamental tenet of Buddhism is that we are all Buddhas, whether we consciously recognize our true nature or not. Therefore *every* action is Buddha-nature in action, whether that is acknowledged or not. Since there is no action you can take that is not the action of this universal consciousness, isn't it arrogant for the "person", the mind, to take credit for it? As Ramana says,

> "Let us not pose as the doers....(Then) the 'doer' disappears, and so also the 'action'; eternal Being alone is left.... So, relinquish the sense of doer-ship...find out *who* the doer is."

And Nisargadatta adds:

> "To say 'I do' is altogether false, because there is nobody who does: all happens by itself, *including* the idea of *being* a doer.... Remain as pure witness, till *even* 'witnessing' dissolves in the Supreme."

So, the dilemma ends when dualistic thinking is seen for what it is: divisive.

To the extent there is allegory in the fable of Adam and Eve,* it would evidently be this: man was manifested "in the image of God": an image is "a counterpart, representation or embodiment". The formless (God: "an immortal, infinite image") manifested as form; embodied as flesh—having already done so as all the other elements of the world and universe.

The generic prototype in the story,† Adam, was aware that there was such a thing as the (tree of) knowledge of "good" and "evil" (dualities), plentiful with sinuous branches and "pleasing" fruit. He also became aware of a portentous message: "if you eat of it, you will surely die (life/death: duality)...you must not even *touch* it". Remain as the nondual *form*-less.

Though man began naming things, there's no indication that he considered himself as apart from anything he named. He named "woman" (archetypal Eve) and considered both to be of "one flesh". Both "were naked and felt no shame" (pride/shame: duality).

A "subtle", treacherous serpent (said to be Satan, which means "adversary")—the mischievous mind?—prompted partaking of the tree, so "you will know good from evil"; *know* duality as a supposition ("assumption") henceforth.

Immediately, "they realized they were naked ("without embellishment"): natural ("uncultivated, instinctive") *versus un-*natural ("deviating, dis-orderly").

---

* Hebrew: Adam means "human"; Eve means "being" (or "life").

† Originally a Babylonian myth.

But the presence of God (known *prior* to duality) is recalled, so "they hid" because (Adam says) "I was afraid." Now among what has become *known* (in addition to shame) is fear. Adam ("I") blames "that woman" (now other than the one personage) for this dread-ful condition. She in turn blames an-other, the serpentine medium of mischief.

So, Eve will henceforth *also know* "desire" and "pain" plus conflict with the *opposite* sex. And Adam, as well, will also know turmoil and death. They are thus banished from the plenteous garden that features the perennial "tree" of life.

But the tree is still there (the story ends) and a flaming sword now "guards the way to the tree of life".

This is the double-edge* sword ("piercing instrument of destruction") that cuts through duality and other mischief of the mind.

Yes, you could say that the ancient texts portray the condition of reality as the "Self seeking (to know) itself", and that consciousness is the instrument.

This would typically be explained by saying that "individuals" are a *manifestation* of the Absolute (Self). When the self is aware of the (originating) Self, sought and seeker are again in unification (one-ification).

How would the Self "exist", if it were not for a self to verify (verity is "truth") its actuality? So, as each Self seeks the Self, this reification of Self-nature continues.

However, to suppose that there is something which can be identified as Self, in *contrast* to something else that can be

---

* Relative (man) and Absolute (God) joined.

identified as self, is a residual dualism—excusable only as a teaching tool.

From the standpoint of nondual awareness, there is but One actuality, and "*all* is (that) One". Therefore, there is *not even* anything in search of anything; nor is there anything which *needs* to have its existence or nonexistence confirmed.

More of the Same

These concerns are addressed in no particular order.

It ought to be obvious to you that any time a question arises, "Is ____ this, or is ____ that?", you are troubling yourself about relative (dualistic) matters. Return to your comprehension of the nondual—"There are no two things", or "All that is, is That" (either phrase saying the same thing)—and any dilemma, any question, is resolved immediately.

"Is there a conscious self, and a subconscious self?" From the standpoint of nonduality, are there any two things, states or conditions? Even if we suppose there are such separate realities as "order" and "chaos", are not all realities manifestations of the same, one supreme reality?

When the teachers speak of consciousness, they are referring to That, the Absolute. They say consciousness simply because you have "tasted" consciousness, therefore it has a familiarity to it: "Gee, I can't imagine what 'That' or 'the Absolute' is. But I know what consciousness is!"

Their point is to get you to comprehend that—just as you are always conscious—you are always That. Therefore, they point out that consciousness is your underlying condition always: in your waking activities; in your recumbent dreaming; in the stupor of deep sleep when even your self-identification is absent.

Their subtler point is that—since "there is nothing *but* That"—what we *call* consciousness is (like every other named thing) nothing more than That, in what appear to be "many forms". Is it not asserted that That (the Absolute) "does not come and go"; it is the singular infinity, *ever present every where.*

Bodies, however, *do* come and go, do they not? So, in death, do you suppose consciousness "leaves" the body; or that "the body" drops away from consciousness?   In deep sleep, does consciousness disappear from the body; or is the body "forgotten about" in consciousness? If consciousness is a metaphor for That, does consciousness ever "disappear"?

There are people attending dharma talks and satsangs (by such as Steven Harrison, Adyashanti, Gangaji, Tony Parsons, etc.) who are awakening to self-realization—every day of the year—who never heard of "gunas" (attributes) or "jnana marga" (path of wisdom). Fifteen years ago, I wouldn't have known a guna from a gumball, and would have thought jnana marga is something you smoke.

Concern for Others

Ramana has said, First set yourself right—*then* concern yourself about others.

Is it clear to *you* that "the relative phenomena we perceive *right now*"—including "our perception of thoughts, habits, words, ideas, opinions, beliefs, etc."—are "not separate from" the "primordial nature of the mind"?

How are you to convey this truth to others, if it is not irrefutably established in your own consciousness?

If it *is* irrefutably established in your own consciousness—that there is *no* separation between our primordial nature and our perceptions, *whatever* they may *be*—then you cease to worry about the "consequence" of any and all such perceptions: they are not disconnected from primordial nature.

Do you concern yourself about your neighbors' "loving" thoughts, "moral" habits, "kind" words, "constructive" ideas, "helpful" opinions, "altruistic" beliefs, etc. Are these independent of primordial nature?

Then why isolate the complementary "negative" perceptions as the object of your concern—which are merely the converse aspects of these relative phenomena?

That Dzochen quote did not qualify "positive" or "negative" phenomena. The point is that such *qualification* leads us into (dualistic) trouble.

The more important point is to recognize that even our *own* negative perceptions ("Bush is an asshole") are still manifestations of that same primordial nature—just the same as the thought, "I'm going to generously give Bush the benefit of the doubt and suspend judgment on his behavior."

One is not closer to primordial nature than the other.

When you recognize this, you cease to obsess on whether the behavior of others is "irrational" or "harmful". Sun-faced Buddha, moon-faced Buddha.

When this is *your* face, you will be in the best position to communicate what is your own *primordial nature* of mind.

...the Buddha mind...is primordially present already...
Simply allow your basic state to be...when all the activities
of dualistic mind dissolve...

– Urgyen

Self-acceptance

"In the beginning was That, and...That was God....
Through That, all things were made...In That was life...
the light of men....

"There came a man who was sent from That...to testify
concerning light, so that...all men might (realize)."

Yes, yours was a relevant observation: in John 1:1-7, a word
substituting for the Absolute (such as That) could replace the
designation Word, or "the Word". In fact, substituting Self, there
are quotes from Ramana that match nearly every sentence.

I agree, too, that "spirit" is a problematic term. It suggests
something "apart from matter" (such as the body)—dualistic:
especially, an entity unto itself (such as Holy Spirit, also called
Holy Ghost).

You Contain Nothing

It should be clear to you that the enlightened do "fall sick".
Ramana died of cancer, as did Nisargadatta. Buddha evidently
died of food poisoning. But what died? This should also be clear
to you. The body died. All of these teachers tell you that what
they *are* is "unborn"; what has not had a beginning point does not
have an ending point.

Why would one consult a doctor, or seek miraculous cures, unless one was identified with the perpetuation of the body? In a "dream" world, there are only "dream" doctors and "dream" "cures". None of the enlightened above (nor Krishnamurti) went looking for a doctor when they were ill. *Every* illness, and suffering, is eventually "overcome"—with the passing of time.

Ramana points out that in our deepest, dreamless sleep, there is no "I" that is conscious of any objective thing. This is our daily (or *nightly*) reminder of our non-relative essence. And we are daily reminded of our *relative* existence, in our waking/dreaming condition: the "I" is an element of this condition, so that we may functionally realize the "purpose" of the organism, during its period of active presence; "I" am hungry; therefore "I" feed the body; then "I" do what this body is inclined to do, etc.

But, at some point, there is no longer the need for an "I", because the aging of the organism has brought it to an end (or some other development has brought it to a premature end). While the "I" disappears with all that it identifies itself with, the impersonal essence (which presents every night in deep sleep) is not dependent on the images of the "I" for its presence; being non-relative, it is not dependent upon anything outside of itself. This was your essence even in the womb, before there *was* an image of "I".

This essence, this "condition of *being*", is not *your* essence; it is the essential condition of all that is, of which you—*and* all else—partake. As in deep sleep, its "*characteristic*" can only be said to be that of *void*: no objective *thing*. No *thing* that is "conscious" of some *other* thing. No "I-sense", because there is not some "entity" to sense any *thing*—form *or* formless. This is your condition in comatose sleep. It was your condition in the womb. Ramana, among others, is saying that this *pre*-conscious condition is the same as (through life-long continuation) the *post*-conscious condition. We come from knowing nothing, to knowing nothing.

So, of what value is it to acquire "knowledge" during the seemingly-real dream between pre- and post-consciousness? Yes, we need to know a few concrete facts of life in order to physically function. But of what value is any "speculative" knowledge? Buddha—for just this reason, it is said—refused to answer "speculative" questions, those that go beyond *here* and *now*. Silence, he indicated, is the door to your non-relative essence. He attuned to it by sitting in non-active quietude under the Bo tree—not by compiling "knowledge".

Lastly. "Truth" is a common synonym for Absolute awareness. Adya is saying that there is only One actuality: therefore *that* is (if there is any *meaning* to the *word*) truth. Live your life from the standpoint of this Truth, is his point.

Purging the Mind

Again, your last letter suggests that you are doing less externalizing and (as a consequence) more internalizing: that is, focusing on the manifestations that are "within" rather than on the melodrama without. Which do you have the best prospect of managing or shaping?

From the Tao Te Ching (c. 500 BC?) on down, the teachings have advised that nonresistance (even to the extent of noninterference) is the wisest course. Your enclosed translation from Padmasambhava (c. 750 AD), the patriarch of Tibetan Buddhism, does not suggest that we resist our emotions—such as anger. Instead, the advice is we contemplatively and objectively observe all that arises on the screen of consciousness ("witness" these presentations) as if we were gazing at a cow and a bull in an adjoining field. We need not pass judgment on anything that transpires.

By raising no resistance to whatever ferment arises in consciousness, we erect no barrier that "holds" it. Whatever comes, will go in due time (emotions of pleasure, such as self-satisfaction, as well). These are merely the clouds, they say, that self-originate and dissipate in the mind even of a Buddha (who was reported to have been visibly upset upon the news of the invasion of his former home province). What *keeps* the buddha mind clear is *allowing* it to empty itself naturally, like those bamboo Japanese seesaw tubes that fill with water, tip, fill again and tip again. It sounds as though you are beginning to allow anger to pass through you, rather than engaging it in a mind that attempts to close in on it. Ramana was once visited by bandits: he did not attempt to bar or delay their exit.

Desire

Desire? If it were not for desire, you would not be seeking the "freedom" that ensues from knowing your true nature.

You are suggesting that you need to contain or restrain desire. Clearly, as long as you have a desire to end desire, you will continue chasing your tail.

Generally, the idea that it would be desirable for one to be rid of desire is based on the supposition that such is beneficial, or even essential, for one to awaken to the truth. And so, this is one of the many proposed "steps" which "lead to" awakening.

Rather than concern yourself with your "shortcomings" and focusing on ways to improve the "inadequate" self, be aware that all steps lead in the wrong direction.

What you are looking for is not to be found in the future. The one who is caught up in the arms of desire, is the "one" you are seeking to know.

You cannot stand apart from what you are expressing, and hope to know your *true nature*. Were you to root out every desire, you would ask yourself, "Now, what next do I need to do in order to prepare myself for realization?"

Realization is a matter of waking up to the fact that you are a dead image, walking around as the purported identity of a live body. The body does not trouble itself about its desires. The image of who you think you are is disturbed by them. When the body comes to an end, desires will come to an end. When the self image disappears, what becomes of the "me" that tortures itself about desires?

You want to excise desires and still be "you". Where there is a sense of "wholeness", are not desires an element of the whole?

If anything, *sharpen* your desire to penetrate through the subject/ object illusion: not "soon", *now*. You and what you seek are not two. That will not be truer tomorrow than it is at the moment you read these words.

Come to terms with what "not two" means, then see who desires what and why. Nothing is hidden from those who dare to look.

Only One Question

From the standpoint of advaita (nonduality), nothing is destined; there is no such thing as destiny. Why? Because destiny is an idea about something which takes place in time. The ultimate condition is one of timelessness; therefore, there could be no application for destiny under such circumstances.

Likewise, from the standpoint of advaita, there is no such thing as God, as a separate entity; in the ultimate condition, not anything can be said to be separate from anything else. By that same truth, there is no "us". Questions concerning "God" and "us" are the bailiwick of theology, not of nonduality.

Regarding Jesus. The truths that Buddha originally promulgated have largely been corrupted by being converted into a platform for orthodoxy and doctrine: organized religion. Even more so have suffered the truths that Jesus elucidated. Within a few generations, the truths that Ramana (and some of his and our contemporaries) spoke will possibly suffer the same outcome. But, considering that there are some alive today who heard Ramana speak, his teachings concerning the ultimate are still vividly "fresh". It therefore seems wisest to concentrate one's study on this source, with reliance on what are *allegedly* Buddha's words and Jesus' words in supporting—though often unsupportable—roles.

When nondual clarity is present, it is possible to read the words attributed to these—and *all*—spiritual teachers and to winnow out immediately the dualistic pronouncements from the nondual teachings.

Finally. In the sense that "truth" (or Truth) denotes the actuality of the nondual condition of our existence, the word represents something which has no opposite: in other words, from the nondual perspective, even that which we might designate as "false" is Truth inasmuch as nothing can be *excluded* from the nondual condition as an *actuality*.

Questions pertaining to the ultimate condition are too important to depend upon the authority of others for their resolution. The teachers of nonduality are not promulgating a religion. They are assuring that you can answer all questions for yourself (no middleman!) by cutting through to the truth of your own true nature.

Bear in mind that the posing of such questions as yours imply that, by gaining enough "correct" answers, there will be a state of illumination that will descend upon the questioner at some point in the future.

What such questions are attempting to discover has never been "lost", to begin with. What the questioner is seeking is *omnipresent*: it does not come nor go. It is, in fact, *inescapable*. Why? Because all things are That. "*All* things", the sages would point out, must *include* the questioner: you *are* That which you are seeking. It is That which asks the question, and it is That which answers it. Every form arises from the formless, interacts with other forms, and recedes again into the formless—at all stages, being nothing other than That, in interaction with itself.

Focus your attention on the question: How could I—or anything else—be separate or apart from that which (by its very definition) is limitless?

Will or Destiny?

Why do you concern yourself with whether your discovery of the truth is dependent upon free will, or whether it is predetermined?

The supposition that there is free will presumes a divinity which grants the privilege of free choice (toward one or another polar consequences); or, a divinity which ordains a predetermined outcome, instead.

In *either* case, the divinity is the ultimate agent for what ensues, so why concern *yourself* about the means provided?

Consider that neither *will* nor *destiny* would likely be tools in the employ of the divine. With nothing that is in opposition to the all-powerful divine, what role would will of any sort ("yours" or "its") need to be called in to play? Likewise, why would an all-knowing divine need to pre-order any developments, when all developments are of its own composition? The divine, being both the evident cause and the apparent effect of all occurrences in the cosmos, cause and effect are nothing more than one stroke of undifferentiated movement.

Thus the past and present (or present and future) are one indistinguishable movement, negating will (the presumed cause of effect) *or* pre-determination (the supposed effect of causation). Any movement, all movement, would presumably have to have been first initiated by the divine.

The premise that there is a categorical 'past' which has an imprint on a categorical 'present' is what permits you to conclude that your identity in the 'present' (the "you" that you think you are) is an accretion from the 'past.' Remove every imaginative memory of the past, up to this present moment, and you are without personal identity: not even a name for yourself. Remove every definitive idea you have accumulated in the past, and what image would you be able to formulate of the divine—or how even postulate the existence of such a thing?

In such a state, free of accumulated knowledge of the purported existence of either "you" or "it", *what* could be in relation (either "apart" or "unified") to *what*? When accumulated knowledge has ended at death, will there be an identifiable "you"? Will there be a conceivable "divine"?

The key to the search is that neither the searcher nor the sought exist as a "thing". When the searching thus ends with this realization, the "unity" which has always already been a fact is revealed as *presence*. Free will or preordination are subjects that are not germane to the point, for that which is unavoidable.

No Entry; No Exit

As per Waley's translation of the Hsin-Hsin Ming, "make an hair breadth difference, and heaven and earth are set apart".

The so-called Pristine or Unborn (Void, or Buddha-nature, to Waley) "is blank and featureless as space; it has no 'too little' or 'too much.'" Neither is there an "inner" or "outer" to it; "For it is not a thing with extension in time or space...it is manifest always and everywhere."

Therefore, there is no way to "enter" it, nor is it possible to be "in it" or "out of it": "In that one Void, the two are not distinguished."

Why think up something you need to *do*, as Bankei would ask.

"The deed disappears when the *doer* is *annihilated*.

"If the mind makes *no distinctions*, the Dharma becomes all one.... Let the thought of the Dharmas as all one *bring you* to the So-in-itself.... In the not-two are *no separate things*...

"At the ultimate point...you get to where there are no rules...to where effect of action ceases.... Let things take their own course; know that the Essence will neither go nor stay....

"Take your stand on this, and the rest will follow of its own accord."

Anything you can "enter", you can exit. Therefore, it will not be that which is "manifest always and everywhere!"

An experiment: Lie down on the floor.

Imagine a heart attack; collapse; and death. *Wyatt* is *dead*.

Let *all* fall away that would fall away for this dead body.

Take as long as is necessary. (You've got an eternity.)

The body has been stripped away. Sensations are gone. The mind is gone.

The past is gone. The future is gone. The present is gone.

Beliefs are finished. Expectations are finished. Memories are finished. Choosing is finished.

Wyatt is dead.

There is nothing.

Wyatt is dead.

As you lay on the floor, with everything that was Wyatt's stripped away, there is nothing left but this inert body. Only someone who had seen its face before would call it Wyatt. Those who remove it will call it "the body". And it will be disposed of.

To this body, laying on the floor without Wyatt, there is nothing. There is not even nothing, because there is not anything to *consider* that there is nothing.

As you lay there on the floor, emptied of Wyatt, what is aware that there is not even nothing? What is it that senses that all that there is, is silent, still, emptiness?

This awareness is more than the core of your being; it is the only *real* being that you have. It has observed everything that has ever gone on with, by or around Wyatt, before there even was a Wyatt. It has remained unchanged throughout. It has remained unaffected by all that it has witnessed throughout.

Every individual embodies this awareness. It is not "your" awareness, or "my" awareness. It is present in every being in common. Awareness must be present even in subatomic particles, because each is evidently aware of the presence of others around it and what its relationship is to each of these. However, it seems likely that a subatomic particle does not consider itself to be an individual, and consider an *inter*acting particle to be an "other".

Out of this ubiquitous field of awareness, the "individual" takes form—each as unique as a snowflake; like you. Good and bad. In each entity where awareness takes form, a renewed evidence of this miracle occurs, a retelling of the eternal *being* story in a never-before-told version.

You are not the story. The story plays-out on, in and around you, as awareness interacts with awareness like a "particle" interacts with a "particle". Wyatt is not awareness. Awareness is Wyatt. Wyatt can be dead, and awareness is still awareness.

First things first. Put everything aside, including Wyatt, and get in touch with what you are—a field of expression solely in the interest of awareness; one of the miracles occurring, while subatomic particles are initiating their miracles.

Bring your attention back to what is aware of this awareness. And every time you fail to do that—which will be continually—be aware that that is what is occurring. Awareness does that. Don't ask *me* why. Perhaps it adds "characterization" to the story.

You needn't be impatient. You have time. And if you don't do it, that'll just be part of the story. The real blessing is that the story will end one day. And then there will be—as there is now— nothing but nothing. The dead Wyatt will know that.

....

No Problem

Your elaboration on Blofeld's translation of the Huang Po quote was well-said. Thanks, too, for your monograph. A few comments:

The interpretation of "not-knowing" as "view-*less*" seems most appropriate. The phrase "not-knowing" can lend itself to the same confusion that the phrase "no-thought" can pose for the unrealized. Both can suggest an imagined, idealized "special state".

It is not a condition in which knowledge or thought is *negated*, but in which both (*and* all other qualities) are "dissipated", as Masao Abe says. When everything "which can be stated" is recognized to be merely a "substantiation of human-made concepts", "knowledge" (or "knowing"), "thought", ad infinitum, are not mistaken for Truth—and therefore *need* not be negated. The "not-knowing" is the absence of relative—therefore dualistic— "differentiations": in that condition, one is then "view-less"; there is "no*thing*" to be seen.

"When the domain of 'thought' has been dissipated, that which can be *stated* (as "object" in a statement) is dissipated", Abe says— leaving only that which is "undifferentiated".

"Reality *prior* to *language*", he calls it, and follows it with the description "emptiness": "emptiness of all *dualistic* notions".

Clearly then, from this standpoint, there is not a "person" remaining, an "individual", who "is not-knowing" (or the possessor of "no-thought"). The "viewless" has no view of "himself": there is no entertainment of a special person who is maintaining a special state.

Abe says, "ultimate reality, in Buddhism, is not Being (some *particular* condition), rather it is emptiness"—the *absence* of any and all definitive conditions.

And this emptiness, he continues, is not in the category of "that which can be stated"—just *another* "substantiation of human-made concepts"—which could also be subject to a negation: it is empty even of "itself". Undifferentiated, it is not relative; non-dual; un-viewable. It is the domain in which thought, knowing *and all else* has dissipated. "*This* emptiness", he says, "itself must be emptied (by the would-be not-knower) by rejecting an *attachment* to emptiness" (such as "not knowing" it). In this emptiness, there is no one *left* to "not know" it.

As Nuden Dorje says, "You don't need to sort out any problems… do not struggle to resist ('knowing', 'thought' etc.)"; return to that "which does not *need* to be…developed…the natural state is there without effort."

Therefore, too, "memory" is not a problem. For the one to whom "past" and "future" have dissipated, what *naturally* becomes of "memory" (even if one *assumes* the "reality" of this phantasm)?

So, the realized do not "struggle to resist" memory, or any *other* appearance that arises in Emptiness. For the one for whom there *is* no "thought", there are no problems for their "thinker".

320

When you gave me Steve Sashen's account of attending satsang with Ramesh Balsekar in January, and you asked for my comment on it, I asked you if you had read Ramesh. How much emphasis ought we to place on a second-hand account of a sage's teachings, when we can read (or hear or see) that sage for ourselves?

One could gather from Sashen's monograph that Ramesh declared that he was "born with" Self-realization. What Ramesh is more likely to have said (judging from what he has said in *Consciousness Speaks*) is that he was born with universal consciousness—which we *all* are born with.

In an interview, he has said that since childhood, he had sought (as many do, especially in India) Self-realization. After college in London, and while working his way up to becoming general manager of the Bank of India, he was for 20 years a devotee of a guru who was not able to enlighten him.

After retiring at age 60, after 10 years as bank president, he heard about—and went to see—Nisargadatta, who had been teaching not far from him. After attending satsang for a few months, he began translating (into English) for the teacher. About a year later, during one of Nisargadatta's daily talks, Ramesh discovered the same clarity. Nisargadatta confirmed Ramesh's Self-realization; and two years after the teacher died, Ramesh began to teach.

So, when Sashen says "(Ramesh) said that he didn't *do anything* to become whatever or whoever he is, that he was just born this way. It was his natural tendency, his innate something or other", Ramesh would have been referring to the fact that he—as are we *all*—discovered that he has never been *other than* Self, or Absolute. There is a vast difference between the fact of this as *truth*, and the *self-realization* of this truth as a *fact*. Which is *why* Ramesh made a *discovery* while considering the teachings of Nisargadatta.

Sashen goes on to say, in his own words, that enlightenment is the "understanding that there is no inherent 'do-er', in our life". *That* is what Ramesh discovered: there is no *person* that "contains" this universal consciousness. In Ramesh's words, "There is no *me*, and there is no *you*, to become [contain] That. Consciousness— Totality or God—is all there is."

This teaching of the enlightened—*That* is *all* that *is*—is what most people listen to, but do not *hear*.

Sashen goes on to interpret, "there is no 'person' who is doing anything…we are not the causes, but instead the effects". No, no. "We" are not the "effects" of anything: if "there *is* no person", there *is* no *we*.

Ramesh again: The seeking, which begins with an individual, cannot end until the "individual" is annihilated—when there is a *total understanding* that there is *no individual* to understand anything, to achieve anything; and that awakening or enlightenment (or whatever the word is), can only happen when this is fully understood. Enlightenment (from my perspective) is the absence of a "me."

The "me" is the sense of personal identity.

Sashen quotes Ramesh: "If you believe that by becoming 'enlightened' you will become free of unpleasant experiences or emotions, you're mistaken…you will get nothing. Nothing."

Why is that? Because—*being* all that *is*—there is no *you* that is an entity that is *apart* from anything that could be gotten.

Therefore, as Ramesh says, "For a *me* to want *enlightenment* is a contradiction in terms.... *as long as* there is a me-wanting-enlightenment, enlightenment *cannot happen.*" The Self, which is all that is, cannot *become* the Self which it *already* is. So the teaching that there is "nothing to do" is predicated on the *understanding* that there is "no one" to "do" anything. All that is done, is done without an "individual" doing it. *This* is what Ramesh understands when he says, "Nisargadatta's basic teaching was that everything happens as a spontaneous functioning of the Totality: the *you* doesn't really exist." So, there is "nothing to do" *when* there is realization of the fact of no "you" who does whatever it is that appears to be done.

The trouble with Sashen's monograph is that the incompleteness of this understanding, of what Ramesh is saying, will merely likely add to the confusion of those reading it. He says, "something I teach people to do (is to) take a look at all the things you do". Does he *go on* to teach that there is *no you*, to start with, and therefore (as Ramesh would say) nothing that *needs* to be *done*? He quotes Ramesh, "there is nobody doing anything... (therefore) there's no need for guilt or blame or shame".

Sashen adds, "I won't get into all the problems with this line of thinking", and he goes on to "point out two". Both are based on assumptions about "your life".

Had he understood thoroughly what Ramesh says about "your" life ("there *is nobody*"), there would be no "problems" for him to "get into".

This is why my comment to you was, "He's only *half* right."

Means to an End

I don't suppose that any sensible person (in prison or out) could help but feel outrage at the institutionalized inhumane developments that increasingly occur. But that outrage *can* be directed into activities that are genuinely helpful to others, to the extent possible under the circumstances. (And the circumstances aren't always very favorable, as Jesus discovered.) What more radical way to positively "undermine the order" than to effectively transmit the Dharma? I, for one, am "permanently ruined", from the standpoint of societal exigencies. Why has China attempted to smother Buddhism in placid Tibet?

The Rusty Key

In regard to your first of two questions, I have spoken with many people over the past (now) about twenty years, under various circumstances. In addition, I have read many accounts of those who've had the experience of self-realization. It seems to be almost axiomatic that the degree and timeliness of this realization is proportional to the dedication with which one pursues it. For those who discover this actuality, typically, they became aware (at some point) that a key does in fact exist which can unlock the truth which all mystical traditions attest exists in a comprehensive form.

Once aware that it is possible for a human, in this life, to access that eternal truth, they comprehend that there is nothing in life which is more critical than unlocking this fundamental treasure-store. As a consequence of the recognition of the vital importance of holding this key to life's purpose, this matter rises to the very top of their agenda of urgencies.

To those willing to offer up their life for it, this truth does manifest. Therefore, as you've indicated, "many *are* called, but few are chosen".

The second part is, of course, related. To die to the self is the price of the key. And what happens when we (normally) die? The mind dies: we are like in deep, dreamless sleep, where there is not even the mentation "I exist", let alone "I exist as…" or "it is my opinion that…" or "I firmly believe in…" etc. So, yes, to discover one's true relation to nothingness, all suppositions about somethingness need to be, at least, suspended.

Not only are our usual dualistic ideas an obstacle, but added to these are the acquired myths about enlightenment and what that condition presents or entails. That is *why* it is necessary to abandon ideas, opinions, beliefs, etc., as a fundamental premise— because *among* these will be lurking the spiritual mythology.

So, there's a vast amount of ego/mind dying that has to take place throughout the entire journey. As you indicated, if those preconceptions about the how and what of enlightenment are retained, one will likely not recognize the true condition *even* when present. "This can't be it: this is too…", or "this is not what…"

What we *hope* for is to proceed from the known to the known. We are not enthused about abandoning the known and engaging the *unknown*. "We fear what we know nothing of," Shakespeare said. Fortunately, for those who *do* encounter the unknown, this transition is the annihilation of fear. After all, you've already agreed to die "going in".

The grace-point for us is that we're not Adam: there have been scores of others who've jumped into the maws of nothingness, well before us. Some of the ones who are no longer living have left their testament as a guide, or manual. And, praises be, there are some others who are alive in our time, whose very presence can convey the message even if they choose not to speak a word.

The key ever lies moldering, and what fool will pick it up? Some do, some don't.

Dualism: "Subject" / "Object" Relationships

That there is "no one who is enlightened" is the message of the teachers. Those who recognize the truth of this statement are commonly referred to as enlightened, awakened or realized. The name Buddha, reputedly, means "awakened", and Buddhist teachers routinely refer to "Buddha's enlightenment". Not until one is "realized" does one realize the paradox of "not being enlightened". Until one can realize this paradox, teachers *continue* to "assist" those who "seek enlightenment". It appears that merely saying to the seeker "no one is enlightened" is not practical; the career of teachers could be much shorter if this sufficed to "clarify" the issue.

Can Pain Be Conquered?

You've asked: "Buddha concerned himself with a response to suffering, pain and death. I can see that suffering can be definitional, a subjective determination; and I can understand that death is something which we are never really apart from. But what about physical pain. Is it possible somehow to vanquish it?"

In the same way that one does not vanquish death, one does not vanquish pain. Pain is a reality; it is not in the imagination (as is, in many cases, "suffering"), and so imagining that it is gone will not help. It did not come at our bidding, and so it will not go at our bidding. In other words, it is not fully subject to our control.

In the same way that we *encourage* pleasure, we *resist* pain. But when in pain, we physically tense and tighten up. One need not *welcome* pain; but when it is present, it does no good to reject it. Resistance to the pain—physically *or* psychologically—only increases our tension. Can you be with the pain in the moment that it is there—even the enduring moment—without wishing that it would end? When it ends, can you give no energy to the thought of dread that it will recur? Can you see that the moment with pain or without pain is always the same moment; can you give your full awareness to all that is in that moment?

Pain is not to be vanquished; pain is of the body, and the body is not to be vanquished. We live with pain, we live with death, we live with suffering. Sometimes we *seem* to live without these. In fearing death, we resist death. In fearing pain, we resist pain. Resistance is itself a form of pain...not a means toward the ending of pain.

Beyond Reason

By the time I finished the first couple of pages of your last letter, it almost felt as if I was reading back to myself one of my monographs. I'm glad that you are beginning to view things from beyond the relative perspective.

And, as you noted, blame (of others *or* self) is a reflection of guilt ("I am not perfect!").

Your musings on the firmament are analogous to a connection that Ramana made a couple of times: the *connection* between Self and the organism can be viewed as the ego. This is why he said it's not necessary to "kill" the ego, but to understand what it is (another of the endless manifestations of the Self): there is no *dis*connection here: Self = ego = self (as manifested Being). He used this equation to suggest that it is *through* recognizing the ego for what it is, that one can discover the Self for what *it* is: self=ego=Self—without manufacturing an artificial separation between each "named" thing. He also used this to point out that it is not "your" ego (or mind, thoughts or will) that is the fundamental source (or "cause") of what transpires, there being no separable you in actuality. In any case, it is the ego's *dissatisfactions* that leads one to the Self.

You (as it were) said something to the effect of, "What could be the purpose [meaning or reason] of all this that's going on?" Any sensible response to that (perennial) question has to be from the standpoint of the (nondual) Absolute. And that is because such a question (if not every question) is a consequence of our dualistic thinking.

When we consider That "which is all that is", how could it have a "center"? This is what was meant when said, "Its circumference is everywhere, its center nowhere." At any and every point in place or time, it is absolutely, 100% present—being an indivisible actuality. It does not operate out of some designated kingdom in the heavens. It is in the *process* of "creating" all that is (itself) right now, being (as it would have to be) *self*-actualizing. It has no *need* of a pre-established "plan" or "purpose" or "reason": to whom would it need to justify itself? No matter *what* happens, it is what is inevitably *supposed* to happen, from the standpoint of the timelessly spontaneous Absolute. So, there is not something sitting at some central point, pulling its beard in anxiety over whether its "purpose" is being fulfilled. What is "unfulfilled" for the Absolute, that it needs to "acquire" or "establish"?

Ironically, what could possibly be a more "intelligent" process: no possibility of "failure"!

So, the evident answer—to the linear mind's consternation—is, "No purpose, no meaning, no reason. You have any problem with that?!"

I don't have any problem with that—merely being "dissatisfied" if I did.

I hope this doesn't screw up your day!

Postscript

When the *divisive perspective* ends for yourself, your meditation gravitates to observing it in other people.

You know *why* they're doing what they're doing, because you've been through it yourself.

But you can't help marveling that they don't see through it, knowing (now) how easy that is.

It will feel to you like watching two other people, arguing in a dream—and wondering why they're carrying on so, considering that it's all just a dream!

Beginner's Mind

Assuming that it is possible that there are functionings of your mind which you have not yet experienced, the question which you might ask yourself is: Have I permitted the *usual* functioning of my mind to subside long enough for possible exposure to *unusual* functionings? What one needs to explore is whether the mundane, frenetic mind can approach a new byway, and at that intersection—as the highway signs read—"yield".

It is not voluntarily, through volition, that the thinking mind will yield to the intuitive, native mind; it will do so only when it realizes that there is no legitimate reason for resistance. And once the native mind has resumed its proper occupancy, the thinking mind will thereafter be in regard of it.

Though there may be a difference, a distinction, between these two aspects of the mind, there is not a severance or division: these are facets of the same phenomenon which we call the mind. But when the logical mind is truly honest in its quest for understanding, it will envisage the limitations of its own perimeters; this calculative mind will admit that it won't ever be able to experience that which can't be known. Once the thinking mind has surrendered to the precognitive, native mind, there is but one integrated, unconflicting mind in operation. This harmonious mind, we could say, is then an entirely new mind… new for that human who now senses mindfulness, or awareness.

For this to happen, the thinking mind comes to a place where it candidly admits, "I no longer know where this is leading", and, without making a choice, moves onward. Thought is then utilized in a different manner: as a sense, rather than as an interpreter or arbiter of senses; no longer is it the judge, but impartially the witness.

A mind which was chronically in passing gear is now in neutral, free to engage in any appropriate direction of the moment. What had previously been a technical, doctrinaire mind, sees the value of flexibility and yields to this practicality, the wisdom in the moment. This perception, this pausing so that yielding may occur, is the only action necessary: a change in momentum is momentous change. Now the brain sees afresh, through aging eyes, and it is the letting go, relaxing, giving up, which has been the pivotal activity: not the *doing*, but the *not doing*.

In this void, in this stillness, is creativity/destruction...the life which is in death. The howling dog of the thinking mind since quieted, the valley of the native mind has awakened to a refreshing new morning. We can now hear hushed voices and not simply the yapping of the watchdog.

The thinking mind will no longer define what it knows in relation to what it does not know: it experiences knowing and not-knowing within the same arena. Now knowledge is not valued as the end product; attention, instead, is given to the endless process of learning. And this thinking mind feels not the impulse to relegate that which it learns to the tarnished bins of "safe/unsafe"; there is but one category, 'what is'.

A Letter to the Self

Judging from recent letters, your mental panorama seems much more settled than it has been. The judgment and anger are still evident, but probably no more so than in the average person.

I hope that while you're carefully noting others' reactions, you are meanwhile observing your reactions to their reactions.

Your reactions may be more "visible" than you suppose. And, even if silent, your evident reactions may incite further, compounding reactions in others. You cannot silently *hate* someone without *something* showing.

These moments of reaction on your part (anger, condemnation, etc.) are an opportunity: while observing others with your eyes, it is possible at the same time to witness what is appearing on the screen of the psyche; the words, the thoughts, the conclusions, opinions, beliefs, etc.

No restraining activity need take place with either the outward display of emotion nor the inward. Merely notice impartially what the body and the psyche are presenting in these instances, these encounters: physically, the tension; psychically, the emotional, inner commentary.

Objectively witnessing your reactions (or lack of them) takes the focus of your attention off of the adversary, first of all. Additionally, it is difficult to continue a negative (or positive) running commentary when your *attention* is focused on the commentary itself.

You are often in confrontational situations. Therefore, you are often on the receiving end of negative energy. Naturally, this does not feel good.

To end it quickly, neutralize it. Passivity on your part will neutralize it quickly. Passivity will be effortlessly present when you focus full attention on what is present in your responsive posture. Objectively observe the arising, expressing and passing of your anger, resentment, condemnation, disappointment, etc.

You will likely notice that these negative reactions are also expressed in relation to your *self*, even when not in the presence of others. Again, passively witness the arising of judgmental (etc.) commentary, give it full attention while present, and observe its dissolution. No need to change anything: non-critical awareness itself is a change.

Your Enlightened Moment

If there is one single thing which the enlightened masters have difficulty conveying, it is this: the "awakened" condition is the condition that *you* are experiencing *right now*! It is not a condition that is *experientially* different from the one that you are aware of right now.

Therefore, if this moment is not experienced as an "enlightened" moment, the difference must be in how this moment is *perceived*. The primary difference in how an enlightened master perceives the experience of the moment, contrasted to how a "seeker" of enlightenment perceives the experience of the moment, is that the seeker is looking for, waiting for, a moment—an experience— that is not present. This ignores what the teachers stress: that what is being sought is present *everywhere, at all times*. If it were *not* present at all times, it could not be perceived in *each* and *every* moment. Yet, there is clearly not a time when it is *not* perceived, by those who perceive it.

So, what is being sought is *here, now*—and is being overlooked. This very, momentary *experience of it* is being overlooked—in being sought *beyond* the present, immediate experience. The "awakening" experience is a truth-full realization that is *summarized* by thought in such a phrase as, "My God, *I* am *That*— right now!"

It is a moment of recognition that the recogniz*er* is phenomenally similar to a subatomic element, such as a proton—which *is both* a particle and a wave *simultaneously*. The organism which perceives "enlightened" Truth recognizes that it is *relative*, in that it is operating in a sense of time. But it is, simultaneously, *Absolute*, in that its *essential* Being is utterly time-less. Put another way, the recognition *of* universal Being is taking place *in* universal Being. This *finite*, momentary experience is the experience of the *infinite* this very moment.

The *perception* of this *Truth*, rather than a dramatically different *experience*, is "awakening". Once "awakened", the precept*or* no longer continues to seek the "experience"—or further evidence— of en-lighten-ment.

Once "awakened", behavior (regarding "me" in "relation" to "others") is subject to change. But relative experience, from moment to moment, is not different for an enlightened master than for that of the seeker of enlightenment. The former is, merely, no longer awaiting an enlightened moment: *every* moment is an enlightened moment.

....

thIS

Yes, the spiritual scriptures speak of That (or "spirit") as "penetrating, infusing or permeating all". But "interpenetrating" would be more accurate. It is not helpful to conceive a *spirit* which infuses or penetrates matter, as if it were an X-ray. The spirit and matter have never been apart, from the very beginning.

(Even the word *That*—representing omnipresence—is misleading, to the extent that it suggests something that can be pointed to. It would be better if we pointed to ourself and said, "This"—since This, which speaks, *is* That omnipresent actuality.)

If there *is* an omnipresent actuality—which words such as *God* presumably describe—it *so* permeates all that is, that it *is* all that is (by whatever name we choose to call its manifold presentations). Thus it can be said that "God is all that is."

But, from the standpoint that nothing exists which can be designated, ultimately, as having an individual or distinct identity, it can also be said that "there is no *God*", as such.

Hence, the meaning of Swami Gitananda Giri:

> *You have two choices open to you, in your attitude towards life: "iti, iti" or "neti, neti". "Iti, iti" means "This is God. That is God. Everything is God." "Neti, neti" means "This is not God. That is not God. Nothing is God." It has to be one or*

the other. Either everything is God or nothing is God. Either
everything is important or nothing is important. Both are
correct. But there is no truth in any in-between.

In other words, whether one concludes that "all is God" or
"nothing is God", it amounts to the same recognition. If—by
"God"—is meant *omni*present, both can be acknowledged as true.

There is still always *this*: this cosmically inter-connected
unfolding; and whatever *this is*—with not anything in the
universe independent of *all* the rest—it is one awesome display!
There is clearly a power which exceeds anything in human
capacity, or even all of human capacity combined. There is an
Absolute presence, to which mankind's presence is consequential;
a presence that produces the body, brain, mind, thought, and
every human action resulting therefrom. The noticing of a passing
thought and the explosion of an ancient star are not unrelated
phenomenon: both the product of a self-creating, self-destroying
ubiquitous capability. Whether or not we identify it, or identify
with it, this source *is* as it *is*; it is that (this) by which is done
either, neither, or both.

You do not exist outside of This which does all that is done. And
among the things that are done is This standing in awe of its
universal, spontaneous profundity.

At one point, the *Absolute* poetically addresses Job:

> "Can you bring forth the constellations in their seasons,
> or lead out Leo with its cubs? Who endows the heart
> with wisdom or gives understanding to the mind?"

The same that "understands" produces what is to be understood.

Deincarnation

Sight-less; eyes closed. Sounds heard, but as meaningless. Nothing separate to touch. Nothing to smell. Not yet tasting anything. Like a fish asleep at the very bottom of the ocean, not aware of any of the defining conditions of life. A baby in the womb.

Not yet breathing, nor sensing light and darkness as defining shapes; not passing air through the nostrils and detecting scent, not experiencing the tongue as taster, not making tactile contact with texture or temperature. All but dead.

Not even *knowing* that it is *not* dead. Not knowing that there is even life. Not knowing that there is a non-liquid space, in which the limbs can move freely. Not knowing that the lungs can expand and contract with air. Or that the body can feel warmed by sunlight, chilled by breeze; can hear chortling and hear crying; and form a sensate circle with mouth and thumb. Knowing no more than if dead.

Not knowing that, within minutes, miraculous transformation awaits. A completely different universe, a radically different existence. A universe and existence in which there are things *of which* to be aware! External objects which can be sensed. Disjointed sensations which can be experienced. An unfolding of uncontrollable conditions, such as helplessness, hunger, discomfort, pain, incomprehension, surprise, fear, uncertainty. A startling reversal of the effortless, unneedy, undisturbed condition previously.

And what if the heart were to cease beating after arriving in this peculiar universe? If the eyes were to close sightless, the ears to register sounds uninterpreted in meaning, the passage of air through the scent-sensing organ to halt, the last taste already tasted, no sensation as touch. No colors discerned, no texture felt, no temperatures noticed. Not knowing that there is air to breathe, space to move within; nothing external or internal, no conditions, nothing of which to *be* aware. No experience of peace, or lack of it. A body in the tomb.

Awareness of Being

At this point, Patricia, it is important that the attention be (or remain) focused. Not as some egoic "practice", but as *present awareness*. This cannot be over emphasized.

Decades of habitual and divisive thought patterns will not disappear overnight. Before, you had no antidote for them: your form of perception was entirely on the relative level. But now that the nondual perspective is clear to you, the persistence of this perspective needs to be firmly established.

Keep attention focused on what arises, moment by moment, on the screen of consciousness. We think in terms of words, and each word isolates some particular thing from the universal field of actuality—whether the word refers to the material ("me") *or* the immaterial ("love"). Words are separative ("seeker"/ "enlightenment"), and this serves a purpose for communication on the relative level; even sages resort to them.

But our dualistic perception is *rooted* in this word-thought divisiveness. The *nondual* perception is rooted in the full realization that every word merely describes a particular manifestation of the ineffable actuality. Therefore, it is important to be aware, in *each* moment, (without making an "aware/ unaware" tribulation out of it) of the divisive, dualistic nature of words and ideas that pass across the screen of consciousness.

One need not attempt to do anything *about* what arises; that would be an effort at further *isolation* ("good thoughts/bad thoughts"). But in being *aware* that each word/idea is pertinent only to relative phenomenon, one is reminded that from the Absolute perspective, *all* that is being perceived is—in its *true* nature—That (Self, Brahman, God, Omnipresent, whatever word you prefer for the indivisible).

As a consequence, the *inter*connectedness, of all that is, will become increasingly apparent in consciousness—rather than (dualistic) "connected-ness".

As present Absolute awareness saturates consciousness, *moment by moment*, the habituated tendency to subscribe to dualistic propositions will be replaced (without making an "effort" to do so). It is merely a matter of where attention is focused. This finally becomes a matter of (automatically) "not making distinctions", as you mentioned.

Obviously, the first and primary distinction we make is "I"; that there is an entity that is in *relation* to each of the word-concepts. And since this word-concept ("I, me, mine" etc.) is predominant among the relative connections which appear on the screen, it provides an in-the-moment flag to arouse introspective attention.

Notice especially the arising of the I-thought (individuation) when it is in *relation* to Oneness, as if Oneness was some condition apart: I, subject; Oneness, object. Oneness is among the many terms used to refer to that omnipresent Absolute, within which there are no "others". That being all that is, the I must *be* that; there can be no *relationship* with what one *is*.

Otherwise, oneness is an *idea* (concerning an immaterial entity), not the inescapable actuality that is (as the Patricia manifestation) self-aware.

What is "freedom in action"? Well, the book-length answer is called the Bhagavad-Gita.

Adyashanti has described three "spiritual" phases, or conditions. There is the "ignorant" period of our life that leads to, or leads up to, awakening to (our *prior* ignorance of) the essential Truth of our being. There is an indefinite *post*-awakening "stage" of *acclimating* to a radical change in perspective. And there is a "period" of unalloyed *clarity* that persists uninterrupted for the *balance* of one's tenure in visible form (or "life").

This latter stage, Adya refers to as embodiment. That is, formless Truth appearing as the form of "an individual". In less lofty terms, it is merely living out one's life in full awareness of one's undeniable presence as an instrument of omnipresent actuality.

During the *post-awakening* phase, there often tends to be a "transitional" process (which is sometimes referred to as "stabilizing"). Generally, it is a period in which one *questions* (typically, through inner dialogue) the certainty of the unremarkable realization that has evidently occurred. All things "known" before are examined under (it could be said) a unique light which casts no shadows: nondual clarity.

This can be a time in which lingering cloudiness, in one's perception of nonduality, can render obscure the unblemished Truth which *had been* revealed. Clinging to dualistic, subject/object bias will make itself painfully apparent. There is no viable position, in realizing nonduality, for a 99% awakening. One percent ignore-ance is ignorance *remaining*. Unclear issues need to be resolved.

The unshaken affirmation (alluded to in Hui Neng's poem, "Where there is nothing from the start, where can the dust alight?") of the unarguable Truth of nonduality will verify the *absence* of an identifiable "personal self", as the sages have asserted. *This* is the "freedom" to which all have pointed. Beyond internal or egoic contradiction, one can recognize the virtue of the statement, "I am not the doer of 'my' actions." If anything, I am that which does *all* actions—*every* action—that is *ever* done.

This fundamental recognition is the sense in which "freedom in (or freedom of) action" is intended. Since it is clear that "there is nothing from the start", the actions, or activities, of the embodied one are without residue. Thus, Ramana says, "Do actions, without caring for the result. Do not think that you are the doer."

The point of all this is that—to the extent that the self is absent, that nonduality has been embodied—there isn't any action (or inaction) which is not an effortless expression of the dharma— even though it is free of intent to be so.

. . . .

"Just As I Am"—hymn

The message of all the true sages is uniformly one, so it is (as you said) "easy and so simple". *Too* simple and *too* easy for most Western seekers, it seems.

Your letter does reflect, to me, that indeed there have been "some changes". You are evidently on a solid footing, and—by being attentive—you can strengthen that. The following are some suggestions as to where to focus attention, at this point.

Every sage has said (in one way or another), "I am *complete*, I am whole." One form in which this is said, is: "I am That (the Absolute)"; or, "I am God."

This completeness, wholeness or "perfection" can be understood in two ways. That which is whole is "one", *unfragmented*. When *this* one is recognized as "one *without a second*" (as the Vedas put it), it is clear that it is an *indivisible* one: there is no *entity* apart that *could* divide it.

The sages are saying that *you* are whole, complete, perfect: that *you* and this One (without a second) are the same *singular* thing.

And not *just* you, *all things* are this One actuality. As such, there is (in truth) *only* That. *You* are That: no *more* and no *less* than any *other* thing. *All* is That.

When this is clearly recognized as being Truth, what happens? The sense of being a *separate* entity, a "self" or "person", falls away. *Identification* becomes *whole*, complete.

Therefore, the idea of being separate or apart from *any*thing dissipates! No longer, in one's perception of actuality, are there *divisions*.

Where there are no divisions, there is not "enlightenment" as opposed to "unenlightenment". In fact, where divisions have fallen away, there is no longer a discrete "me" to *be* enlightened *or* unenlightened.

Then things are just *as* they *are*, and one is completely satisfied with that. *There* the seeking has ended: there *is* no longer a "seeker" or some thing *apart* to be "sought". There is but One thing: *even* seeker and sought are *That*.

Now that this is becoming clear to you, you are beginning to relax. You are not waiting for something "special" to "happen"; you are not looking for some thing beyond what is actually *already* present. And, what *is* actually present? That! (As are "you": what a co-incidence!)

And what *is* the guru? Isn't the *guru* That? How then are you and the guru different? When you've recognized that (there *being* but *One* thing) there is no "me" and "other", you and the guru cannot even *claim* any differences.

You say: "Is awakening happening? If not, it doesn't matter (anymore)." That is the *guru's* recognition: how then are you different from the guru?

The reason why "this got missed in previous readings" is because there was a "you" (the "reader") standing apart. When the you *disappears*, what could be *missed*?

I want to proceed to a couple of points which you may not have as yet considered.

When wholeness, completeness, is present (as one's awareness), "all is well", as you said, "as it is. I and everything is perfect as it is, and nothing *need* be done." You have heard the sages say this many times: now you understand it.

If that is so, does it make any difference *what* the "ego" does, whatsoever?

If all is That, doing what it does—isn't the so-called ego That, doing what it does? If there is, in actuality, no "you", *is* there such a distinct entity as an "ego"? (*Ego* is the Latin word for "I"; what becomes of "ego" when "I" evaporates?)

What is it that is *aware* of this supposed ego? "You"? or That? If the ego is, in reality, That's creation (as are all creations), let That concern itself with the workings of the ego!

You spoke of "tricking the mind". Re-read the previous four paragraphs, and substitute the word "*mind*" for "*ego*". Is there, in actuality, a distinctive entity (which is not *That*) which can rightly be called "mind"? "Mind"—the *idea* of that—is itself the "trick"!

Yes, you *will* notice "fears" dissolve. *Who* is there to fear *what*? There is only *That*. If there *is* fear, it is That doing what it does—just an additional part of the completeness, wholeness, the perfection. As they say in Buddhism, "That *too* is It."

As Krishnamurti would say, "Think on *these* things" (as I'm sure you will).

There is no "you" to awaken, and there is no dream. Realizing *this* is "to *awaken* to the dream"! There is just what there is: That. All that is, is That. Isn't this what all of your gurus have *told* you?

If "you" are a "sleep walker", it is That doing what it does. Perfectly. Why make an effort to change what is perfect, as it is?

All the "seeker's" agony you have gone through has brought you "here". Now, forget what had happened to the "you" which *wasn't*, really, in the first place.

And, while you're at it, don't look for anything more special in the future. *Rest* in peace. Now just "view everything from a different [non-dual] perspective". That's *all* the guru does!

....

Forsake Deliverance

We spend the vast majority of our temporal time at an imaginary intersection, where the boulevards of What Was and Could Be meet the avenues of Better and Worse.

Still, there is no way around, no alternative to, the What Is.

All one need do is to seriously contemplate what one's situation *is,* to realize that there is nothing which needs to be thought about.

When there is nothing which one needs to think about, there is not any thing which need be fretted about.

However, we constantly keep trying to wind things into (or out of) the skein of reality.

We want not only solutions to our problems, but elegant solutions. There can be *solutions* only to that which are viewed as *problems.* Is death, for instance, a "problem"—for which there is a "solution"?

Consider, if you will, how much of our energy is continually absorbed in attempting to delay or resist death. But death is, itself, nature's final reminder that we must, from moment to moment, let go.

There is no requirement, in this universe, that you must like or dislike what happens to (or around) you…or that you must not like or dislike it. It is our sense of self, of its "likes" and "dislikes", which lead us into situations that jeopardize our health.

Whether we like it or not, if there is anything which is constant with the body, it is change and readjustment. To expect to be "chronically healthy" can not be realistic; it is an ideal, and ideals are resistance to what is. As with anything else in life, illness can be the abode of present awareness.

If all things change—as they do—then all things are the same. Anything which is involved in the movement of change— including the mind—can come to a rest, to stillness. And anything which has come to a stop, is free to move in a new direction.

It is time for us now to outgrow the notion that to head in one direction (or its opposite) is the only alternative. A person has not only the prerogative of voting Yes or No, but also of abstaining. Choosing no direction can, for most of us, be a new direction.

Few of us have even considered that giving up all of our ideas can make all the difference in the world. To give up our ideas is to give up our ideals; such as finding contentment, or perfect health, or a painless and peaceful death.

It means abandoning the search for techniques, for deliverance from what is.

To *expect* is to await; what is there to be awaited, when everything is undergoing constant change? Who is there to await it, when there is not even a self which can be taken for granted?

Abandon what you think of as your identity, and that which you identify with. Consider that there is no "person I was", no "person I will be", and no "person I am now". There is nothing which was yours to start with, and so it ought to be clear that you must relinquish everything which you *think* of as yours. You neither need to want to be, nor to want not to be.

If you are to do the important things first in life, the first important thing is to discover if anything *is* important. This discovery will predicate a departure in your present mode of living. It will mean the cessation of your protection of the routines of security.

Free your self. Perception is an immediate response, and response is what is. Through perception, the self will vanish—as it appeared—like ice on the pond.

The meaning of *nirvana:* "dying out", extinction.

That the truth of our existence is that (despite appearances) "there are not two things" is a difficult realization to transmit. Therefore, teachings of nonduality have taken various approaches. In advaita, the emphasis is perhaps the most direct: you and the Absolute (all That is)—generally referred to as the Self—have never been two different things, and can in no way be apart.

In Dzochen (the "zen" of Tibetan Buddhism), the emphasis is more indirect but, in some ways, more ascertainable to the enquirer. Everyone is familiar with the phenomenon we refer to as thought; after all, it is by the locution of thought that we conclude that there is a me, on the one hand; and the Absolute, on the other.

Likewise, it seems to be a universal experience that we conclude that the conscious thought process is a product of our fundamental consciousness, which we *refer* to as the mind.

Dzochen teachings make the point that this fundamental consciousness—which all of we who are conscious experience (and is experienced, though we are not conscious of it, even when we are unconscious)—is our primal, or "true" nature; it is our common essence, the only thing with which we will ultimately identify.

This essence, which is at the root of our animation, is typically referred to as Buddha-mind (or simply Mind, with a capital M), equivalent to the Self of advaita, or the Absolute.

Therefore, thoughts—including the thought that you are a separate being (the "I-thought", Ramana calls it)—are the product of, or are an appearance or phenomenon of, the Buddha-mind.

Thoughts have no substance, the Buddha-mind has no substance; and when it is realized that both are the same, it is recognized that "you" have no actual reality. Nor does the Absolute. Ideas (thoughts in the mind) about both then dissolve; a "union" remains, which had always already existed. Only by attaching significance to thought could the proposition of the separation of "me" and "Buddha-mind" have arisen in the first place.

The discovery is the same as that in advaita: you and the Absolute have never been two different things, and can in no way *be* apart.

The greatest difficulty that teachers of nonduality have is making it clear that there is not some point at which "you" merge or *unify* with "Buddha-mind", but that there has never been a divergence from the start. (Hui Neng's famous line: "If there is nothing from the start, where can the dust alight?")

The dilemma for most seekers of divine awareness is that if their thoughts truly originate in Buddha-mind, then "my thoughts" are not *my* thoughts: "I" am not in control, nor *ultimately* responsible. How, then, am I to fulfill my sense of duty, and perform "good" deeds; if "I am not the doer" (as Ramana points out), what is to prevent this organism from engaging in "bad behavior" or "evil acts"?

The concerns, or values or image, of the I is still preeminent in such considerations. To the extent to which that remains, there can be no "dissolution" of the small self into the infinite Self— even in the sense of realizing that neither exists as an objective entity.

So, much of the teaching points out that where there are "no thoughts" (no thinker [no I] = no thoughts), there are no considerations or judgments concerning "good" and "bad"—or any other of the dualistic polarizations.

There is, in essence, but one thing (if even that), Buddha-mind. *All* that evolves (from your petty thoughts, to a cataclysm in the cosmos) is attributable to the nature of the primordial presence, known in Dzochen as the Buddha-mind. When you are "one" with that, you need ask no questions; omniscience means infinite intelligence.

Hence, much of the teachings are reassurances that one need not worry about the nature of one's behavior, in fully surrendering the I- or ego-thought. *Whatever* one does is Buddha's doing. Or, as Ramana would say, all that *is* (actor and/or its action) is That.

In the mature Dzochen mind, the continual focus of awareness is on the Source of all phenomena, not on the phenomena itself; on the *nature* of Mind, not on the fleeting expressions of that nature.

Looking for What *You* Want

What you suppose that you want is not what you *really* want. What you want is a discovery that will enhance your life. The discovery the sages are pointing to will *end* your life as you know it. It is because you suspect that this is so, that you continue to look for a *different* kind of discovery. When you discover what is being referred to here, the "discoverer" is annihilated. *Life* goes on, without you as you now know yourself to be: but it may not unfold in the way that you would *now* like it to unfold.

An element of this discovery is the surprise that you (the discoverer) were not born. Nor was Buddha born. Jesus was not born. Not Ramana either. As *unlikely* as it seems that you could ever imagine that Buddha, Jesus or Ramana was *not born*, you find it unlikely that it could possibly be that the you that you know so well was never born. That's how life-shattering this discovery can

348

be. The you that you suppose is you does not *want* its life shattered.

And that's okay: you still were never born, even though you prefer to think otherwise.

But since you *were* not born, you have nothing to lose in discovering that self-immolating truth. You have, if only you knew it, no individuated life, to be shattered. Though in the spiritual literature the death of the "individual" is referred to—from the would-be discoverer's point of view—the discovery itself involves the awareness that what has not been born does not die.

What is not born and does not die does not "live a life". The life that you are living now—from that unlikely-seeming standpoint—is not within an actual, meaningful context: that you think you are living a life is a false supposition.

So how could the "discovery" *possibly* enhance your life? All the discovery could do would be to free "you" from "your life". That doesn't sound too appealing to most people. That's why most people continue to suppose that the "me" that they think was born will discover something that will leave their life intact as it is now.

Annihilation doesn't fit the bill.

Dzochen: (the) "Great Perfection"

Dzochen has a particular emphasis: perfection. *Natural* perfection. That is, that all things are already perfectly okay just as they are. (Think about it: they *have* to be, or the universe—and its workings—would be imperfect; and if there is any such thing as an Intelligence in operation, it would then be a flawed

Intelligence. Dzochen masters do not allege that they are in touch with a flawed Buddha-mind, rather a *flawless* nature.)

Therefore, everything that everyone does—from *this* point of view—is inevitably "an expression of a state of complete fulfillment" (as Peter Fenner puts it.)

When one understands, as the Dzochen masters profess to do, that *all* is already perfect as it is ("there is nothing *but* Buddha-mind"), one must—by extension—apply this to one's self. (And, by further extension, to all "other" selves.)

Therefore, one realizes that a person's every activity is "just as it should be".

Recognizing that one's every activity (physical, mental or otherwise) is already just as it should be—in reality, *must* be— why would (an enlightened) one make any concerted effort to try to change anything whatsoever? Hence, Fenner's phrase, "one (consciously reflecting Buddha-nature) doesn't intervene in or meddle with one's [moment-to-moment] experience…"

As a consequence of this surrender of volition (doer-ship), one's behavior "is natural, unaffected, unmanipulated and free from contrivance". We could suppose that someone who met Buddha might describe his demeanor with just such a phrase.

When your viewpoint is that everything is perfectly okay just as it is, and you decline to interfere and meddle in the way things *are* developing, would we describe this *absence* of involvement as a "discipline"? To someone who is essentially "doing nothing", it could hardly be considered a discipline (apart from the root of the word: disciple; in which case, yes, he's a disciple of Buddha). To someone who has no comprehension as to how the Dzochen master has assumed such equanimity, she would probably suppose that awesome discipline was involved!

Fenner points out that "the only discipline in Dzochen" is to *remain* in your *original* condition: that is, the state of your mind before you ever had any conceptual ideas such as "imperfection" as opposed to "perfection". He refers to this as the "natural and *unfabricated* state of bare awareness". *Not created* by discipline.

This is all that any of the Dzochen teachers are asking anyone to do: drop all the ideas about everything. Witness the perfection of Buddha-nature in all that occurs—inwardly or outwardly.

Buddha claims this condition is bliss, peace, perfection.

. . . .

Nondual in Christianity

We all walk this earth as mortals, yet we are all—in our essential nature—that which is eternally omnipresent.

The early Christian Church sought to understand the meaning of Jesus' teaching, "The Father (God) and I are one": Should Jesus be referred to in the context of God, or in the context of man? or both? or neither? To say that "Jesus is God" is not to say that Jesus was also, at the same time, a man. To say that Jesus was a man does not emphasize his simultaneous godliness. To say that Jesus was God-man (or man-God) does not emphasize the person who acts as both, always, at once.

We all, like Jesus, live in the relative world of life and death; we all, like Jesus, are living expressions of the birthless and deathless Absolute.

The Council of Chalcedon (451 A.D.), in its *Definitis Fidei*, resolved the matter by suggesting the nondual nature of this man —who wanted all who heard him to apprehend that "you and the Divine are one, not two". As these prelates put it, Jesus was "made known in two natures (which exist) without confusion, without change, without division, without separation..."

Your nature is no less the nature of Jesus: one with the Absolute, "without division, without separation".

No Exit

You've commented:

> "Although Buddha-nature is ever-present, there are conditions that can obscure it. So even though Buddha-nature (or Buddha-mind) is ever-present, one can lose sight of it (and it happens). To me, this suggests that one can easily fall into duality; and, in fact, it happens. The fact is that people do make distinctions, and so they lose sight of it. Is it 'manifest always and everywhere' to everyone? Is everyone awake to Buddha-nature? What if one does not sense the presence of Buddha-mind...? When we are making distinctions, Buddha-mind is present—but not manifest."

Taking these statements as given, consider:

If something is *ever-present*, it is present *in* the obscurations as well. Being ever-present, it is present *in every* such condition that presents.

One cannot 'lose sight' of that which is never not-present. But, more accurately, that which is ever-present cannot be 'seen' or viewed as any separate or particular thing. That is *why* it *is* the 'obscurations", and any contributing 'conditions' as well. Even if Buddha-nature could be 'lost sight' of, the 'losing sight' of it is a reminder that *this too* is Buddha-nature!

Yes, one can 'easily fall into duality,' as indicated *above*. When you allege that Buddha-nature is ever-present *but* that something can somehow be apart or estranged from it, you have established a dualistic proposition. By the very fact that Buddha-nature is not absent *anywhere*, it is not absent *even* in the deluded mind. It does not fail to be present 'due to unfavorable conditions,' nor is it ever present only in part or by degree. Those who fall into, or out of, duality are falling into or out of the *ever-present*!

So, even if you say that people make such dualistic distinctions and fail to comprehend the full meaning of non-duality, that occurs within the province of the never-not-present.

Tsen Tsang reportedly said it is "manifest always and everywhere". No equivocation, no ifs or buts. No, "However, it's here when..." or "It's not here if we're talking about a deluded person who makes misguided distinctions".

Some can be said to be awake to it; some can be said to not be awake to it. Buddha-mind makes no distinctions: it rains on the deluded and the not-deluded.

One cannot *sense* as *separate* that which is always everywhere. In any case, whether one sensed this presence *or not*, it is present always everywhere—like it or not.

Whether we are making distinctions or making cheese sandwiches, Buddha-mind is present in its entirety everywhere— whether or not we know it or acknowledge it, fret over whether it happens to be present or "fails" to be present. Buddha-mind is relentlessly impartial to our concerns, or to our lack of them. It does not manifest on the basis of how well one follows each stanza of the Hsin Hsin Ming or the myriad books of the Dalai Lama. It was here first, and therefore has taken up all the space that anything else occupies. Anyone who's unsatisfied with it can move somewhere else. (But it will be *there* too.)

Inherent Buddha-nature has never been damaged or corrupted by *sin* or *error*; its nature remains the same whether we are an enlightened Buddha or an ignorant, sentient being, says John Mydhin Reynolds (with the approval of Namkhi Norbu).

Whose "Will to Live" or...?

(An exploration does not necessarily lead to a discovery. Consider this an exploration.)

In the spiritual literature, there are enough corroborative accounts that one need not personally experience the consequence of deep meditation in order to garner a sense of the condition that pertains. The general and universal description of the deepest state of meditation is one in which the awareness of one's body disappears; the awareness of mind and thought disappear; the awareness of the individual's *being* disappears; and simply pure awareness remains—without subject or object, without an awareness of being aware. However long this empty, "cosmic" condition might persist, it eventually ends (according to those who, once roused, report on it) with the awareness that one has experienced a timeless, center-less immersion in that eternal presence commonly referred to as the Absolute.

Yogis who for centuries have cultivated dissociative processes to access this condition (as a means of authenticating the truth of this spiritual actuality) say that this transcendental, impersonal consciousness—which is not conscious of any thing in particular —is our most basic, underlying life force.

In recent centuries, awareness *as* this universal presence has been reportedly accessed by other than *meditative* means (for temporal periods lasting approximately as long—or short, depending on your valuation); particularly through the ingestion of psychoactive drugs.

In this "mindless" condition, one could not function indefinitely in the material, relative environment. A veil evidently obscures this transcendent condition from our normative, interactive, person-al consciousness for most of our generative moments throughout the days, as a natural provision.

Yogis say that it is this condition which prevails when the eyes are closed, with the body in restful relaxation and the physiology submerged in the deepest level of sleep—a complete, subjective unawareness of the unlimited awareness that is present.

The only thing which evidently distinguishes this death-like, unconscious torpor from the physiological state which we pronounce to be death is the automatic, involuntary continuation of pulsation and respiration.

All life forms seem to have a predilection for self-preservation (self, in this sense, meaning bodily: the organism or physical entity). From the standpoint of an intelligent nature, if each life form did not have an inclination toward self-perpetuation, forms might tend to endure for such brief periods that they would not mature sufficiently for progenitive replication. After a robust period of vitality, which peaks beyond the reproductive phase, organisms weaken, become more susceptible to predatory forces, and eventually surrender the self-sustaining life impulse.

But until circumstances are naturally ripe for the senescence and dissolution of each form, animative energy persists as an essential element.

That this preference for the continuation of purposive existence is self-sustaining can be concluded from a particular phenomenon. From the death-like, identityless state of deep sleep, awareness of our body, mind and persona return routinely. From the cosmic, limitless expansiveness of drug- or meditation-induced egolessness our consciousness eventually resettles in the functional, individuated mind.

Even accounts of those who declare near-death experiences often report than an intuitive awareness informed their disembodied presence that consciousness is not yet resolved to relinquish its bodily identity.

But, presumably, for those for whom the death experience is nearer than near, the intuitive resolution is otherwise: bodily functions cease and the unconscious, timeless, unitive state continues undiminished.

That the veil between personified awareness and impersonal awareness is tenuous is attested by eyewitness descriptions, over the years, of life surrender by Buddhist monks (in particular, since they have given this occurrence a generic name: powa).

Usually (though not always) at an elderly age, a monk announces that on a given day hence, he will vacate this life. While sitting (or, in some reputed cases, while standing), he will lapse into deep meditation. The only visible indication of death will be when respiration ends and the body slumps (or, in the case of standing, falls). To outward appearances, there is no difference in this death and that of a person who dies in sleep, or of a narcotic overdose, or on an operating table.

Of interest (in this connection) scientifically is the recent conjecture by quantum physicists that there are operative elements in the brain (as disclosed by neuroscience research) which are so minute that they likely function at the quantum level.

A reason that this is of particular interest is that a principle of quantum physics is referred to as "wave function collapse". This principle has been demonstrated in scientific experiments. Basically, the principle is that events, at the subatomic level, exist as a multitude of potential possibilities until—evidently—acted upon by consciousness. Physicists characterize the catalytic interaction as "observation", or "measurement".

For a simplified example, if a physicist sets up an experiment to measure (thus observe) subatomic elements as particles, they will present (appear in measurements, or observation) as particles. If she sets up her experiment to measure such elements as waves, they will present in wave form.

Is it wave function collapse—live/die—which is the operative principle in whether consciousness returns to bodily form after absorption into the cosmic realm? Why—in deep sleep, entranced meditation, narcotic torpor or anesthetic suspension— does consciousness resume in some personas and not in others? And if it is wave function collapse, who or what is the catalyst?

If there is no subject in the vacuum of Absolute awareness, whence then the catalyst for wave function collapse?

Being in our true nature the Absolute, do we have the capacity (potentiality) to determine when consciousness necessarily returns to bodily form—from deep sleep, narcosis, severe illness? Is a form of wave function collapse (*of* consciousness, *by* consciousness) occurring in the brain, nightly or while in meditation or when in chemically-induced unconsciousness— directed by the cause of all effects and the effect of all causes, the Absolute (which you are)?

Do we carry "within ourselves" the determination of life/death (as intelligent, expedient, occurrences) at every moment?

Neti, Neti: Not "I", not "God"

There are a couple of obstacles to employing the Bible as a vehicle for spiritual wisdom.

1. Virtually any statement found in the Bible will be contradicted by some other passage in the Bible (similar to the Koran): thus the saying, "Even the Devil quotes the scriptures."

2. More importantly, biblical writers (unlike those of the Vedas) were not non-dualists: why look to dualistic literature for a comprehension of the Absolute?

If you are going to peruse the New Testament; you need to be aware of the unreliability of what is reported there. Read *Misquoting Jesus* by Bart Ehrman, and *Beyond Belief* by Elaine Pagels—at least. (I also have some audio tapes available to you on this subject.)

Regarding your last question: every sage says that subject/object perception is a barrier to enlightenment. Where a subject is perceived as an entity and an object is perceived as an additional entity, dualism (two-ness) is present. For example, "I" is the subject in the thought "I seek God." "God" is the object which the I is seeking: this presumes that I and God are two separate, or different, entities.

Enlightenment is, simply, the ending of the dualistic perception. This means the recognition that I and God are so *inter*dependent as to be *inseparable*—one existence. Thus the saying, "The observer (that which is looking for the essence of God) is the observed (the essence of God which is being looked for)": both (subject and object) are the same thing, despite the *appearance* of distinctiveness.

When "I" and "God" are recognized to be the same, one thing, the "seeking" part has clearly ended. What remains is not even "*I* am *God*"; no "I" persists as an entity apart, and no "God" exists as an entity apart (no subject *or* object)—all that pertains is just "am": *immediately present*.

(You would be better served spending your time in *contemplation* of what is said here, than *reading* the Bible.)

The Essential Principle

It is not uncommon to imagine this Essence as something that is within us—but we are, as thoroughly, in it.

Since it is not contained by anything (being infinite, or omnipresent), it must be understood to have no locus: it is *nowhere*. But though not contained *in* anything, there is no place, or point, at which it is not—since it is not confined to location.

Yet it isn't that this Essence is merely transcendent: it transcends transcendence, in that it is imminently ever-present. All this may make it sound sterile or abstract; but substitute the word *love* for *essence*, if you prefer.

Not having a center from which it is constrained to act, it manifests in all places at all times. Its nature being emptiness, *all* things emanate freely from it, and return to it. And yet there is no separate space from which things come, nor destination to which they go.

Being empty, it is always undiminished. Since it cannot be diminished, it can be said to be ever full, or bountiful, or superabundant. Yet the fullness/emptiness is without containment; that is *how* it is in all things, while all things are generated in it.

Putting it another way, it has been said: "From the principle of a mathematical series, we can generate numbers indefinitely. But the principle does not *need* to generate any of these numbers—although it contains them implicitly....The mathematical principle does not *cause* the instances that illustrate it....It would not have cared if they had not come into being."

The point is that the mathematical principle could be said to be saturated or abundant with possibilities; and the consequence of its abundance is that abundance is possible—whether it is manifest or unmanifest; and whatever is manifest is not different from—or apart from—the nonactive principle, or the essence.

The essence is ultimate emptiness, and that is "your" essence.

Mind is Buddha

One of the teachings you sent is true, one of the teachings is false. I trust that you can tell which is which.

The unsigned thesis states,

> "...only after years of arduous training...badgering the brain until it tires of seeking answers to questions...this ultimately...permits 'instant' awareness of the world... by the emptied mind": the writer adds, "but not in all disciples", and goes on to refer to "those who succeed".

Can one hold to an objective of succeeding through years of arduous training, without establishing the fear of being one of the disciples who fails? Is the concept of success versus failure not a dualistic distinction or comparison? Is one not choosing, or opting for, 'success' over 'failure'? How is the mind to be emptied, while it tirelessly seeks answers to questions? Is not badgering the brain an activity enforced by the mind? What awareness of the *world* could a completely emptied mind have?

Continuing:

> "How do you empty your mind? One road is through...
> understanding that you must cease thinking.... Then
> you may experience enlightenment...(where) all
> perceptions are received...without comparison,
> without censoring..."

If there is one road to emptying the mind, is there *more* than one road? How is the *mind* to choose which road insures its *absence*? Can the thinking mind dictate the cessation of thought? Can the mind maintain a preference for no-thought, as opposed to thought, while avoiding comparison or censoring? What, or who, is it that understands that one must 'do this,' or must 'not do that'; that maintains the desire or preference for *one* condition over *another*?

Further:

> "This mind is simply a passive brain...uncritical,
> receiving all perceptions...without recording any...you
> do not label anything, you do not discriminate or
> censor...you internalize one world directly."

Sounds ideal. Does the mind that does not label anything know itself as a mind? Does it refer to *itself* as a passive brain? Is it the *mind* that no longer records, or is it the *brain*? Can the *empty* mind even discriminate between these two? Does it care? To the emptied mind, is there a 'you' or a 'world'; 'internal' or 'external'?

And:

"...once you have achieved passive, choiceless awareness ...you will know...how to enter the state...without memory of that experiencing."

Where there is *choiceless* awareness, are there preferable states which one hopes to enter? Is there a 'you' to have an 'experience' that is not remembered? Does an emptied mind, with thoughts ceased, entertain ideas of achievement/non-achievement?

The clue to inconsistent teachings is that they are grounded in dualistic distinctions which cause them to be inherently contradictory.

In the other article, Masao Abe (*Fundamentals of Zen*) quotes Daito Roshi, regarding Buddhahood (as a synonym for enlightenment): "He neither practices 'good' nor commits 'evil'": indiscriminately choiceless. "He has no attachment to his mind." Whether 'thinking' or 'ceasing to think,' he could care less; he is not intent on achieving some ideal, concerning must/must not.

Pu-Yuan is quoted for the reasoning: "*ordinary* mind is Tao". Does one need to *try* to *attain* choiceless awareness? "If you try to direct yourself toward it, you go away from it." Effort is *ineffectual*.

The 'enlightened mind' is embodied in this present moment. It is a *confused* mind which *hopes* for 'emptiness' in some *future* moment. As Masao Abe points out, there is no enlightenment that is *apart* from "the absolute present". Wherever there is separation, division, duality, there is confusion—*not* an 'emptied mind'. An emptied mind permits of no subject nor object: "freed from all kinds of duality, including dualities of self and other, self and the world, one and many, time and space, being and non-being". Empty or not empty. Thought or no thought.

Abe: "The realization of no-thingness, and no self, is essential..."

"The valley stream"—*mindless*—"is preaching the Dharma." It is not concerning itself with some supposed mind that has 'ceased thinking'.

Where There's Smoke

Alcoholism. Assassination. Bigotry. Censorship. Corruption. Crime. Crowding. Disease. Exploitation. Famine.

Greed. Homelessness. Narcotics. Nationalism. Overpopulation. Pollution. Poverty. Racism. Recession. Rioting. Smog. Starvation.

Terrorism. Tyranny. Unemployment. Urbanization. Violence. War.

Is man's house on fire?

Letting in the Light

I'm pleased that since your awakening you have done very little but to contemplate; to, as you said, let it all sink in (or out).

As you indicated, the realization deepens of its own accord ("Self deepens"), like something that submerges in the depths as each (air) bubble is released.

The energy which is freed with the release of self concern will find its appropriate channel, or outlet.

First the fermentation. I can see, by what you say, that each day is bringing a more greatly expanded view.

The less stirring, the less distraction, the better. Ramana soaked up illumination for several years, after his enlightenment. When duality ends, the whole of existence is re-viewed, and one's own *reality* as that whole. *Then*, from that wholeness, one moves and acts.

It's good that you are uncovering these things on your own, without dependence on an "other".

Your True Identity

That which is purely the essence of all things is sometimes spoken of as "unitary consciousness", Mind, Brahman, cosmic intelligence, etc. And it is sometimes said that "out" of this essence, this one actuality, all other things are manifested.

But it must be clearly recognized that this essence is not something which has a center somewhere. And so, when it is said that plurality "manifests" from singularity, this is not to say that something is "coming out of " something else (as in childbirth). There is not a One standing apart in readiness to impart the Many.

The One is infinite, omnipresent: it has already always been all that is. And in its infinity, it is "outside" the pale of time; knowing nothing of duration or sequence—nay, only simultaneity—it is not the predecessor of any other thing. To *manifest* means to "make evident", to express, not to manufacture. And, in this case, that which expresses is itself expressed by the expression. That which is giving birth, to put it another way, is itself always at the same moment being born; neither womb nor fruit is more fundamental or preliminary than the other.

A nagging idea—which even the most ardent of the religious thinkers have difficulty surpassing—is that the Absolute "existed" before (and, in that way, apart from) us, and that out of this pre-existing condition we were "created" or "manifested".

Even if we were to take as a provisional *composite* that essence which is present in every iota of matter and energy, and at every point of form or void, it would form a singular, whole connection —the only *denominator* of all things.   As the basic, common identity of all things—the Hindus would call this Brahman—if we were to ask what any particular "thing" is, primarily, we would have to answer that it is primarily Brahman. (Or whatever name we choose to give it.) Principally, we would have to say that—at the "bottom line"—it is the *only* thing which does actually *wholly* exist.

In other words, it can be said that essentially all things (the Many) are this essence (the One). That which truly *is*—whether we speak generally *or* specifically—is Essence.

That means that you are It, I am It, all things are It. Therefore, in this context, there is not any "thing" which is *apart from* any other "thing": all things are It. (Brahman, Mind, Essence, ad infinitum.)

And this is the point which many have failed to grasp. *Being all things*, it has no separate or particular identity *of its own*. It occupies no special place or center, it exists in no particular sequence or duration, it has nor holds not anything to itself. In short, it *has* no self. And in fact, in this sense, it can be said to be Void, Nothing or Empty (and, frequently, is said to be all of these).

When this aspect of the Absolute can be comprehended, a startling discovery can unfold. This, which has no identity of its own, in a peculiar way does *not exist*: this Absolute, in other words, has no choice but to eternally be unknown to itself. Put another way, if all things are Brahman, there is not anything outside of that condition which can recognize that there *is*

Brahman. Brahman, we could say, does not exist, unless some aspect or entity of Brahman manifests its existence.

Is that where *you* appear? Your capacity to recognize Intelligence *is* this Intelligence in re-cognition of itself. The Absolute, being all things (including *you*), anything which any aspect of it contemplates is It contemplating Itself. Put differently, it is only through your unitary consciousness that the One can be conscious: even when you are merely conscious of yourself, you are conscious of "more than" yourself. Though you may not be *aware* of it (although you *can* be), you are always supremely, wholly conscious. *You* are consciousness *itself*, to the extent that there is any consciousness in existence in the cosmos.

As Shankara says, It is not the "object" of anything "but its own self".

. . . .

Floor-painting Experience

Half way through a lifetime of trying to improve ourselves, some of us notice that we are painting ourselves into a corner. It is a task which can never be satisfactorily completed. We find that our ego (or idea we cling to of who we are) is planted squarely in the middle of the remaining portion that would be eradicated

The question is, can I (the ego) acknowledge this, and gracefully leave the scene even if it means tarnishing the lustre of my colorful reputation which is still drying?

Zen tried to warn us that the floor never needed painting from the start. Now that we're in a corner, we begin to realize the wisdom of inaction. Some would call this "insight"—and *continue* painting until their ignor-ance forced choice upon them. But some few will realize the nature of what they have realized, and will surrender, will let go of their compulsion to emerge with an intact ego and an ideal outcome.

The sooner we awaken to the true situation, and surrender to it, the less "touching up" we will be in a position to do.

This is Freedom

Wayne Liquorman (now an advaita teacher) was dependent on alcohol and drugs when he met Ramesh Balsekar. Complaining about his sorry condition to Ramesh, the latter said, "It took that to bring you here!"

Your many years of incessant seeking have broken the ground to permit a shoot to spring forth.

Any time that we are desperately in search of anything, anxiety will be companion. When the search has ended, there is inevitably a release. You are evidently noticing this, in the extra 3-4 hours of sleep that you are getting.

Aside from a relief of unconscious tension, there is usually a noticeable quieting of mentation—without any effort for such. Many erroneous ideas are involved in the quest for enlightenment (I know from experience); when the truth is experienced, these ideas evaporate like dew.

Both the physical and psychic relaxation result in a generation of released energy and contemplative space. As if the development of a laser, these can now be used to focus on present awareness.

As this awareness deepens, you will recognize that it only tangentially has anything to do with what is going on in the body or psyche. For there to be concern (positive *or* negative) with what is transpiring physically or mentally, there is an "I" which identifies with these particular phenomena. In present awareness, you will merely observe what was (previously) "subjective", objectively. That is, to witness—without having *transferred* a personal (I) identity from the body/psyche to the witness. The witnessing itself is witnessed as (equally) impartial phenomena. *Awareness* is present, and that's all that can be identified.

You spoke of "missing certain aspects of my being". *Being* is not "yours": it's a condition which is present whether there's a sense of self or otherwise. There being no you, not anything is yours. Even present awareness is beyond "your" control. Toward this truth is where the laser of always-present attention, awareness, can be tuned: not a matter of doing something positively, but simply a matter of not doing anything *in particular*; ceasing trying to do. The "zen" of Tibetan Buddhism, Dzochen, focuses almost exclusively on these teachings of "non interference" (in awareness).

This implies not looking for, or expecting, a better or more preferential condition to arise, or result, from awakening. "Why do you want enlightenment?", Ramana asked someone. "You might not like it." A test of awakening is whether even the most subtle conceptions of (such dualities as) "better" or "worse" have been abandoned.

Where there is no better/worse, there is no concern for whether "I" am awakened—or not. Thus, the life-long search collapses in a heap! Attention, awareness, then is focused simply on 'what is'— *however* it is. (And, from the *relative* standpoint, "What a relief!")

Finally: yes, you will notice that this transition does not leave you (from the standpoint of the witness) a "normal person". An enlightened person once remarked on "pretending to be normal". But that does not mean that anyone will necessarily be aware of your realization: in Buddhism, they speak of the taint ("smell") of enlightenment (as a sign of unfinished enlightenment). People often remarked on how "common" Suzuki Roshi seemed.

At this point, it could be wise to put the books aside. This must be *your* realization, not second-hand from others. The time could best be spent in mere present awareness. This is what is meant in Buddhism by shikan-taza: "Sitting quietly, doing nothing." Quietude, or so-called inner silence: *attending*, without an *intention* to attend. This is freedom, freedom from the "known".

. . . .

The Sole Revolution

From the relative (worldly) point of view:

The word *society*, at its Latin root, means "companion"; any society, of which we speak, is a collective group of *people*. We could say that as soon as two people interact, their society has its beginning. But we could also say society had its beginning even before their interaction—because of what each person brought to the interaction. In other words, where two (or more) people are gathered whose predisposition is hostile, for instance, we will likely have a hostile society.

So society is dependent upon each individual; so much so, that where there are not individuals, there is not society. In this sense, I "am" society—or, at least, have a full share of responsibility for it. And you, too, are society—and have a full share of responsibility for it.

Therefore, society can (realistically) be expected to change only to the extent that I can be expected to change. Put another way, change in society *begins* with me. Conversely, where there has been no radical change in me, there has been no radical change in society.

Generally speaking, changes in an individual can be from forces within or from forces without. That is, one might be inspired or self-motivated to make a change; or one might be coerced or outwardly constrained to make a change. In the former instance, it is usually because of a conviction that this is the proper or correct thing to do; in the latter case, it is usually because it is the presently expedient or temporarily acceptable thing to do. In other words, we believe in the rightfulness of our self-motivated changes; but this is not often the case with changes that are imposed upon us from outside forces.

Therefore, we will tend to implement and to sustain those changes we personally endorse or accept; but we will not typically propagate or perpetuate those ideals or propositions of which we are not inwardly persuaded. And, thus, we have those for whom no law is needed, and those who are lawless despite the societal consequences.

So societal change is not only dependent upon *your* change, but upon *inward* change as opposed to outward pressure. Only the former is real change, because it will be sustained even when it appears *not* to be expedient.

A truly changed society will be a society of changed individuals; truly changed, inwardly changed.

When we realize this, we end our external speculation as to how the society might function if *others* were to change. We focus all of our attention on our individual *internal* change—so that what we personally bring to society is of a radical *departure*.

This, without even intending to do so, sets an example for the inward revolution of other individuals, for the only hope for change that there (realistically) is.

Once we have personally ceased to externalize societal "problems", and have taken full responsibility for our own contribution, we are *then* in a tenable position to discuss this dynamic with others. But all such discussions are didactic: they can only be meaningful to the extent that they are an *explanation* of what we *ourselves* are already *doing*.

It is the example, that we bring to society, that has the greatest potential to change society—not what we enunciate or propose. For instance, it might merely be the example of not attempting to coerce others; or of not tending to externalize an "improved behavior" on an abstract "society"; or it could be a commitment to resolve social malfunctioning at its source—in one's *own* behavior.

When we observe how difficult it is to truly make change within ourselves, we have a more realistic attitude about effecting even outward changes in others. This can generate compassion, or at least an objective detachment.

Only out of such a radical inward revolution can outward action be taken with purity, or "righteousness", or clarity.

Clarifying the Natural State

In Dzochen discourses, lamas speak of the mind in its "natural state". This is referred to by various names (by different teachers), such as rigpa.

Rigpa is the condition which exists untainted by conceptual thought. One can argue that all thought is conceptual, inasmuch as thoughts are normally recognized in the form of words which have meaning to the thinker (we do not think in a "foreign" language, unless the "words" in that language express definitive meaning). It has also been posited that *every* word is expressive of a concept; each is symbolic of an idea, thought or notion, which is the meaning of the word "concept": a conviction, opinion or image that forms in the mind. Clearly, the only thing which is not a concept is that of which the mind cannot conceive ("give birth"). Even for that which we cannot fully conceive, we have designated a *word* (concept) for that which we cannot fully conceive ("non conceptual").

The condition of rigpa is not dependent upon any of these words: anything which we can refer to—conceptual or nonconceptual— is "beside the point", as far as rigpa (the "natural" state of mind) is concerned. We cannot even describe rigpa, because it is a condition antecedent to words. Words have a relationship to each other as a consequence of the individual (or class of) things which they describe; this is what establishes each its meaning, "significance". Every word, and each thing it describes, is relative —comparatively dependent upon some other thing. It is this realm of separative identifications that is referred to as "duality", or (in terms of the process involved) "dualistic thinking". The classic example, of course, is the word "I", which by definition separates the speaker and the spoken to.

The condition spoken of as rigpa is "prior to", or free of, duality. Rigpa is not something which we conceive: it is not created by thought. It is the unmoving field, as it were, in which the movement of thought (arising, dissolving) appears. Even the designation "rigpa" is merely a reference to that which thought cannot conceive (cause to give life). Rigpa is not influenced, in one way or another, by thought.

While it might be possible to be without thought (for whatever interval of time), it is not possible for a conscious (or even unconscious) person, say Dzochen teachers, to be without rigpa. It is our "natural" state (L.: "by birth; existing by nature; uncultivated"). One may or may not be cognizantly aware that this is so: the teachers consider it their duty to assist each student to *be* aware of his or her "true nature".

Were it not for the field or ground (fundament) from which thoughts are free to arise, we would be incapable of the comparative (relative) thought which makes possible our form ("intelligent") of life. Whatever purpose an ocean wave serves to nature, it would not be provided were it not for the ocean. Clearly, the wave is in no way apart from the ocean; the wave is merely a manifestation or "activity" of the ocean. It is neither superior nor inferior to the ocean. Only through language can the two even be separated conceptually. That which we call a "wave" is water; that which we call an "ocean" is water. (Even "water" is just another term for parsing the unity of the cosmos.)

Thought and rigpa are not different (mutually exclusive) "things", except to the extent that we have artificially and arbitrarily designated them so. In fact, from the non-discriminatory standpoint of rigpa, there is no such independent reality as "thought": it has no more reality than the word "poof" points to anything identifiable.

That is, not the case, of course, from the standpoint of the relative. In that context, we speak of (ephemeral) "thought" as "different" from (inconceivable) "rigpa".

The teachers urge you to see through this artificial divisiveness, and to recognize that whatever thought you have is an expression (manifestation) of the "natural" mind. Since the natural mind is perfect as it is, you need not bedevil yourself about its expressions.

When that kind of anxious, divisive, polarizing habit or pattern of thought subsides, through allowing every manner of thought to arise and depart *unhindered*, what then remains?

The End of "Reconciliation"

These are excerpts from a letter, in which the writer—who took the phrase "all that is, is That" as his meditative "mantra"—for the first time referred to himself as That; and "God" as That; and the person he was addressing as That: finally recognizing the truth of the omnipresence of the Absolute actuality! Bracketed interpolations are mine.

There's a "shift" taking place.... All of the concern about "reconciliation" [guilt for his "sins"] *seemed to have went south....*

"That's" [his] *activity has been immense these last few days.... "It" was meditating and...got up to open the window and let air into That's cell. Don* [he, objectively] *noticed that things were not as they seemed when he had last pondered them* [as a "seeker"].

Everything was suddenly "finished"...I have no need to [harmonize] *with "what" (That) I have never been separated from. That* [he] *even understood how to write That* [the addressed] *about That* [Absolute awareness]...*I am sure That* [the addressed] *knows that That* [he] *can't really explain what That* [Self/self] *seems to be experiencing here, but it is all coming together in one place, at one time, for "all time" (Eternity). That thinks "it" finally gets it!...*

Your [last letter] *"confirmed"...the "big change".... You are used to dealing with those on the upper slope of the mountain* [but reached one] *below the timber line.... It seems to me that I have had no interest but* [seeking] *THAT "place" for longer than my* [12 year] *incarceration....*

From everything that I seem to now understand, [the anguish which prompted self-realization] *was a "necessary" distraction—and even up to this point where I thought I needed "reconciliation"....*

It's pointless to try and explain it to anyone. I understand perfectly, so there is no need to. How can they understand what it has taken me over 30 years to even scratch the surface of [the] *insight that ushered in this spiritual awakening?...*

Things sure have changed "materially" from when our communication first began!

Death: Where To From Here?

The Ganges loses its identity in the ocean. It no longer can take its previous form.

But even in the form of a river, its fundamental nature—water—was the same nature as that of the ocean.

Our individual consciousness is inseparable from universal, or cosmic, consciousness. Reverting to its non-individuated form, there could be no residue of distinctiveness to re-emerge again in its previous unique form.

The Absolute—being all that is, and nowhere that its not—does not move from place to place: there is nowhere it could go that its not already present. There is not a reservoir in a perimeter somewhere to which our essential consciousness retires, awaiting future recall. The Absolute presence which is unbroken is without distinguishable parts; form-less. Nor, being ever-present, does it appear sequentially.

Though it manifests as the myriad impermanent forms, it is not merely *within* each form but *without* each form. Its transcendent form is in connection with all that is in its immanent form, an unbounded whole—*in* which all things exist and it exists in (or as) all things.

Although 'your' consciousness may regain its transcendent form, free of any consideration of separateness, no essential change or movement will occur. Change and movement are determinations in the form we call the mind. Your true essence is the formless. Unlike the cognitive mind, you are unlimited.

To One Who Understands

Once nondual awareness is present, one finds that one no longer has the same motivation to read advaita (or "spiritual") texts. Before, one was a "seeker" (subject) in quest of the Absolute (as object); the texts have said all along that seeking is fruitless, because what is sought turns out to be the seeker itself. So once it becomes clear that, verily, the seeker *is* the Absolute/the Absolute is the seeker, there is no further need for reading the instructive texts.

But one may discover a new motivation in reading (or re-reading) such texts. Firstly, they will now be appreciated and comprehended in a new light: what before had seemed puzzling or paradoxical is now meaningfully understood. ("Of course: 'the observer *is* the observed'!")

Secondly, there may arise at some time the inclination to communicate to others the nature of one's (personal) realization; as they say in Buddhism, "the mind-to-mind transmission of the dharma". Toward this end, it can be instructive to read (or re-

read) the texts to observe how others have communicated the substance of the message (e.g., Buddha's "Four Noble Truths").

In terms of both impulses, few sources are more direct in summarizing the essence of non-duality than Ramana. And, though not often as succinct, Nisargadatta too is a clear exponent. Reading pertinent excerpts of the teachings of these two adepts will permit the reader to notice any areas of residual unclarity. If there are any comments made by these teachers which are unclear, these are subjects for deeper contemplation.

There are also some good sources for reflection from the Zen tradition. There are many translations of the Hsin Hsin Ming; a careful, contemplative reading, of one or more, can be very helpful.

The Zen Ox Herding Pictures are also instructive, in that they refer to the real-izing process from pre-enlightenment to post-enlightenment. There are still other materials that can be of benefit (though *none* of these are *necessary*), even after such materials as these have been assimilated.

But it is important—as it was initially—to read these materials slowly enough to comprehend the implications, and to clarify the contents in one's own awareness so that no further *reliance* on the *sage's* insights is necessary: that's what en-lighten-ment is all about!

So, post-awakening is the time to read those teachings which are best understood by one who under-stands.

"What you are saying seems similar to Zen or Tao," you remarked. And you ask, "When one arrives at the central core of the teaching, is it 'love' then to teach it to others?"

There are several elements here which you might look at more closely.

The idea that there is some fixed body of doctrine which comprises a "teaching'" is to suppose that there is vital information, somewhere, which is separate from the "individual" who is "taught"; it, similarly, implies that there is a meaningful teaching, or lesson, apart from the presence of the "teacher".

When we ask ourselves why, say, Buddha or Jesus said some of the things they said, is it possible that they were explaining to those around them the nature or basis of their noticeably unusual actions—rather than intentionally "teaching" moral or spiritual lessons?

Were you to *awaken* someone, would you be teaching them anything? Can you guide another to a place which neither of you has ever left?

Even if there were a teaching which had a definable central core, does one who is constantly attentive to learning ever "arrive" at any such place? To arrive anywhere implies that the journey is finished. Are you embarked on a journey which envisages a future destination; are you seeking to identify the core of the apple, or are you consuming the apple bite by bite, moment by moment?

Were you to have the core of the teaching in the palm of your hand, what could it be *compared* to—another intellectual doctrine? And if so, how would it essentially be different?

When you have left preconceptions where they originated—in the past—what is it of Zen or the Tao which you are employing to measure your observations in this moment? For knowledge, we need to make comparisons; when you perceive truth, it compares to nothing.

Whether or not there is a teaching to be understood, is love something which originates in and proceeds from that place which some might "attain" and some might not? Does one "understand" love, and *then* love; in what way could love and awareness be apart from each other?

Love is the expression of who and what you truly are in this eternal moment—and you are nothing, except perhaps a living organism which is itself constantly learning. You are not even particularly unique in your openness to learning, and so you observe that you have a common ground with all living consciousness. When you are aware of this, others are aware of it. What is there about it that could be taught?

What Price Freedom?

Buddha considered that there were two possessions which he personally owned. If you were to take something away from Buddha, it would have to be either his robes or his begging bowl.

Jesus, too, was homeless. He reportedly carried not even a begging bowl, and possessed only his robes and sandals.

Ramana Maharshi had but one item that was acknowledged as his own: a loincloth.

Krishnamurti considered only one item to belong to him: a wristwatch, given to him as a gift, which he wore.

All four of these sages were adopted by those whom they met and communicated to, and they drew these supportive acquaintances into a community. They each urged their audience of acquaintances to, like themselves, relinquish all attachment; to be free of temporal concern and calculative fear.

In regard to personal security, they were heedless and impractical. None asked for more than what was willingly offered—and in exchange they gave of their time and attention unsparingly. None considered that they were lacking anything, or needed to await something before proceeding.

. . . .

True (troo), adj.: As It Is

You wrote:

> "My feeling, which may not be correct, is that if I am caught up in deluded thinking, it would be a mistake to equate that with my true nature."

You *are* caught up in deluded thinking:

It is "deluded thinking" to deduce that there are "deluded" thoughts.

Your true nature cannot be *equated* with anything. It is whatever it is, in any moment. If delusive thoughts are *present*, that *is* your true nature—actual, in this very moment. Your *true* nature is not something which will come or will go: it is your present condition at *any* and *every* instant—deluded or enlightened!

"It would be a mistake to equate" an ice cube with water. It *is* water—was and will be. Water is an ice cube's (whether clear or cloudy) fundamental condition, its *true nature*.

Your deluded thinking is self-delusion. There is no self apart from delusion. There is no self apart from its true nature. Your separative thinking—"I"..."deluded thinking"..."true nature"—is the creator of the subject "I" that describes the object-ionable "thinking".

Bankei: "Abide in the unborn Buddha mind *just as it is*." Just. As. It. Is. (Or "You'll never have a moment's peace!")

It's your true nature (unborn Buddha mind) that is the source of *all* thoughts you think. Abide ("reside; go on being") therein; delusion dis-appears.

Surrender of the Ego

It is dissatisfaction with one's ego-centered life, generally speaking, which leads one to inquire into the spiritual teachings. After having experienced the conflicts, tensions and strife resulting from the convention of self-centered orientation, one may read or hear of the condition commonly referred to as "awakening", "realization" or "enlightenment". Typically described as an "egoless" condition or a "state of oneness", it is attractive by virtue of being contradictory to one's current condition. Thus one may be motivated to direct one's attention toward the possibility of enlightenment.

At some point after this direction has been initiated—and the earlier, the better—it is imperative that the seeker come to a crucial confrontation with himself. Simply stated, if he honestly examines his motivation for seeking a profound change in consciousness, he might discover that he is interested primarily in improving, or alleviating, his personal condition of suffering: in other words, his real concern is the state of "number one", rather than the "state of oneness". The change of condition which he *fundamentally* seeks is a change which puts in order the life around him but which leaves his *ego* intact.

Spirituality, succinctly described, is the *surrender* of the ego. To expect to be "whole" while remaining *apart* is delusory.

The Mystery Revealed

Enlightenment is a matter of perspective. If you are lost on snowy peaks, the world is white. If you are lost in the jungle foothills, the world is green. But viewing the landscape from a remote location, the white and the green are not sensed as separate worlds.

The shift in enlightened perspective is like that. The familiar perspective of the subject apprehending an object is eclipsed by an unfamiliar perspective in which both subject and object evaporate as discrete entities.

It is a development in the subjective mind which provides the discriminative perspective; and the shift in perspective is a corrective development—as when one physically shifts one's perspective for a clearer view.

Once the shift in perspective has been thoroughly noticed, it is constantly accessible. And whereas previously one had access to only one perspective, one now has access to both, the familiar and the (initially) unfamiliar.

If you were decoding an unfamiliar passage, at first the passage would appear to be an impenetrable mystery. Once you had broken the code, there would be nothing further that you would need to do to decipher any and all related passages.

Once you had deciphered the symbols and thoroughly apprehended the cryptic content, you could have no doubt of your comprehension. It would be clear to you that there was not anything further that you needed to do in order to exercise your understanding. And it would be clear to you that this understanding was not something temporary, but that it was permanently available.

At various times and places, the key or keys to this shift in perspective were regarded as secret. As such, one had to demonstrate a sincere commitment to unraveling the mystery before the presentation of the keys was granted. Today the keys are openly displayed, and their value is not taken seriously. They are not energetically viewed as the precious keys to the kingdom that they are.

Time Depends On "You"

Q. I arise in the morning, bathe, dress and eat breakfast. I sense the continuity of these activities, the change from one event to another: and, to me, that is the experience of the passage of time. How can it be that there is no such actuality as time?

A. To experience the passage of time, one envisions oneself *in* time, as if one were a boulder in the stream. The "you" who is involved in the first activity—arising—is not the same you who engages in the last activity—eating: where there is a you which is engaged in continuity, the you is *itself* continuous; the you which participates in change is itself changing. There is no fixed entity *to whom* change is happening: you are not apart from the change or continuity you perceive. Put another way, there is no you without continuity or change. And so there is no fixed "you" which stands like a boulder and "experiences" the passage of time sweeping past you. Arising, bathing, dressing and eating are not occurring on their own, independent of your participation. You are the time that you perceive, and there is no time apart from you: there is not, in other words, a separate you. When you see this from an obverse perspective, you see that there is no separate reality which can be designated as "time".

If there is a stream in movement and you are the stream and time is *also* the stream, you are *both* the same actuality—there can be no perceivable relationship *between* you.

Q. May I give another example? In the morning, I feel the warmth of the sun. By noon, it is hot. In the evening, it is cool. That, again, is continuous change, which I feel that I am experiencing as the progression of time.

A. At this moment, this day is not "warm" or "hot" or "cool": it is simply whatever it is. If you conclude in the morning that this moment is warm and then you isolate the moment—as a separate moment, apart from this boundless moment—and later *compare* it to another moment which you have isolated, you will conclude that the "morning" was "warm" and the "evening" is "cool". The cooling of the morning to evening represents to you the progression of time. But to the moment —which is always whatever it is, at "all times"—there is no distinguishable point from which to measure "progression" or "regression". There is no change or continuity, to something which is always only simply what it is. Without your imposed conception of time, you are always only simply what *you* are. Without your conception of time, "you" are nothing but change. Being change itself, there is no change which you can designate as apart from yourself and give it the separate identity of "time".

The condition of which the enlightened sages speak—hold on: you're going to resist this—is the condition you are in this very moment, wherever you are and whoever you are.

The only difference between you and the "realized" is that you're expecting—hoping for—something more than what exists for you in this present moment. The only difference is that you do not accept your Buddhahood in its naturally occurring—ever present—state: the condition you exist in this very moment.

In examining your condition this very moment, you will identify some positive aspects and some negative aspects. The presence of the negative aspects is your grounds for conviction that you have not yet discovered the key. It is your supposition that when the key has been found, the negative aspects which you can identify in the present moment will be replaced by *positive* aspects. "A moment ago, I had it: I was sooo peaceful and unperturbed. Now I've lost it: my mind is tumultuous and all I can think of are my petty concerns and irritations!"

When you identify the condition as positive, you desire to remain there. When it revolves to the *negative*—as it definitely will—you prefer to be someplace else. Samsara and Nirvana are *the same*, says Buddha. *Both* are the dharmakaya. The mind *present* in both is the Buddha mind.

That's not the dharmakaya you want. So you continue to look for it elsewhere.

The sages aren't looking, aren't seeking, for anything beyond that which lies in this very moment—which for every sentient being is *alternatively* positive and negative.

This could be said instead:

"A moment ago, I was peaceful and unperturbed. Now my mind is agitated with some petty irritation. The Buddha mind is *all minds*, all conditions. My mind *is* the Buddha mind!"

The (agitating) thought that your mind is *not* the Buddha mind is *also* the Buddha mind. But you won't accept that. You desire a mind which never has a negative thought or doubt. So you pass over this mind which exists in this very moment, preferring to discover a condition of mind which you presume will exist somewhere in the future. Thus the Buddha mind is *not* your present mind.

Why do the awakened exclaim, "It was here all along! I overlooked it!" Because they *were* doing what you *are* doing right now. Overlooking that your present condition—*this very moment*—*is* what it *is*, and will not ever be otherwise no matter how enlightened you get. Buddha stopped comparing what his condition *had* been, or what it *could* be. He contemplatively witnessed what occurred in the moment—positive *and* negative—without any idea that he should be in some other place than he was.

That's where the difference lies.

But you will likely conclude that this is not a positive message, and will continue to look elsewhere.

The Critical Question

On the occasion of receiving a Nobel Prize, some years ago, Mother Teresa was asked, "What would happen if everyone in the world were to do what you do?" She did not attempt to answer such a general question with a rational reply: "Hmmm. Well, I guess I'd be out of a job!"

Questions, such as the above, are often the self's defensive gambit, a form of resistance which poses as reasoning. For example, there are implications in the question which was cited: a) for the first time in human history, a majority of the world's population might find themselves acting in unison, as the result of one person's example: and, b), if they did, might not such a revolutionary imbalance create chaos in the social tradition?

Put into the form of a statement, such a question is often arguing, "I am impressed with your example and would similarly order my life, but there is no guarantee that it would offer a perfect solution to the world's problems."

When we are confronted with a proposition that offers promise of inner peace—but at the cost of the surrender of the sovereign self—the mind immediately responds with, "Yes, *but...*"

The human mind can manufacture justification for *any* form of irrational behavior, at a whim; but when the sanctity of self-image is at stake, the demand for a *rational* explanation is ceaseless.

The mind says, "If you are influenced by another person's example, there is a risk that you will be misled." And the mind is correct, to that extent. What the mind does not admit is that you are continually influenced by others, in every *conventional* aspect of your daily behavior, year in and year out. And *are* misled.

The truth of life—and death—is to be found everywhere, and no one has to be lead to it. Who awaits a leader to blaze the trail is not seriously intent on the journey of truth. The question which pretends to probe is often merely an attempt to delay an *unequivocal* response to truth. There is no guidance to the core of your true self, save for your own.

When his father, finally established in California, sent for his family in the Azores, Manuel was seven years old. Manuel, his three brothers and mother, arrived at Ellis Island, New York, and traveled across the country by steam train ("A lady on the train gave me a piece of a chocolate bar. I spit it out. I thought it must be chewing tobacco."), and by logging train to Fort Bragg. He learned English in school, in Cleone, and eventually went to work in the woods. "We got laid off; the company said they went broke. That was the best thing that ever happened to me. I borrowed $250 and bought a fishing boat."

Shortly after the bay at Pearl Harbor was filled with sunken boats, Manuel was called before the draft board, but was quickly given an exemption. His renown locally as a fisherman was such that one man said, "If we send Manuel away, the army ain't gonna have no fish."

Manuel built a house on the hill overlooking Noyo Harbor, and one across the street for his daughter. He fished until fifteen years ago. Now, a few weeks from his eighty-first birthday, he sits in a recliner chair near the front window—when not weakened with emphysema and lying next to his oxygen tank—and watches the moon rise over the water beyond the jetty.

I asked Manuel what was one of the important lessons he had learned.

"For a while, I owned a boathouse in Sausalito. I fished San Francisco Bay while they were building the Golden Gate Bridge. Lucky I'm still alive!

"Did you know *that* cable weighs one ton per foot? How do you suppose they got that up there? Ain't no force in the world could lift that kind of weight! You know what they did? They raised that cable strand by strand, one strand at a time. You can do a lot, when you do a little bit at a time—but do it day after day. You don't have to try to do anything mighty."

I was reminded of an interview that I had once read about. A polar exploration party had lost all forms of their transportation, and the group surprised the world by walking three hundred freezing miles to the safety of a base camp. The interviewer asked the group's leader: "How on earth did all of you find the courage to walk three hundred miles of the most forbidden terrain in the world?"

"We didn't try," the leader replied. "We worked up the courage to walk one mile, three hundred times."

The root of the word *effort* is "to force". How many of the important things in our lives require great effort, force? When I am trying to lift the cable with a mighty effort, I might be wise to ask myself if there is order in my life: am I neglecting to lift strand by strand, day after day? Am I imagining the hopelessness of a three hundred mile walk, or the possibility of walking one more mile?

Let future "results" take care of themselves: live moment-by-moment.

Unbroken Awareness

The word *realization* means 'to make real,' to reify. The meaning of *real* is 'existing, actual, true.'

What is made real, in Realization, is the abiding awareness of Absolute presence, that all is That (always has been, always will be) and not anything is ultimately apart from, or independent of, it.

Once this awareness, this Real-ization, is established, it does not at some point become *more* real, or *less* real. *True* means 'constant, certain,' not ambiguous or tentative.

It could be compared to a shift in perception, in which a fourth dimension is indelibly visible; while one continues to see three dimensions as had been customary, in this example, a perspective is now recognized which had gone unseen before.

However, this dimension (to continue the example) is the matrix of *all* dimensions. It is the fundament of any other of the dimensions that you see. Therefore, you recognize that any of the customary dimensions you perceive exist within, and dependent upon, the context of this over-all dimension.

But whether or not you focus on this fourth dimension, it remains ever present. Having recognized its existence, it is as persistent in your experience as the three dimensions have constantly been.

This is analogous to the permanent condition of Absolute awareness which is present with the establishment of Realization.

To develop a related metaphor, it is like comprehending that no matter whether the sky is covered in the darkness of midnight or the sunniness of noon, the sun is continually shining without interruption.

Whatever arises in the awakened mind is comprehended to be merely a form (a dark cloud; a ray of sunshine), the fundamental nature of which is the formless. Put another way, it is the abiding, persistent awareness that everything which is relative (impermanent) is the expression—a 'subset'—of the omnipresent Absolute.

This effortless awareness, once established, is the 'meditation' to which awakened sages point. It is, one might say, a consistent state (or condition) of being—similar to the sun's unbroken effulgence. One's awareness is like a mirror which ceaselessly reflects the true, fundamental nature or dimension of any item that passes before it.

Since the recognition is that "All that is, is That," the particulars upon which this awareness automatically reflects may be 'material' or 'immaterial'; whether one is conscious of a child, a thought, or oneself, the true underlying dimension is simultaneously discernible.

The awareness of the 'relative' and the 'Absolute' are conjunct: it is simply the clarity that the relative *is* the Absolute, and vice versa. It is like perceiving a third dimension and recognizing its relation within the fourth-dimensional matrix automatically.

Due to this inclusive awareness, meditation (or contemplation, whose word root is *temple*) is an on-going 'mindfulness' or consciousness. Whatever arises on the screen of consciousness is recognized to be a form (whether a 'material' form or an 'immaterial' form), while the formless screen remains unaltered. One can momentarily be attentive to the *screen*; to the *images* passing before it; or to the co-existence of *both*—but all are interrelated in the mindfulness of meditative awareness.

Under these circumstances, one is 'in meditation' regardless of what activity (or absence of it) one is engaged in. Whether one is thinking (a projection on the screen of consciousness) or not thinking (the absence of projection), there is no discontinuance with That Which Is. Were awareness itself to disappear, 'meditation' would disappear; so something apart from awareness is not what the awakened sages have referred to as meditation.

You Before You Were Born

Why are the enlightened sages adamant that comprehending the Great Mystery involves neither time nor space (nor a distinction between cause and effect)?

You, as the mystified, think of this Essence as something which existed prior to you (even prior to the existence of the world)—which places a distance between you and that (and between the world and that).

But, the sages insist, you *are* that. Your very presence is *its* very presence. *Because* it is present, you are present.

It is only in *your* awareness (whoever you are) that it certainly exists. And your awareness is its awareness.

The reflection does not exist prior to the mirror. The mirror does not exist prior to the reflection. The reflector, the reflected and the reflecting are all one indivisible phenomenon.

The mirror and the reflection are not separate.

Yet, we have been conditioned to think of That as the "Creator", existing independently of the created—as if an artist who stands apart from the canvas; the artist the cause, the painting the effect: the reflector existing before the reflecting or the reflected.

The true "creator" (being without form and being all forms simultaneously) is the creat*ed*—creat*ing* in the very same instant. This is not a spirit, hidden somehow *in* the creation. It *is* the creation, the creator *and* the creating; all at the same instant. It is, likewise, the destroyer, destroyed and destroying—*also* the *same* as its "counterpart", at the very *same* instant.

It is not that it stood before you were born, or that it will stand after you die. It is that it is the birthing itself, and the dying itself —and anything that could possibly be "in between".

It *is* both existence (in any and all forms) and nonexistence (in any form possible).

Any idea that it exists somehow independent of your existence (or nonexistence) is to fail to recognize your complete inseparability from it.

There is no "it" and "you". There is only one thing, whether you call that "self", "God" or whatever.

Being *one thing*, there cannot be a separation in time or space.

Before you were born, you were your creator; you are creator still; and after your destruction, you will still be creator and destroyer. Creator of *all*, and destroyer of *all*—without a time when you were or weren't.

· ·

One Friend to Another

X. I finished out my college years, and I got my degree. But immediately after graduation, I reduced all of my belongings to what I could carry on my bicycle. I then bought a tent and packed that on my bike, and reduced my belongings to the barest of essentials.

I had "been around" in my college years, and so I knew what I was looking for. I am now living in my tent on the property of an "extended family" I've located; it's nature is that of a small, mellow commune of about a dozen men and women of varying ages, backgrounds and origins. I'm in the midst of putting in a vegetable garden there; meanwhile, I work part-time in the village, in a bookstore.

I'm right where I want to be in my life: free of obligations, responsibilities and most all attachments. My mother is vice-president of a large computer company; my step-father is a successful consultant who travels all over. My biological father is also a very successful businessman. They would all like to see me utilize my college degree; and, in various ways, they could help me launch a promising career.

I met a young woman, about the time of my graduation, and we were able to spend some intimate time together. We write to each other, and she would like us to get together again, to explore what might become of our relationship. But, so far, I'm able to maintain my independence.

Y. It sounds as though you are just beginning to feel the kinds of pressures that militate throughout our lifetime to direct us into the normal patterns of conformity. It also sounds as though you perceive where such conformity leads, and that it is your intention to live your life in an atypical manner. I'm wondering how you will manage to be consistent with your intentions, and not find yourself conforming to common societal pressures?

X. Yes, I wonder about that too. I know what those normal values represent—I'm able to see, and hear, and think for myself—and I feel that *my* deepest values are definitely different than those.

Y. That is true of many people, like you, who are starting out into the years of their maturity. Obviously, the majority of them sooner or later—mostly sooner—choose to modify their "non-worldly" values to accommodate a satisfactory career and a comfortable homelife.

X. Why, do you think, is that so?

Y. Having myself experienced, in my previous years, a business career and the satisfactions of marriage and home ownership, I would have to say that the common denominator was a desire for acceptance and security—that is, conventional, comfortable self-esteem. If I were to succinctly characterize my basic values throughout that period I would have to say candidly that it was purely "self interest".

X. It seems to me *that* is the only basic value that most people appear to know.

Y. Are you saying that you are operating from a different fundamental value?

X. There must be more to life than living solely for one's self-interest, isn't there? Even my years in college showed me the limitation, the hollowness, of that kind of life.

Y. Yes, but what is the central reference that one operates out of —if one chooses to not habitually operate out of the frame of reference of self-interest?

X. Well, I hope to discover that it's *wholeness*.

Y. What is "wholeness", to you?

X. Non-fragmentation. Recognizing the interconnectedness of all things.

Y. In other words, that *true* "interest" goes beyond *self* interest? You are presently living your life "in the moment"; that is, moment-by-moment, without concern for your future security. Your parents, and possibly your prospective mate, would probably say that this is not what one does when one "looks out for oneself" (or one's family). How will you be immune to the pressures on you, day-by-day, to become ambitious, to compete, to establish a respected name or reputation for yourself? Can consistent integrity to your values be maintained *along* the way, while you hope to discover *someday* that the only true value is wholeness? In other words, even if your life, your behavior, isn't dominated at present by self-interest, are you *grounded* in the actuality of wholeness—and presently operating out of that central point of reference? Or are you operating out of a place of fragmentation—that is, yourself not "at one" with wholeness —even though it is not the *particular* fragmentation which we call "career" or "householding"?

X.   I'm not sure I see what you mean...

Y.   It seems to me that while we may perceive that self-interest is a *false* value, then whatever *transcends* the value of self-interest needs to be clearly and operationally in place. Otherwise, we are operating from a central point of reference that is merely a vacuum. If the falsity of self-interest points toward the truth of wholeness—or non-fragmentation or "non-duality"—then our first priority would appear to be to experience the actuality of nonduality in our awareness in the immediate *present*, not as a hope of realization at some future point down the line. When that first priority is realized, all other priorities will then take their natural order.

X.   Are you saying that it is because the "first priority"—which I take it to be *firsthand* recognition of the interconnectedness of all things—has not been attended to, that this allows one to slip into a modification, or fragmentation, that ends in a career or other general pursuit of self-interest?

Y.   If you are not initially operating—acting—out of a consciousness which is not fragmented, not in contradiction within itself, how are you to respond to all of the conflicting, bewildering choices that so many others before you have found themselves overwhelmed by?

What I am saying is that, it seems to me, it is important for you at this time to arrive at complete clarity as to what it means to be "one without division", to *be* "whole". That is the fundamental item on the agenda. When that matter has been completely, wholly attended to, then every other subsequent matter has *already* been attended to. Short of this full clarity at the outset, conflict and confusion are normal throughout the average human lifetime.

Pain and Liberation

Ultimately, our fear of (and aversion to) pain is usually even more predominant than our fear of (and resistance to) death. This appears to be the case even in the non-cognitive condition of babies and animals, and is particularly evident among the terminally ill. There is likely not anyone who, at some time, has not felt pain and associated fear.

Whatever one's thoughts about, or reactions to, pain (such as "suffering"), physical pain and discomfort seem not to be dependent upon thinking. In other words, pain appears to be "necessary" to the fulfillment of the process of life and death.

And, so, we face in our lives not only the inevitability of death but also the unavoidance of pain. And both—being interconnected, according to our observation—are resisted. Yet, though we know we can't postpone death, we hope to avoid pain.

With the onset of pain, there is the fear that it will not end; or, if it ends, that it will reoccur. And there is also the foreboding of pain as the harbinger of death. Yet, when the pain is intense, death is welcomed. So, pain does always end, permanently, at some point.

Anything which can have a beginning at some (relative) point, must have an ending at some point. That which can end is impermanent. That which has had neither beginning nor ending is the only thing which can be permanent.

Our breathing had a beginning and will have an ending. Our thoughts, and consequent reflection on ourselves, will have an ending just as it had a beginning. But the awareness, or "consciousness", with which the body functioned while still in the fetal form, had no discernible origin and will not discernibly end.

With the ending of thought, our "personal" identification will end. But personal identity was not our original, *true* identity (which arose at no particular point and will recede at no particular point).

We cannot be attached to our original identity, by the very nature of its nondualist inseparability. Attachment could only be possible with our personal, subjective identity. With attachment, there arises the fear of loss, and psychic pain. With non-attachment, there is freedom.

Our drive to be secure—lastly, in our personal, even pain-ridden identity—is restrictive of ultimate freedom. When we can relinquish our false identity, in life or in death, we can dissolve our attachments and allow liberation.

The very idea of security—in our identity; in avoidance of pain; or in postponement of death—leads to our attempt to control circumstances, and to fear those circumstances which cannot be controlled.

When one is welded to the helm, one at the same time sacrifices liberation.

No Experience Necessary

Among our endless desires is the desire for experience, for the accumulation of experience is the backbone of the self. From the experience of another orgasm to the experience of unitary enlightenment, the drive for experience propels our everyday life.

Experience is viewed as a form of completion, of somehow improving upon our present situation, such as "preparing oneself" for future eventualities. Experience is the avenue to becoming. We plan for experience, and any plan is a plan for becoming, for somehow improving upon, or influencing, the 'what is'.

Particularly, experience—whether pleasurable or painful—is viewed as a means of improving the self. It improves the self, with its accumulation, by expanding the self's sense of identity. Experience feeds on self-image, and self-image feeds on experience. Were there no self to seek comfort in the extent of its experience, there would not be pursuit of experience. The self is the accumulation of the past, of past experience. Can we continue to seek experience, *any* experience, and yet anticipate a transition to selflessness?

No Disconnection

From the time that human beings have first become aware of the mysterious, supernatural phenomenon that is beyond our control —that nature which thought is incapable of creating—the overriding question has been, "What is my relationship to that?"

But, apparently, the supernatural was present before there were any human minds to ponder relationship. In fact, since the human being arose from the stardust in the cosmos which is a supernatural manifestation, the human being and its mind and thoughts are no less an extension of the supernatural *itself*—another *aspect* of the same origin, not different in origination.

What is your relationship to your face, seen in the mirror? The source and its manifestation are essentially the same, although the appearance is of multiplicity.

All that we experience with our senses is a manifestation of, an extension of, the same supernatural source—as are, of course, the very senses that we sense with.

Since everything is ultimately the manifestation, the reflection, of the same supernatural source, all things (and all their aspects) are ultimately that.

So, when the human mind produces the thought, "What is *my* relationship to *that*?", it is (in the most fundamental sense) "that" reflecting on "that".

When you look at the cosmos, you are looking at a product of the supernatural. When you look at human beings, you are looking at a manifestation of the supernatural. When you look in a mirror, you are looking at an appearance of the supernatural. When *you* look, again, at the *cosmos*, it is an aspect of the supernatural "in relationship" to an aspect of the supernatural.

For the purpose of manipulating the material world to serve our life functions, we can—and do—give various aspects of this underlying reality descriptive names: "me", "tree", "cosmos", "God", etc.

But when we allow these manufactured descriptions to obscure the truth that *all* is *That*, we are no longer in direct relationship with Truth.

For in Truth, there *is* no "relationship". The tree is an aspect of the supernatural. The cosmos is an aspect of the supernatural. They are, in their fundamental essence, the same thing: they have not been *un*related, ever.

You and the supernatural are not unrelated. There is no relationship to be found among those whose very presence is the same. What is your relationship to that image reflected in your mirror?

The names we give things, though useful practically, are divisive. When it is fully realized that all things are That, regardless of the name, division ends. No longer is there "me" at one end of the spectrum, and "God" at the other. There are not "two things": just That. There is no longer a disconnection from the supernatural; there has *never been* a disconnection from the supernatural, since you *are*—and have always been—that.

This is the realization which is referred to as "nonduality" or Self-realization, and which "enlightened sages" have referred to since the beginning of the written word.

. . . .

Quenching the Candle

> "Saying that *I* am the *body* is the dual state. Saying that I am the witness of *all*, is the witness state. Saying that I am the *one* Supreme is the undivided state. Rejecting two out of these three…Be of the nature of the said *undivided* state." – a Gita verse

Saying that "I am the witness" is the 'witness state.' One has finally moved back from—at least tentatively—the 'doer state,' the condition of viewing oneself as the independent *cause* of the observed daily *effects*.

Now one simply monitors, without judgment or attachment, the activities of the organism which embodies the witness. One notices how the Absolute actuality unfolds its creative and destructive presence in our everyday experience, beyond the control of any human doer. It's a source of fascination.

But where there is the witness, there is the witnessed. The 'object' of awareness is a reflection of the 'subject' of awareness. This gap can yet be closed, leaving no separation remaining; no object, no objective and no residue of doing.

The deep realization that the Absolute is utterly indivisible is the simultaneous disappearance of all that has been witnessed *and* that entity which has witnessed it. The candle which *defined* the darkness has itself been quenched and all that remains is a condition devoid of any definitions. The 'witness' is no longer aware of the 'witnessed.' There is but that one undivided nature, which—with nothing objective apart from it—is all that is. The 'observer' and the 'observed' are the one, same reality. All definitions have dissolved in the ineffable Absolute, along with the definer: no more an "I", or even "that". Gone as well; "am" or "am not".

No Thought

As I recall, in Satyam Nadeen's second book (*From Seekers to Finders*), he performed the service of deflating many of the myths concerning enlightenment. One of the most confused conceptions has to do with a) the nature of thought (in the general, "unrealized" mind); and b) the nature of thought in the "realized" mind.

Because sages have sometimes declared (by way of stating that thought is not a condition which is indispensable to consciousness) that the activity of thought can be suspended entirely, the novice sometimes interprets this to mean that the sage, once enlightened, relinquishes all thought for all time. The suspension of thought merely demonstrates that natural processes continue whether we think about them or not. Just because it is possible to suspend thought does not mean that there is any imperative—or practical—point in doing so interminably.

Even Ramana, who presumably disassociated from the thinking mind for long periods of time, reverted to the thoughtful condition when there were relative, practical matters to be attended to: he translated and wrote poems, read his mail (aloud), authorized building plans, occasionally read the newspaper, etc.

Thought, like any other phenomenon, has its rightful function in the operation of actuality. Its function is to focus awareness on some particular point(s) in the time-space lattice, for the sake, primarily, of the physical survival of the organism. Self-preservation, we might say, is the brain's major priority; thought, memory, imagination serve its purpose.

But the very focusing of awareness on particulars isolates them from their general, ambient field. There is an operational dis-connection which breaks an "it" down into elements of "this" and "that". Such analytical cognition is valuable for relative, mechanical pursuits. In our dependence on these serviceable qualities of mentation, we forget or overlook how limited its capacity is.

When we attempt to envisage a possibility which absolutely has no parts, thought is stymied. Operating in a field in which there is neither subject or object, or no here or there, is not its venue. Therefore, if we rely solely upon the scope of thought, there might be some things—the sages say, *important* things—we miss.

With our focus on the linear *action* on the screen, we fail to notice the presence of the *screen*. That screen, we might say, was present before anything which is being projected on it. And, by comparison, the screen is stable and unchanging, while all that appears upon it is transitory. The thinking mind has plenty to occupy itself with, regarding the images, but has little interest in the unembellished screen.

Thought's role is to identify each thing in relation to other identifiable things: the tree is closer to the house than to the barn. The sage has recognized that the self identity, which he had previously taken for granted, is merely bestowed by thought. In the absence of thought, he discovers by experiment, consciousness is not dependent on thought. Separative identifications—"me", "mind", "thought", "brain", even "consciousness"—are incident-al to consciousness. "Thought", and all that it identifies, is a product of consciousness; even the idea of an identifiable "consciousness"—or "one who is conscious": *me*—is merely a projection arising on the screen.

So, the sage has dis-associated from the entire process of substantive identifications: all identification is seen to be illusory, including the self identification of the seer.

This is not a momentary "fleeting thought" on the part of the seer; it is a disruption in the accustomed pattern of thought. The process of thought now has a different function. Whereas the *images* were seen before to be real, it is the screen which now is customarily recognized to be the fundament. There has been, if you will, a reversal, a change in the *form* of thought: not the absence of thought, but the presence of the consciousness which is the ground of the named and the unnamed.

In the sense that the "reality" of thought now no longer is dominant, this could be described as the condition of "no thought", just as when the illusion of separate self has evaporated, we can speak of "no self". But this does not indicate that the sage cannot, or will not, employ thought in its analytical, comparative form when appropriate.

"How Much?"

In the history of mysticism, there are sages whose one-pointed focus after enlightenment has been the measure of their transformation; for example, Buddha, Jesus, Ramana, among others.

While reported details in the lives of each vary, it can be instructive to study their similarities.

Their lives, after their awakening, were their instruction. But the manner of the movement that led to their awakening is not disconnected from that instruction.

Buddha is said to have engaged in something like six or seven years of various extreme ascetic practices in search of truth—without success. In abject surrender, he then sat under a Bo tree, vowing not to move again until fully awakened: this for a matter of weeks.

Jesus is reputed to have consigned himself to forty days in the desert, before he appeared on the shores of Galilee to begin his ministry. In biblical terms, "forty days" is a general phrase which means "a very long time". That long time might have been many more days of self-imposed incubation than a mere forty.

Ramana, after what might be called his near-death experience, sat alone and silent for several years—without interruption—in and around various temples, near one mountain in India.

These sages did not later say that one had to duplicate their feat of endurance and deprivation in order to arrive at the ultimate truth. On the contrary, they emphasized that this truth is immediately realizable.

But all spoke, in their own way, of commitment, surrender, and attentive one-pointed focus on the challenge of transformation.

Their own examples of isolation—which occurred before their awakening, though not after—were evidently directed toward one purpose: to remove every conceivable distraction from their focus of attention. There was one question, and one question only, apparently on the mind of each: what is my true nature? And none was willing to bestir himself until the truth was a revelation.

That is commitment, that is surrender, that is attentive one-pointed focus on the challenge of transformation.

Distractions are likely far, far greater now than they were in the time of Buddha, or Jesus, or in the environs of a remote Indian mountain. Today, it would be difficult to even find a place where you *could be* isolated for as long as forty days. But it was not the external panorama that was critical in this focus of attention, it was the internal.

Indeed, the discomfort of deprivation can be the greatest distraction of all. So the focus of the attention of these seekers was on contemplation, contemplation so urgent and insistent that the distractions presented by deprivation could not allay it and may have even served to foster it.

If the gate could be easily and casually opened, who would not have already done so? Jesus spoke of "the pearl of great price"; a "merchant" sold "all that he had", in exchange for that *single* item. In exchange for that pearl of great price, the sages turned their back on life as they had known it. Their transformation began *before* the discovery of their transformation.

Those merchants, who sold *all that they had,* left little room for the *typical* distractions.

....

Just Another Hymn

All things are manifestations of the one thing, the Absolute.

Among the things manifested is what we call the ego, the sense of being a separate, individual self.

Among other things manifested are such things as what we call a tree.

What we call I (ego) concludes that among the things which it has apprehended is what is known to it as a tree:

The Absolute, in one of its forms, is in relationship with itself, in another of its forms.

The same ego has the capacity to apprehend its own source.

This comprehension is what is called awakening, or illumination, or realization.

But it is not the ego which recognizes; it is the Absolute, recognizing itself as
itself—as it is in all things that exist.

All that is manifested is impermanent. Only the manifesting is endless,
eternal, permanent.

That which is manifesting is what we call the Absolute.

Your body and ego are impermanent. The intelligence which is aware of
your body and ego is the intelligence of the Absolute. This presence is
ever-present, present in (and as) every manifestation … the formless
former of endless forms.

There is something which is eternally present, and not impermanent. All
things are manifestations of this one thing, the Absolute.

Killing Buddha

Yes, of course: the sages ("enlightened masters"—though they're
masters of nothing) of advaita, Zen, Tao, et al, are perceiving the
same actuality—*because* there *is* but one actuality. Put another
way, they all refer to it as the formless; therefore, how could any of
them be apart from the same illimitable essence? Standing in a
rose garden, would they not all smell the same perfume,
regardless of what word they used to describe it?

The fact that realization is as simple as breathing is difficult to
envision—until it is real-ized ("made real"). As the sages have
said, after realization nothing has really changed except for one's
perception of that which is present. Thus, the saying of the roshis:
"nothing special". Thus, such observations as this comment by
someone who knew Suzuki Roshi: "He was a surprisingly

ordinary person." Thus, such comments as can be found accompanying the Ten Ox Herding Pictures: "no smell [taint] of holiness about him"; and (in the 10th picture), "The gate to his cottage is closed, and even the wisest cannot find him."

As a Buddhist teaching has said, "*This* mind—*this very* mind—is the Buddha mind." *Whatever* your mind is doing *right now*: *that* is the Buddha mind. Nothing Special.

When that is understood, one essentially becomes a mere observer (a "witness") of the Buddha mind: the sense of its "ownership", and doership, subside. This watchful meditation ("choiceless awareness") is a continual meditation which perpetuates itself without "personal" effort. Since it does not rely upon self-motivation, it does not diminish. (Since one particular day, about twenty years ago, that meditation has been unending for me; it is an awareness, a "presence", which does not "come and go". It is as undeniable as breathing, as effortless as seeing. It can be said to be, descriptively, the *way* one sees; as in, "absolute *perspective*".)

Because this awareness is our "true nature", we begin to see— through this awareness—that *all* that we (and others) do is our true nature. Nothing special.

(Therefore, all that we do becomes special, because we are not looking for anything *more* special.)

If this very mind—your very mind, as it is right now—is the Buddha mind, your very actions (whatever they happen to be right now) are Buddha's actions; "mind" and "actions" are not separate, are they?

This "nothing special-ness" is very difficult for people to grasp: it is much, much too simple. (So, let me invent a koan for you.)

Chen-Chi says that for those "identifying the mind Essence" (that is, realizing their true nature), "those who have already entered [the "gateless gate": the one that no longer needs even to be entered, in the Tenth picture], this ["choiceless awareness"] is the easiest of all meditations....

> "In activity or in quietness, the illuminating void-consciousness will always shine brightly within him....
>
> "Once the 'gateless gate' is entered, meditation will no more be a 'practice' or an effort. It now becomes a natural and spontaneous act of life. Sitting, walking, talking or sleeping—*all* activities *and* conditions of life become marvelous meditations in themselves. ["Wow, this *too* is It!"]
>
> "No effort need be made, and no object[ive] *or idea* need be worked upon."

So, if there is nothing to 'practice' once the gateless gate has been entered and "closed" behind one—there is nothing special that needs to be done—is it possible that there is nothing special that needs to be done on the *other* side of the "gateless gate", the "barrier" which is really nonexistent?

"How Are You?"

Here in our Western culture, where we are accustomed to attempt to exert maximal control, it is difficult for us to bear in mind that things are always unfolding in the way that they are bound to do.

As could be expected in a culture which so emphasizes the value of human life (as, for example, over the value of other species'), this tendency is particularly evident in our reaction to the manifestation of chronic or terminal illness—in us, or another person.

If the condition of health changes for the "better", we can accept that. If it changes for the "worse", we *can't* accept that. The only unfolding of life events that we meet with equanimity are the *positive* ones. The implication in our attitude toward *negative* changes is that they must be met with resistance.

Sooner or later, every fact in life *must* be accepted.

Each of us will do whatever it is that we do, when the time comes. And nature will do whatever it is that *it* does, *regardless* of whatever it is that we do.

Yet notice the implication in the reaction to a change in health: if you are ill, you *shouldn't* be: if you are not anxious about your condition, you *should* be.

"The dark threads are as needful, in the Weaver's skillful hand, as the threads of gold and silver in the pattern that shall stand," if I recall an old poem.

Can we relate to what is, as it is—for ourselves and others—even at the most pivotal junction?

. . . .

Energy Is Energy

The particles of which living matter is made are cells, and cells are composed of molecules which have an atomic structure. An atom is a microcosmic universe, with various energetic elements in constant motion, or movement, around various other elements of energy. And so the basic *structure* of matter is not material, in a substantial sense, but it is elemental energy.

The elements of energy in the atom circulate or pulsate around each other in a spatial medium, in a manner similar to the celestial bodies in our observable universe. The space *we* are familiar with is saturated with air, and air and gases in general are combinations of such things as hydrogen and oxygen, which themselves are molecular or atomic in structure. And so even space is fundamentally another expression of energy.

And then, in addition, there are such active forces as the energy of light, which can be measured (depending upon the instrument) much like matter, as particles; *or* like spatial energy, as waves. Indeed, the energy of light, under certain circumstances, behaves predictably like matter.

Matter, such as your body, is composed of atomic particles, which are themselves elements of energy, including that medium of energy which we call space.

A raven calls, and you hear its call. The raven is energy, the waves of sound are energy, the air they traverse is energy, the ear which detects the sound waves is energy, and the brain which interprets the sensation is energy. Aside from movement or change in the universal field of energy, nothing is happening.

"Your" body is an expression of energy, "its thoughts" or emotions or sensations are an expression of energy, its actions or behavior are an expression of energy—all taking place in a field from which it is not divided: energy.

When nothing is affected but energy, and nothing is the cause but energy, can it be said that anything really makes any difference?

I regard what you are experiencing now as a promising development.

Awakening is a (sometimes unsettling) disruption of the status quo: as is the trauma of birth.

Disassembly is prior to renewal. There must be an emptying before there is to be a refilling. The house is demolished in order to construct the temple. In other words, a dying to all which has gone before.

You have been, in the past few months, untying the moorings: putting yourself at risk; drifting further into the unknown present. No busy agenda now, to distract the attention.

It is an opportunity to let go of ideas *about* things: not knowing (or analyzing) what might occur on the mental panorama. Just observe what arises (or doesn't arise).

A lizard, sitting at my feet in the sun this morning, was entirely attentive to the moment. He was watching for insects, and even if his mind was on his hunger, it was even then focused on the present. I spent a moment considering all of the things which he was not troubled to think about. In the lap of the Absolute, there was exceedingly little that need trouble this lizard's mind.

Forget everything you know, and start afresh; seeing without retaining. As Krishnamurti would say, "no residue". He titled a book *Flight of the Eagle*, meaning that the bird's passage through the air leaves nothing in its wake.

On the Adyashanti tape, the first person to come forward with a question (or concern) was a woman, in tears. She indicated that she is in the midst, for the first time, of experiencing what it means to live in the "emptiness" of unconditioned existence. "How am I to relate to the world now?" was basically her question, now that I have no platform of assumptions to stand on. She was feeling this falling away of supports (some would call it a demolishing, some would call it a conflagration, some would describe it as a collapse) that accompanies freedom.

It is not just the psyche which is transformed. *Trans*: from Latin, "passing through". *Form*: "the configuration of". *Transform*: "to change the condition or nature of something". Death is a trans-form-ation. Birth is a trans-form-ation. Transformation represents a changing of condition: sometimes a painful changing.

Dialogue

A. Who are you?

B. I am myself.

A. My-self. So there is something which is in possession: 'This is *my* self'. Who is the 'I' which, 'am myself'?

B. It's impossible for me, then, to be both 'I' and 'myself' at the same time?

A. The 'self' is projected—held out at arm's length—as a representation or characterization of that which speaks as 'I': it is a mask of identity. *You* are not your *identity*.

B. We could say that if the 'you' is substantial, the image of the you, the 'self', is insubstantial?

A. The self is an illusion, the creation of the speculative mind. The mind builds a castle in the air, and then occupies it as an isolated fortress.   The human mind has the power of imagination, and can imagine division or separateness where none exists. The tendency of the human mind is to partition itself off as a fragment particular to each human individual. It projects the image of an identifiable self, and remains a thoughtful patron of the self. Was there an 'I' there, before there was an identity?

B. There was only a consciousness, and it was not individuated.

A. We would say, by way of definition, that to be alive and to be aware—such as, of your environment—is to be conscious. All human beings are commonly conscious. We could put it another way: primarily, consciousness is general; secondarily, to each human who views himself as an individual 'person', it is individuated. Is this consciousness an exclusive property of mankind—or is that perhaps another presumption of man's divisive intellect?

B. Animals, and even plants, are alive and responsive to their environment: intelligent response is the equivalent of consciousness.

A. And does not all of nature, of itself, exhibit intelligent response? In other words, if consciousness and intelligence are related, would we not say that man possesses natural intelligence or consciousness: that being an aspect of the natural world, any intelligence of man is merely an extension of the intelligence of the natural world, or universe?

B. You're saying that there's a universal consciousness, which man shares.

A. Let us say that there is a consciousness which precedes or antedates the human mind's consciousness of its self. We could say that the real you is the you that existed before you identified yourself as you.

B. So, the real 'I' is…'It'.

A. Can you see that if all that the human mind designates as separate, individual and isolated—such as 'I' or 'my self'—is actually It, there is no division (except that which the mind *envisions*)? In other words, there is not even an It—as a separate, identifiable entity. When all things are It, who is to identify it…but for the human mind?

B. 'I' and my 'self' are attempts of the fragmented human mind to identify It—something which it is impossible to separately identify, because the human mind itself is an element of It.

A. That is why 'your' mind cannot admit to 'your' true identity. To encounter the true you, remove the 'self' limitations from your mind.

Ungrasping

To say that something is omnipresent is to say that it is always (all ways) in existence: presence implies existence in time *and* in space. That which is always in existence would be eternal (a word whose derivation is "always"). The dictionary defines *eternal* as 'without beginning or end; timeless'. Anything which is without beginning or ending is infinite (derivation: "not limited"), defined as without bounds; endless; inexhaustible.

(The dictionary gives as an example of infinite: "such as space, or time". It defines space as "distance without limit", and time as "an interval of existence"—the word *interval* meaning "gap, distance" and the word *exist* meaning "be present". An added definition which the dictionary gives to infinite is "beyond comprehension". An added definition given to eternal is "always true", true as in "certain".)

So the very existence of omnipresence nullifies any possibility of a when or a where. This is presence which cannot be confined in either category of "then" or "now", nor in either category of "here" or "there". It is here and now, there and then... or here and there, then and now—or any other designated arrangement. In truth, it is incomprehensible ("ungraspable").

When we say that there is that which is in all possible places at all potential times—omnipresent—this (ungraspable) thing would have to be (logically) thoroughly and entirely without any parts, pieces, fragments, appendages, residues or remainders: unequivocally whole and complete, without any division, seam or separation whatsoever. (Be aware that whole and complete are weakly illustrative words: this wholeness and completeness has no borders or edges, no beginnings and endings.)

So if this that is purely without division is present in *any* place, there is not merely a *part* of it which is present in that place: it has *no* parts. Since it is present everywhere, it is not stretched over something, like a mist in a pine forest. Being itself *every where* (a word which is derived from "who"), there is not anything or place which it does not occupy or inhabit. That which is omnipresent is, by definition, every "part" of any pine forest, and any "part" of every mist.

And never being anywhere other than in its entirety, if you could designate some particular point and assert that it is there (which would not be truly accurate), it would be there (as well as at all other places at the same time) in its *absolute entirety*.

As with space, so with time (which, even as concepts, are not legitimately divisible). That which is ever present (ever's derivation is "all time") has, by implication, not ever not been present. Its presence transmutes anything which could be conceived of as time. Therefore there is not some part of the "everlasting" which has been *here*, while at some other time another part of it has been *there*. That whose continuation is indefinite ("no limits"), eternal, has no discernible or identifiable "parts": no *then*, no *now*. To impose the concept of "time" on that which is eternal is to impose a calibration on something which offers no point at which to begin, and no hope for a place to mark an end. Time is "an interval of existence": to that which never started and will never stop, there is no interval; to that which knows not of non-existence, existence is a superfluous idea. And so, omnipresence is as unbroken in "time" (despite man's attempt to section it) as it is in "space". At any point in time in which you can refer to it, it has been there fully, in its unbroken entirety. There never has been a time when the omnipresent was not present—otherwise, it would not *ever* have been omnipresence.

So, that which we refer to as omnipresent cannot but be present at any and every time and place, simultaneously at every and at any point which one (who presumes that he is separate) might choose to designate. ("Cleave a piece of wood, lift a rock, and I am there", Jesus is reputed to have said.) This "thing" which we call omnipresent is in every place at all times: that being so, clearly it itself would have to *be* all things. If there is not anything which it is not, there cannot be anything which is in actuality divided from it, separate, apart ("distant in space or time").

Being itself all things, it is all events. Even if there were, under some conditions, an interval between events (which supposes a continuum of time), "it" would be the interval as well. Being itself all things, there is no spatial disconnection (distance) between one thing that it is and another thing that it is; if there were such a *thing* as "distance", it would have to be this omnipresence, too.

If this omnipresence is indeed any and all events or things (which distinctions then become meaningless), it itself is both the actor and the acted upon among all things—*and* the acting, as well. Therefore, there is not anything which happens ("random occurrence") without it being the happener of. Everything that knows to do what it does is this thing. Put another way, anything which does what it does, does so because "*it*" does. Since it knows to do anything and everything which has been, is, or will be done, it is perforce the "knower" of all "things" (be aware that this construct automatically sections the "knower" from the "things"). In other words, being omnipresent is to be omniscient—not in addition, but as a consequence.

The omnipresent thing which moves (or event that happens) is the same as the omniscient mover that presents movement. Since it represents totally the moved, the mover and the movement, there is not one of these singled-out elements which is of a higher order or position than any other. This thing is equally (a separative word) the leaf on the stream; the stream; and the energy which moves the stream and the leaf. One cannot accurately say that the essence of the transaction rests in the energy (without the water and the leaf), or the leaf (without the water and the energy).

Assuming that omnipresence means that this presence is present in a molecule in your body (bearing in mind that it means more than *that*), omniscience is also—implicitly—present in the same molecule in your body: indeed, the molecule *is*, by its very nature, omnipresence and omniscience in material form (remember, however, not particle-ularized). It is not divisible into "omnipresence" and "omniscience"; it is, in its very existence, *both* equally (in our manner of speaking). In other words, the prime mover is not the "intelligence" or "energy" of the molecule, anymore than it is the "matter" of the molecule. There being no division, there can be no elevated distinction between omniscience or omnipresence, between "intelligence", "energy", "matter", "molecule" (or "body", etc., and so on).

Put another way, no "part" has any more (or less) potential or capability than any other part: no element is more in "control" than any other element. Any and all elements are fully and equally capable at any or all of the time—omniscient, yes, omnipotent ("all able") as well.

For the sake of obfuscating and commercializing that which can be referred to (inadequately) as the omnipresent, omniscient and omnipotent, the church fathers disqualified another aspect of this un-graspable, indeterminate presence. That which is omnific ("all making") is all-creating. If it is the "creator" of "all" (which, again, is a subject/object deception), it has to thereby be its own creator. The omnipresent, omniscient omnipotence is, in its all-pervasiveness and indivisibility, the creator, the created and the creating itself. Not ever having had need of something to create it, it never was uncreated. All things are the creator of everything, simultaneously, at all times.

It has always been present, independent of anything; independent of anything, there is no reason why it will not always be present. Being always present, it is present wherever there is presence—in all of the present places. Being self-generating, it has never not known what to do, or how to go about doing it.

All things, not anything excluded, are omnipresent, omniscient, omnipotent and omnific. Not at time's, not in places, not in part, not by some external design and not through some remote control. No element is more present, more eternal, more infinite, more intelligent, more a cause or more an effect than any other element, anywhere, has ever been, or will be. No division.

The supposition of cosmologists is that the material elements of our cosmos are the debris of an explosive combustion—the Big Bang, it has been called.

Should this be the case, there was presumably in initial existence only that which exploded: in other words, there was not anything "else" (there being only one thing entirely).

There being no distance—inasmuch as there was not anything separate from anything else—there was no point at which anything could happen ("take place") at "another time". In other words, with no arena for comparative "events", there was not anything which could be identified as time.

Where there is not the advent of time, there are not such continuous processes as "cause" and "effect". The implication of this is: for that which was in existence, there could have been no such development as "cause", not even a First Cause.

That which is without cause must be without meaning, without intention.

In fact, in a situation where there is no such thing as time, it is erroneous to even refer to "existence": the designation of "existence" has no relevance apart from time.

And in a situation in which there is no such reality as distance, there could be nothing which was separate, or apart, which could have "created" an existence.

Our ideas of meaning are the product of a fragmented imagination, and not of the sense of wholeness.

"Accepting" Bliss

Among the many misconceptions which are related to awakening, perhaps the most pernicious is the notion that it involves a movement from the negative end, of life's spectrum, to the positive.

Many who are attracted to the mystical, of course, are motivated by their personal acquaintance with suffering. Indeed, there are those who historically have had an illuminating breakthrough at a time of deep anguish or disappointing sorrow in their life. Pain and worldly torment are frequently the catalyst which motivate the search for a profound change in perspective.

Then, too, enlightened sages speak assuringly of their own freedom from the bondage of suffering. And, in fact, they sometime's speak of a generally-undefined condition which they refer to as bliss: "sat chit ananda": being-consciousness-bliss. Such references suggest to the unrealized that the awakened condition is one of unremitting pleasure, unexperienced pain. Indeed, the dictionary gives the contemporary meaning of 'bliss' as "intense pleasure".

The real movement in awareness, which the sages describe, is not from one relative polarity to another—such as negative versus positive—but instead a profound transcendence of *all* polarities, all dualistic concepts, all relative (and thus limiting) points of reference or identification. It is not a matter, in other words, of 'bettering' one's life; it is a matter of accepting life as it is, and placing no higher value on the positive aspects than on the negative aspects.

The consequence of this shift in attentive-ness, or awareness, happens to be a smoother experience of life's vicissitudes, free from the customarily perceived emotional ups and downs. This condition, when it is truly present, is the traditional, mystical meaning of references to bliss.

But the difficulty for the seeker is in appreciating the full implication of this condition. In essence, it presents a perceptual absence of psychological "pain". It *also* presents a perceptual absence of psychological "pleasure". *Both* the interpreted "negative" phenomenon *and* the interpreted "positive" phenomenon are annulled.

This, in many cases, is not what the seeker is actively seeking: the absence of psychologically experienced pleasure *along with* the absence of psychologically experienced pain.

Transcendence of such evaluated dualities is Ramana's (among others') core message: "Accept with equanimity whatever happens. For pleasure and pain are mere mental modes."

And, "Pleasure and pain are relative, and refer to our finite (limited) state…(the awakened) ceases to have relative, temporary pleasure and enjoys perfect peace (equanimity): bliss."

"He looks on everything with unconcern (whether positive or negative) and remains blissful himself."

So, the paradoxical truth is that even bliss is not a 'positive' condition to be sought. It is the condition of peaceful nonattachment which pertains for those who have transcended the dualities and preferences. Bliss is a presence which one accepts, when all else has been accepted without preference.

Consciousness Is…

It has been said, "Consciousness is all there is." This is meant to say that the Absolute is all that there is. "Consciousness", like so many other words that are intended to stand in for the ineffable Absolute, is prone to suggest an image which can lead to misinterpretation. Indeed, in New Age literature, it is not uncommon to see "Consciousness" in a context where it is merely a substitute for the concept of an enthroned God (Jehovah) who is located some *where*, directing cosmic affairs through *time*, as the *cause* or "creative principle".

In addition, the average person tends to identify "consciousness" with their thinking process or "mind"; after all, the Latin root is defined as "knowing". Were a sage to say, "consciousness is all there is", she does not mean "knowing is all there is".

To understand the meaning of consciousness as it is used in spiritual literature, one must be cognizant of what is also said of the mystical nature of the Absolute in general usage. Consciousness in this sense will be seen to be something other than "knowing".

First, it would be evident that from the standpoint of That Which Is, anything that is "happening" is happening *now*; there is no time (when we remove human concepts or ideas about time) *other than* now. Everything which is happening, has ever happened, or shall happen will occur in the endless moment that we particularize as "now".

Secondly, the *"base* of operation" of anything which occurs is *here* —*wherever* "here" is designated as *being*. All that arises, arises spontaneously: there is no *precedent* for it. Events are not following a pattern whose design has been established elsewhere in the cosmos; creation originates in—and as—the very activity that is created or generated.

Consciousness, as a metaphor for the Absolute, is not a static quality that stands apart from that which it enables. It *is* what it *does*. For an approximating analogy, it would be more akin to a penetrating field of gravity, or X-rays. Not only are we speaking of something which has vitality, but vitality as in *life*: it *is* vital; it *is* alive. In the sense of its all-pervasive presence, all things are conscious and entwined in the same "life". Consciousness, in mystical terminology, is more closely related to "essence" or "actuality": *presence.*

It is due to its presence that it has no need of "knowing". One of the descriptive words often used in connection with the Absolute is "omniscient": *all* knowing. This does not propose that there is some *thing*, some *where*, which *possess* all knowledge of all things. It suggests an "intelligence"—consciousness—which *is* all things and therefore has no *need* of (or *use* for) extraneous information. Being thoroughly, 100%, informed in its nature, it *is* the information which could (that is, might otherwise) be known.

Further, consciousness—as an aspect or element of the eternal now—has no relationship to time: "then" as the past, or "then" in the future. There is no time in which to acquire or accumulate specific knowledge; "knowledge" of what is happening is present *as* it is happening, and is the *basis* of what is happening. There is no cause which stands apart from the caused: the cause and the caused are the same phenomenon.

This consciousness has nothing to do with "knowing" as its function. Where apart from itself could acquired knowledge be stored for "later" use? To that which is at the root of all that is taking place all of the time, there need be no plan for "later" use.

For this omnipotent consciousness, no matter *what* happens, nothing can go wrong. Whatever is, *is*—and that's *how* it is. This is the consciousness of the Absolute.

Love Letter

What could be more loving than the Presence which requires no recognition, and which is what it is unfailingly, regardless of the circumstances? Which loves in so much infinite detail that it even *is* the circumstances? That leaves not anything unembraced, least of all Itself? Is in opposition or resistance to absolutely no thing, including destruction and death? Which even provides abundance for the non-existent "you"? The you which cannot acknowledge this love even if you try. The you which is busy writing love letters to yourself. The you which disregards even its own face.

Is this not transcendent love?

This love does not even single itself out. It is not bestowed upon you: there is no burden. There is nothing to repay, even to be grateful for. This love is so much "you", that you cannot be separate from it. Your being, alone, is nothing but sheer love. You remain as love even though (in your folly) you seek love. Love, truly, is blind.

Blind or not, the honeysuckle is fragrant!

Beyond Thought

In some of the spiritual literature there is reference to a condition of "no thought". At the broadest level of understanding, one can take this to mean that where one has realized that all conceived forms are hollow, thus meaningless, there is in actuality no such isolated activity as "thinking thoughts". From the standpoint of advaita, the sage would ask, "Who is the doer that is assuming responsibility—origination of—the activity?"

426

Thus the condition referred to as "no thought" would suggest that, to the awakened, the idea that "I am thinking thoughts" is realized to be merely another dualistic illusion—based on a "thinker" who is the subject of the objectified "thoughts".

If one takes seriously the relinquishment of desire and attachment as aspects of enlightened perspective, it ought to be clear that a sage would hold no preference for, or concern with, one state or condition over some other—such as the conceptual polarities of thought as opposed to absence of thought.

Indeed, thoughts come and go. If there were a condition of "no thought", it would be an alternation with the condition of "thought". Like all phenomenon, which have a beginning in time and an ending in time, it would simply be another finite experience—to a "separate individual" who stands in relation to a passing event. That which is finite and impermanent is "not worth seeking", as Ramana would say.

In addition, if one were to pursue an attempt to experience a condition of "no thought" as a noticeable occurrence, it would either be intended as a means to an end, or as an end in itself. If such a condition were not already naturally present in one's experience, why would one abandon the actuality of the present moment for some presumed advantage in the future? Is there some ideal condition which we are to suppose will bring us closer to our 'true nature'? Or as a behavior—of experiencing no thought—do we have some ideal of behavior that we ascribe to an awakened person?

The ultimate teaching of the spiritual lantern bearers is: "you are That"—unconditionally. Awake, dreaming or in deep sleep; knowingly or unknowingly; while thinking or not thinking; you are That which is perfection itself. There is no achievable experience which can bring you closer to your true nature— which you fully abide in this very moment, just exactly as you are.

In a poetic reflection, the 13th century Zen master Keizan Jokin wrote: "Most people want to have pure clarity, but sweep as you will, you cannot empty the mind."

Halleluyah

Halleluyah! There is one joy that I have left in life, and it is to get a letter (or statement) like yours.

You are not any longer, judging from your letter, presupposing a dis-location between "you" and "others" (or "other things").

And you also comprehend that it is possible to effectively operate in the relative world—as you are used to doing—while simultaneously recognizing that the relative is merely a subset, or manifestation, of the Absolute.

The dramatized dialogue between Krishna (voicing the Absolute perspective) and the mortal Arjuna, in the Bhagavad Gita, is what this is all about. Take the most extreme case, it says: to kill ("cause" "death"). *Who* is it that is "ending the life" of *what*?

I was pondering this, one day, when a dog next to me snapped at a pesky fly and swallowed it. It occurred to me that a human organism kills life forms all the time, intentionally and unintentionally. All forms of "creation" are perpetually being "destroyed". That *is* "what is".

It is a physical fact of the very cosmos. "What" is it that is *doing* this? When you've discovered what the *doer* is, then you can (if you choose) concern yourself about *what* is being done.

Your sentence could have come from the mouth of Krishna itself: "*That* is *responsible* for *everything*—period!" Or, the biblical phrase that you followed it with: "It is (That) Father that doeth the works." The coming. The being. And the going. All an unbroken actuality.

As you, later, remarked: "How is it that I am the one in prison?" Don't try to "make sense" of it, any more than the fly questioned "How is it that I am the one the dog swallowed?" *I* could have been the one "the dog swallowed" myself, for some of the things I've done.

"That" moves in mysterious ways, "its wonders to perform". Negative as well as positive. To That, its all the same. And, lately, to "you" as well.

....

From Origination, to Decay

Let us set reason aside for a moment, in order that we might have an insight into something which may not seem apparent from a strictly linear point of view. Physicists sometimes have done this: Einstein occasionally used to "experiment" in this way.

Suppose that you were to form some green knitting yarn into the likeness of a life-size caterpillar—with mouth parts so realistic that when you set it upon a rose leaf, it would chomp away at the leaf.

Who would we say was the original source of the rose-pruning activity: the caterpillar, or you?

If you were to, further, endow this ersatz caterpillar with the capacity to think, and it *decided* to devour another rose leaf, where would we say that this action ultimately originated: with the caterpillar, or with you?

If you were then to free this caterpillar to *choose* to eat rose leaves or to choose to not eat rose leaves, as its circumstances seemed to be most proper, who would we say was the ultimate source of its movement toward one direction or the other?

In other words, if one were to assume that there is an all-powerful Creator, who created man—and this man had the capacity to think, to make decisions and to act upon them pro or con—the Creator who is responsible for creating this man must finally be considered to be the "cause" of this man's thoughts.

If the Creator created humankind, then it follows that the Creator is the ultimate originator of all of the thoughts of all humans.

The One, we could say, has manifested as plurality: it is not only the All, but the all in All. In its manifest form, it is everything which ever has been, is, or will be. It is the origin of the spectrum that is inanimate and animate. It is the source of the man; the man's capacity to think (even to think the thought that there is no source); the man's thoughts; emotive behavior; and consequent activity. And this is so, for all humans who were likewise created.

If a group of these humans meet and agree upon collective behavior (the basis of "society"), this is one of the Creator's activities, or manifestations.

If the agreements of this society are handed down from generation to generation and become the conditions upon which each human governs his actions, the Creator is the real actor.

When one has been conditioned to (or even arrives at it "outside" of conditioning) love his neighbor and treat all beings with respect, this can be (and is) said to be the activity of God.

But when one acts contrarily (whether as a result of societal conditioning or individual thought) and selfishly disregards one's neighbor, is this not also the activity of the originator?

If not, then there is a power in force which is not the creator's power.   In other words, the Creator has been rendered *not* all-powerful.

Adyashanti, in a taped talk, made some insightful pre-Easter comments.

That guy on the crucifix was *crucified*.   He gave his life, in the unfolding of his enlightenment.

Nor was he, meanwhile, a guy who was constantly happy, cheerful, upbeat.   Read the accounts and notice how many times he barely avoided a stoning.

Did being a Jew among Jews help him?   Being regarded as a Rabbi?

Did all of his good deeds help him?   Even being, no less, the Son of God?

And did he die willingly?   Or with reluctance—because there was no choice?

And, all told, what was the message?   His body died.   Two thousand Easters later, the message is that his spirit didn't die.

And the message, right through the "resurrection"?   From formlessness to form; from form to formlessness; from formlessness to form; and back again to formlessness.

"Good" Friday is the day he passively drank from the cup of oblivion.

This isn't just Jesus' *story*, it's suggested as your story.

- -

Political Activism

"When one gives up all ideas and ideals, one gives up political or social activism. It seems to me that to give up on the struggle for human rights and dignity is escapist."

Or is it reform that is an escape, "a way out"? We object to the form of conditions around us—politically or socially or whatever—and so we re-form them. We improve on capitalism with socialism, and on socialism with communism. Perhaps the only *ism* which hasn't seriously divided mankind is witticism.

The root of the word *revolution* is *revolve*, "to roll back". Can we roll back the hands of time? Can we consciously roll the hands of time forward? Can the hands of time truly be bound in any way?

When we take the pattern of our left foot and turn it over, do we have anything that is newer or more revolutionary than our right foot?

Until something has been completely ended, and not continued, where can the freshly new appear? When we have finished with every historic *ism*, perhaps we will be ready to face the timeless *is* —not defect into what "could be" or "has been", but directly face what genuinely is.

The truth is that there are many things about reality which humans do not like. Reality continues to change, and that disturbs the status quo—and that is one of the things which we humans most dislike, whether we are leftist or rightist. When the conditions which surround us in this world are not felt to be changing fast enough for us, they are felt to be changing too fast.

Humans, too, change; but they do not appear to be changing their resistance to the nature of reality.

If it is a reformation that I'm after, am I more likely to make progress in reshaping others or to shape-up myself?

And if I am to radically change my ways, do I not need to tear up my old patterns and break the worn molds? Or do I continually "improve" on, simply modify, what has been effective in the past?

One may concentrate on oneself to the neglect of all other things; or one may concentrate on all other things to the neglect of oneself. Either way, there is a difference between concentrating on oneself as the center of the universe, and of being attentive to oneself as an element of the universe. There is no symbiosis without you.

It is while you are aware of the juggling balls, that they stay in the air. It is when you concentrate on one of the juggling balls, that they fall to the ground.

One need not busy oneself with anything, to be attentive to oneself. To be attentive is to be observant, to be fully present. If attending was synonymous with busyness, it would be redundant to "attend to business".

Activism is activity as a means to an end; action is the means and the end. Observe your need for security, attend to your fears for the integrity of the self, and that will activate a change which will transcend—"go beyond the limits of"—ideas, ideals and idealism.

There is always an I at the start of idealism.

"Untitled"

There are few words which are more loaded than the word *God*. Yet, definitionally its interpretation is uncomplicated: "eternal, infinite; omnipresent".

And these three descriptive words are likewise rather simply defined:

Eternal: "without beginning or end, timeless".

Infinite: "without limits or bounds; immeasurable".

Omnipresent: "in every place at once".

By contrast, time and space are not normally categorized as limitless—being measurable.

Time (whose root means "to part or divide"): "a period of existence, or the interval between events".

Space: "a continuous expanse in all dimensions or directions, extending between or within things".

Simply by definition, God—being limitless, immeasurable, infinite—is not bound by time's "period of existence" or by being bracketed in space "between or within" any other entities. If there is that which is without any limit or bounds—in every place at once—there would be, obviously, only *one* such thing; it would necessarily extend to and beyond any other such thing. Put another way, if there could be two things (or more) that were equally omnipresent—being in every same place at the same time —they would, for all intents and purposes, be the very same thing.

One could say (as some do) that God is "it" (or It, if you prefer); *it* (whose plural is *they*) singles out the specialness of "this one":

"it" is defined as "an unidentified, but commonly understood, object; or the ultimate or final thing".

But in this case, there can *be* no It—and this, of course, we find inconceivable. This immeasurable quantity or quality (defying identification) has *no center*, is limited to no discernible space, and cannot be confined within any particular period of time. There is not a particle which can be pointed to as the object which discloses fully the identity of this thing: it is emphatically *not* "this one" *or* "that one".

Being limitless, immeasurable, infinite to the extent that it permeates and embodies all that is (and isn't), it is *not even one*: there is no unit, no "thing". *Thing* means "a single entity"; *nothing* means "nonexistent". This thing, "God", being in all of existence —completely and entirely—*is all* of existence, all things *as* they exist, and therefore has no *separate* identity or existence.

There being not anything separate, separable or special, there can be no center from which this (which is Nothing from the start) can "operate". There can be no separate entity which intends, plans or directs: that which is without beginning or end, and which would extend beyond any temporal or spatial limits, would already include any actuality which could be intended, planned or directed.

There is, implied in this, complete freedom from relativity. Put another way, there is no thing upon which all other things are finally dependent. This cosmos, this world, this life, this you— none more permanent nor significant than any phase of the moon. Nothingness is, ultimately, mere absolute sameness: and all things are, unspecially, the same thing. This "thing" does not manifest forms: anything which could form would *be* this sameness, and this *sameness* can have no explicate or implicate forms.

The statement is inaccurate which says that you—as well as "all things"—are It. There is no you, no things, nor It. To say that all That Is is it, is simply to say that it is nothing in particular.

And, so, what could there possibly be to be aware of except that there is not anything which finally is individually aware of anything?

There are no walls to the mind: there being no personal you, there is no individual mind. Furthermore, there is no *other* mind which is apart from any particle which is (or isn't). There being no "mind", and no mindful cause or effect, each thing, each form, is self-generating—as it were—and self-completing, without any intention or motivation for either. There is not anything which has any lasting control over anything else.

And this, dear friend, you cannot conceive. Why? *Because* there is no separate thing to conceive it, nor to be conceived.

There is no authentic "God"—or Isness—which *can* be *conceived*.

Still Life

To truly "sit quietly, doing nothing" is to realize that there is not anything more urgent which needs to be done. This is the complete ending of personal ambition. One cannot be enjoined in such a simple inactivity without having brought profound order to one's daily life. One cannot be engaged in such an inactivity without having surrendered oneself to the insecurities of living in the moment. One cannot engage oneself in such activity without a confrontation with the purposive self.

Genuinely "doing nothing" implies to be without purpose, beyond "usefulness". It is to be without expectation, to suspend the yoke of cause/effect. It is to be unassailed by the desire for experience.

When one can thus sit quietly...for even one minute...one can live quietly and simply. One can then return to one's "normal" daily life with a radically renewed perspective. When one's mind has completely come to a standstill, the self is no longer in a subject/object relationship to consciousness. One recognizes, with finality, that there is not anything which really needs to be done...not even stilling the mind. One is then free to love more than one's life.

Soul Talk

Take away your name. Take away your memory and your imagination. Take away all of your interpretation of sensual perceptions. Remove all feeling, emotion and personal experience. Remove every trace of anything which makes you separately unique. Whatever remains, when you are clinically dead, is what mystics have referred to as the soul.

How then is your soul different from anyone else's soul?

And when your soul joins those other souls who have vanished before you, what is it joining?

The Irony of God

Early Christian writers spoke of a "Godhead", as the source or ground of all that is. This Godhead represented what in Eastern religions would be referred to as "nonduality". It included the polarity of the unmanifest universe (emptiness) and the manifest universe (form), in somewhat the same way that an electromagnetic field comprises the negative charge and the positive charge.

The depiction of the Godhead also contained a third element, which represented the movement or change from emptiness to form (and vice versa). The analogy, in the above description, would be somewhat comparable to the energy we call electricity.

In simple characterization, Jesus was considered to be the manifest embodiment. And the space of cosmic creation—out of which all that is material arises—was viewed as the unmanifest, the dominion of God (as an element distinct from the Godhead). The *arising* itself, the manifest*ing* or forming, was considered to be the nature, or province, of the Holy Spirit. (It was the Spirit that "moved upon the face of the waters", in Genesis, when "the earth was without form".) This formative energy—like Jesus and God— is viewed as a separate distinction, *within* the Godhead.

It was through God, in conjunction with the energy of the Holy Spirit, that the material world made its appearance—and the "son" of this union propitiously added to it, according to the catechist. When the faithful revere the Father, Son and the Holy Spirit, they are acknowledging their awareness of the Godhead, it is deemed.

In terms of a visual depiction, if you were to join three triangular units at their apex—so that their bases and sides were joined to form a three-sided pyramid—you would create a consequent area: the empty, cone-like space designated by the prismatic outline. This defined "center" could be analogous to the Godhead.

The three triangular facets "rest upon" each other, and are interdependent for the existence of the pyramid. Remove any one

438

of these three aspects and you no longer have the pristine configuration which imparts reality to the center, Godhead.

In the sense that sides A, B and C *comprise* the Godhead, this trinity could be said (as it generally is) to *be* the Godhead. In this regard, also, Jesus could be said to be equivalent with God. However, in this context, Jesus is *not God*—does not replace or supplant God. Nor is God (though even many of the devout are confused on this point) "the same thing" as the Godhead. It is the Godhead which gives God *form* (through Christ-*consciousness*, the Catholics would say) *and* the power of holy creation through spirit (breath). The Godhead is the ground, it might be said, upon which God would be found.

Put another way, the ground precedes, or supercedes, even the unmanifest God. But not anything precedes or supercedes the ground itself. So, if one were to refer to God and Godhead interchangeably, one would be missing a dimension or ignoring a subtlety or nuance.

The general purpose of the doctrine concerning the Godhead is evidently to give meaning to the description of "Absolute". While *God* is often referred to, by even some theologians, as the Absolute, it is obviously the Godhead which is referred to. In the context of the *Trinity*, God is relative—as Father viewed apart from Son and Holy Spirit. And these three configurations stand in *relation* to their source or ground. Since each is by definition, in this symbolism, dependent upon its relationship to the Godhead, only the Godhead is considered to be beyond their intrinsic limitations.

In other words, the Absolute is not meant to be the opposite—at the opposite pole—of the relative. It is meant to include or encompass all that is relative—and yet to remain as a dimension more. "Relative" *and* "nonrelative" are, we could say, the Absolute; but the Absolute is not ever—in the real sense—

relative (*or* nonrelative). To say otherwise is to erode the meaning (the only significant meaning it has) of the word "Absolute". If the Absolute is, at any time, nothing more than relative, we might as well simply refer to all that is (and is not) as "the relative". The Absolute is intended to mean (as said in sentence number one) the ground or possibility of all that is—inclusive of, but not limited to, the relative, nonrelative and any other possibility. Unlike the relative, there is no other, other than it: not-two; not even in relation to anything else.

The significance, of all this, is that it is—theologically—from the *relative* point of view (I-Thou) that one recognizes the existence of God (or the primacy of Jesus). From the point of view of the Absolute, there would not be any distinct *entity* to recognize, describe or define. The Absolute, being all things already, would have no particular or distinct qualities to recognize or define: it is not locatable, having no locus. From the standpoint of the Absolute, there is not anything that has ever been apart: *within* it is all time, all space, all causation. Not anything comes together or is united in or *with* the Absolute, since not anything could have stood apart from it.

Obviously, the sages would say, this is what you are. This is what *all things* are. Therefore, you are not separate from anything: you are That.

However, the rishi would add, you are not the Absolute. And *yet*, it can be said relatively, "you" and the "Absolute" are inseparable.

The Absolute is the "relative"—and *all else* that exists. But the relative is not the Absolute, *and all else that exists* ... or it would not be "the relative". This is the supreme irony which the Trinity/ Godhead is meant to suggest.

Hillary Rodrigues has written that Krishnamurti was the proponent of "religion as encompassing a way of being, a quality of life, which is neither personal nor impersonal, where individuals can course in anonymous, free-flowing and direct communication with the sacred ...."

"What is remarkable about this religious teaching is that it does not require people to follow any spiritual guide, to form or belong to any religious organization, to perform any rituals, study any scripture, build any church or temple, perform any pilgrimage, or commission any priest."

Instead, its essence "is in the radical transformation of one's own consciousness from its illusory and destructive notions of individuality or community, into a wholeness which is genuine, and utterly related to the ground and substance of all creation."

This transformation is "an abiding with Truth, which apparently only reveals its presence when the mind of the individual is free from the trappings of tradition and conceptualizations of any kind."

He quotes K:

> A man who is passionate about the world and the necessity
> for change must be free from political activity, religious
> conformity, and tradition—which means, free from the
> weight of time, free from the burden of the past, free from all
> the action of will: this is the new human being. This only is
> the social, psychological, and even the political revolution.

And further, from a discussion with representatives of all of the Foundations:

In this chaotic and disintegrating world, what is of the greatest importance is how each person lives these teachings in his daily life. It is the responsibility of each human being to bring about his own transformation which does not depend on knowledge or time.

Krishnamurti pointedly asked:

What is the responsibility of each member of the Foundations?...is their responsibility... to understand the teachings fully, not partially?

He answered, to the International Trustees, that *the members of the Foundations should be... centers of light; (they are) totally responsible to see that they themselves are—in themselves—light.*

Go into it, he urged the KFA Trustees. *That's not interpretation.*

What would Buddha do?

Two things. First, he put an end to his own suffering, by aligning perfectly with the all-powerful Intelligence (dubbed "Void"). *Then*, he spent the rest of his life—24/7—pointing to his own liberation as a means by which to eliminate suffering.

Jesus, evidently, did the same. Suffering for humanity, he entered the desert. Suffering as humanity, he exited—to spend his time (24/7) communicating the good news of the possibility for salvation, human by human.

And Ramana. *Self*-awakened, he *then* dedicated the adult years of his life to responding (24/7) to the endless suffering that presented itself at his door, detailing specifically the manner by which he had ended his own suffering.

So, it's abundantly clear when and how to do the second task, as soon as the first requisite has been resolved.

Have you ended suffering for yourself? If not, how then are you to show others the way?

Yea, Listen to the Mockingbird!

It is June 21 (The First Day of Summer) one hundred degrees in the shade, and completely open to the blue skies on this hilltop. Standing out in the pure sunlight is a pine tree about fifty feet tall. Perched at its very top, and overlooking the hills of this ripe green valley is a mockingbird. Singing.

It has been singing since about 7 A.M., when the sunlight first hurdled the mountaintops, and it will continue until the sun is gone; that is, about one half of the day. The mockingbird will fly away for brief periods of this time, during which its absence will be noticed in the quiet.

It sings for several minutes at a time, and then—still singing—it will leap into the air and flutter its wings in a semaphoric display of black and white, settling again on its prominent perch and continuing its plaint. Its song is not desperate, but it is insistent and unrelenting. It is designed to carry for a considerable distance over the hills.

As one listens, on this day in which few creatures are active, the song itself is astonishing. Though repeated, literally, for hours, it is not repetitious. Though one can hear, at moments, the mimicking of a cricket, a frog and the call of other birds, it is nonetheless inventive. What startles the human ear, as it listens, is that each note is sung with an intensity as if it had never been attempted before. Each refrain ends with the urgent sincerity and enthusiasm with which it began. Indeed, as the day wears, the mockingbird renders each passionate soliloquy as if every one of its previous efforts were completely forgotten. There is never a tired, worn or half-hearted effort; each effort is as if it were the first—nay, the only effort. The bird and its song are in no way divided; each breath and the expression of each note are inseparable. The potential for each moment is ever richer than the moment before. And all, and everything that one is, is in that rapturous moment. Nothing more is to be attended to than that.

The author may be contacted at:

Robert Wolfe
℅ Karina Library
P.O. Box 35
Ojai, California 93024

Website: www.livingnonduality.org

Coda

Hi Robert,

As I was heading towards the door, at the conclusion of our last visit, I remarked that I wanted some time to contemplate the matters we had been talking about. And you said: "You're not going to find anything out there that isn't right here."

Odd that such a simple statement should resonate as it has.

I take your meaning as "There is nothing to get."

It is a subtle shift of perspective—from identification with a thought-constructed persona, to clear seeing as no-thing.

And from the all-encompassing perspective of no-thing, your statement could not be more true! There is nothing to get—here, there or anywhere. Nothing to add. Nothing to subtract. No modification necessary, or possible.

Thank you,

Ronald O.
Ojai, California

Help others discover this work by leaving a review online, or creating a link to:

www.livingnonduality.org/book

Alphabetical Title Index